STANDING on the PROMISES

STANDING on the PROMISES

THE AUTOBIOGRAPHY OF

W.A. CRISWELL

CONTENTS

CONTENTS

1
In the Beginning
Eldorado: December 19, 1909

"Honor thy father and thy mother:
that thy days might be long upon the land
which the Lord thy God giveth thee."
Exodus 20:12

TYPHOID FEVER!

The dreaded news raced like prairie fire through the little town of Eldorado, Texas. Cases of typhoid fever had just been reported in Texas and Oklahoma. People were dying.

It was spring, 1903. A new century had dawned, and hopes were high. A twenty-six-year-old cowpoke named Wallie Amos Criswell was busy working on his uncle Charlie Neeley's cattle ranch near Eldorado. Rumors of the deadly disease didn't trouble him.

Five years earlier, Wallie Amos had married a beautiful young woman from Eldorado. While he enjoyed working for his uncle, W. A. and his wife dreamed of buying their own land and building a home for their growing family. They had three beautiful children, and their fourth was due in a few days. Times were hard, but the Criswells had a lot going for them. They were young and strong. They were deeply in love. They had their whole lives stretching gloriously ahead of them. And to them, nothing seemed impossible.

"What's wrong with her, doctor?" W. A. asked with a growing sense of desperation in his voice.

"I don't know," the old country doctor replied as he felt the young woman's forehead.

"And what's wrong with my son?" W. A. asked, staring at the beautiful young baby who had just been born.

"It might be the fever," the doctor answered. "We'll have to wait and see."

"The fever?" The very word itself was terrifying to the young husband and father. He must have whispered it over and over to himself. "The fever? Typhoid fever? It can't be the fever. She's so young, and the baby's just been born."

The country doctor was helpless against those relentless, raging fevers. He had bathed the young woman and her child in tepid water and rubbing alcohol in an attempt to cool their fevered bodies and bring them some relief.

Grasping his wife's damp hand, the young husband watched and waited in desperate silence. For a while, mother and child cried out in pain. Then, both of them were silent.

Friends and family who attended their funeral in the little Southern Baptist church in Eldorado told me many years later that there had never been a funeral service like it. Wallie Amos Criswell's beautiful young bride lay in the casket with their baby cradled in her arms. On the front pew, near the casket, W. A., his eyes red from crying, tried to control his own grief and at the same time comfort his three young children.

In the decades that followed, I never heard my father speak of his first wife, the child, or the tragedy they shared. But I could tell that the fragments of his grief lived on, buried somewhere deep in the hidden places of his heart.

Abandoned!

Somewhere in the wilds of New Mexico, a young woman named Anna Currie was facing her own tragedy. Anna was the daughter of privilege. Her father, Dr. David Currie, was a respected surgeon who had served the Confederate Army with distinction throughout the Civil War.

When the fighting ended, Dr. Currie returned to his beloved Texas. His successful practice enabled him to buy thousands of acres of grazing land east of San Angelo, where the Concho River flows into the Colorado. Patients traveled from farms and ranches all over central Texas to seek his care.

Anna Currie's life began on that great Texas ranch. From earliest childhood, she was her daddy's darling. With her long, brown hair trailing in the wind and her dark brown eyes sparkling, Anna was often seen riding across the ranch at breakneck speed. She had the spirit of the pedigree filly Dr. Currie had given her and the bright, active mind of her father. He must have dreamed great dreams for his precocious and determined daughter. There was nothing he would not grant her. But Anna had her own plans. At sixteen years of age, she met a young salesman named Glynn and fell deeply in love with him.

"Please, Anna," Dr. Currie pleaded with his only daughter. "Don't let your heart rule your head."

"But I love him, Daddy. Everything will be okay. You don't need to worry."

How often that same conversation has taken place between a father with his hopes and plans and a daughter with her dreams and visions. And how seldom anything good comes of it. They say love conquers all. In fact, love based on infatuation, without the miracle of God's presence and blessing, can ruin lives and destroy dreams forever. Anna Currie left her home and family in Texas and moved with her young Mr. Glynn to New Mexico. I have often wondered if it broke her father's heart.

In New Mexico, two precious daughters were born to Anna Currie Glynn and her ambitious young husband. For a brief time, it looked as if Anna had been right and her father wrong. Then the young woman's dreams collapsed as her father's worst fears came true. No one knows exactly how or why it happened, but one winter day, Glynn just disappeared. Apparently, he left New Mexico en route to Arizona or California and was never heard from again. Anna, still just a teenager, cared for their two daughters and waited.

Every day she went to the mailbox hoping that there would be news of her missing husband. Every night she knelt beside her two daughters and prayed with them for his safe return. There were occasional reports that Glynn had been sighted and plenty of reasons to believe that he was alive and well. Finally, his young wife had to deal with the awful fact that Glynn had abandoned them. He would never return.

Wallie Amos Criswell and Anna Currie Glynn

Anna did not go back to her father's ranch near San Angelo, Texas. Perhaps she was embarrassed by her failure and, unlike the prodigal, too proud to return home. Perhaps her father forbade her to come. Father and daughter were both children of the frontier. Like the land, they were tough and hard to tame.

Early in 1905, when Anna finally admitted that her husband was gone forever, she and her two daughters, Edith and Ruth, moved to Eldorado, Texas. Anna's older sister, Clara Currie Thompson, was married to the town's sheriff. They had a small, two-story home, but they gladly made room for Anna and her little daughters. There is no love more powerful than the kind of love that opens hearts and homes to those in need.

It wasn't long before Anna Currie Glynn met Wallie Amos Criswell. I don't know how they met. Neither ever spoke much about their courtship or romance. But it isn't difficult to imagine how their marriage came about. Eldorado was a frontier town of no more than a few hundred people surrounded by thousands of acres of undulating grazing land and some brave fields of wheat and cotton. The young widower with three small children and the abandoned wife with two daughters of her own were probably drawn together more by their loneliness and grief than by some great passion. I like to think they met each other at a Sunday morning service at the little wood-framed Southern Baptist church. They had gone to find God's comfort, and God, in His great love and understanding, gave them to each other.

Shortly after the death of his first wife and baby, W. A. Criswell had met the Lord in Eldorado. Wallie Amos was twenty-six when he was converted. I imagine that from that day, he rode into town every Sunday to worship with Eldorado's congregation of Southern Baptist believers. Anna Currie Glynn had been converted when just a child in her father's home on the ranch near San Angelo. After the grief and disappointment of her first marriage, Anna, too, must have been all too willing to return to her spiritual roots, attending church faithfully, sitting in the pew with her two daughters, her sister, and her sister's husband, Eldorado's only lawman.

Somehow, Wallie Amos and Anna found each other in that great open Texas space. They were married that same year. And four years later, on December 19, 1909, I was born in their home in Eldorado, Oklahoma.

Little W.A. Criswell, Jr.

The Ranch in Eldorado

That's right, I would have been born a Texan but for a decision of the United States Supreme Court. In 1905, the court decided to change the Texas-Oklahoma border from the north fork of the Red River to the south fork just four miles south of Eldorado. Suddenly, Eldorado, once a hearty little Texas town, found herself a part of Oklahoma. It was the moment of truth for my father and the opportunity of a lifetime to begin a cattle ranch of his own.

All the newly acquired Oklahoma territory between the north and south forks of the Red River was opened by the state for homestead filing. When W. A. heard the good news, he rushed to claim three hundred and twenty acres, a half-section of undeveloped grazing land. He borrowed money to build a ranch house for his family. He built his own fences and bought his own livestock. And from sunrise until dark he rode the range.

There was little chance of developing a great Texas ranch in Eldorado, although my father and my mother gave that dream their very best. First there was drought. The grass died and the dust blew mercilessly in the strong northern winds. Fences went down. The price of feed went up. Then came winter cold. Snow drifted. Cattle were lost and stolen. Some died. For years, Wallie Amos Criswell fought to keep the fences mended and the cattle safe and fed. It was a difficult and heartbreaking task. To supplement his meager income, my father learned to use barber's shears to cut the cowboys' hair. He soon discovered that there was more money in barbering than in cattle ranching. Eventually, he sold his land, moved his family into the town of Eldorado, and built himself a barbershop. So, because of the Supreme Court's decision, I was born a barber's son in Oklahoma instead of a rancher's son in Texas on that cold December day in 1909.

Roots

Although I still consider myself a "Texahoman," our family roots go back to Ireland. In the 1720s my father's ancestors moved from their farm near Dublin to Chester County, Pennsylvania. There they established a dairy farm and a blacksmith shop. There were at least seven Criswell sons born to these new Irish-Americans, whose roots in Protestantism reached back to their origins in England.

My great-great-grandfather, John Y. Criswell, a son of those first Criswell immigrants to the new world, was born in 1786. When John was forty-four, he and his wife, Eleanor, packed up their six sons and two daughters and wagon-trained to Texas from their home in Kentucky. In a letter dated June 1831, John asked for permission to buy some land in Texas at Matagorda, a settlement near Austin.

"I am not wealthy," he admitted, "but I can say to you I came to this country clear of any debt or bad fame."

John Y. Criswell, Jr., my great-grandfather, was born in 1824 while his parents still lived in Knox County, Kentucky. John was just six years old when his family migrated to Matagorda, Texas. When John was eighteen, he joined an independent company of Texas Rangers and, according to his obituary, "engaged in desultory Indian fighting." In 1845, he entered the service of the Republic of Texas and "served proudly in the company of G. H. Bell." For the duration of the war between the United States and Mexico, my great-grandfather served under Captain M. B. Gray of the Sixth Texas Rangers.

Sue Ragland Diggle, a dear friend and the source of almost all my information on my father's family roots, discovered a letter of commendation issued by my great-grandfather's commander in the Texas Rangers.

"John was in the main a good soldier," the letter reads. "He was fond of running horses . . . and participated in all the little amusements legitimate in camp. He was considered a wild young man, but generally esteemed a fit associate by his fellow soldiers."

Although my ancestors were not among the brave one hundred and eighty-seven volunteers who died in the siege of the Alamo by the Mexican general Santa Anna, John Sr. and John Jr. both had exciting stories about the Alamo from their own personal experiences.

In the restored Alamo fortress near San Antonio, a framed letter referring to my great-great grandfather hangs in a place of honor. John Y. Criswell, Sr., was fifty years old when the battle began. He wasn't called upon to fight, but he offered his home and hospitality to the fighters. The last squad of volunteer Rangers heading for the ill-fated battle stopped by his home en route to the Alamo. "Being out of provisions," the squad's agent wrote, "John Y. Criswell Sr. fed us in his own house with his own provisions for the night and next morning breakfast . . . ."

Apparently, John Jr. went on to fight for the Confederate Army in the early days of the Civil War. In 1862 and 1863, he was appointed to distribute War Tax Script among the destitute families of the soldiers from Fayette County. John Jr. and his wife, Mary Rebecca, had six children. Their oldest son, L. H. Criswell, was my grandfather.

L. H. "Leander" Criswell was the postmaster of Dumont, Texas, for twenty-three years. He also was the first journalist of record in the Criswell family, serving as a correspondent for the Post City *Post* in Garza County for a dozen or more years. Grampa and his wife, Emma Adaline, had thirteen children, seven boys and six girls. Both my grandparents were devout Christian workers in the Southern Baptist church in Dumont.

Southern Baptist roots grow down deep on both sides of my family. My mother's grandfather was a Southern Baptist preacher from Kentucky, and all the Curries back for at least four generations worshipped in little Southern Baptist churches in towns and cities across Texas.

In 1909, the year I was born, my father, W. A. Criswell, was a deacon in the Eldorado Baptist Church. Two years later, in 1911, my brother Currie was born. My father was proud of his large, noisy family. There were seven of us children. Each Lord's Day we were dressed in our finest Sunday clothes and paraded down Eldorado's main street to the Southern Baptist church in the heart of town.

The children my father brought to the marriage were Leona, Theo, and Gladys. The children my mother had were Edith and Ruth. They all joined in to take care of Currie and me. We sat together squirming in the front pew at worship services, prayer meetings, and revivals.

My father's little barbershop was prospering. The cowpokes were lined up to get a Criswell shave and haircut for twenty-five cents. The barbershop was the social center of Eldorado. His collection of old newspapers and magazines was the primary source of information for those men who spent the daylight hours riding the range and their evenings in bedrolls beneath the open sky.

During those years before World War I, my father prospered. He paid off his debts. He owned his Eldorado home and barbershop free and clear. He even joined the two million Americans who invested in the stock market. He was one of Eldorado's leading citizens, with respect from the townsfolk and money in the bank.

The Second Plague

Then, once again, my father's life and the lives of our family were altered unexpectedly by rumors of another plague. This time it was tuberculosis that turned my father's world upside down. I don't know exactly what happened that day almost seventy-six years ago. I just know that one chance conversation in my dad's barbershop nearly ruined his life—and headed our family in an entirely new direction.

"Wallie Amos?" the town doctor began as he settled into my father's barber chair. "I have to warn you . . . ."

"Warn me about what?" my father answered, stropping down the razor and reaching for a bowl of shaving cream.

"TB!" the doctor answered firmly but quietly, leaning forward in his chair and looking my father in the eye.

"TB?" my father replied, "You mean tuberculosis?"

"Of course tuberculosis," the doctor groaned, leaning back into his chair. "It's invisible, Wallie, and it spreads from person to person through the air, in a cough, a sneeze, or just a gusty conversation. Once inside your lungs, the disease begins to spread. Then comes lack of energy, weight loss, and a nasty, hacking cough. The next thing you know your lungs fill up with fluid and you die."

My father must have been stunned. One plague had taken away his wife and child. He could not risk another.

"You need to be out of doors, Wallie, in the fresh air," the doctor urged him. "Who knows what you're going to catch being locked up in this small room with all those cowboys coughing and hacking away."

Until that day, the idea never dawned upon him that barbering could be dangerous to his health or to the health of his large, young family. How could he know which cowboy might be infected with the dreaded disease? How could he avoid catching it with all that shouting and laughing, coughing and sneezing? My father could not risk becoming the carrier of that terrible illness from his barbershop to his home.

"We're moving," he suddenly announced one day. "We're going to sell everything we have and take a chance at farming."

Looking back, I am convinced that my father made a grave mistake. He was happy in Eldorado. He had a good life there surrounded by family and friends. He had fought the land once and lost bitterly. He was about to fight the land and lose again. But if his decision was costly, it was also a loving, generous act. My father gave up his good life in Eldorado to save his family from the possibility of disease and death. I am sure that friends and neighbors tried to dissuade him. But young Wallie Amos Criswell had already seen one wife and baby struck down by an invisible, deadly force. He would take any risk or pay any price to keep that tragedy from striking once again.

We lived in Eldorado until I was five years old. I can still recall my father's barbershop, the sweet smell of tonic, soap, and after-shave lotion, the boisterous sounds of cowboys stomping and shouting, and the wondrous sight of my father putting down his shears and reaching out his arms to welcome me. "Hey, fellas," he would say as I toddled into the noisy, smoke-filled room, "meet my son. He's going to be a cowboy-barber just like his dad."

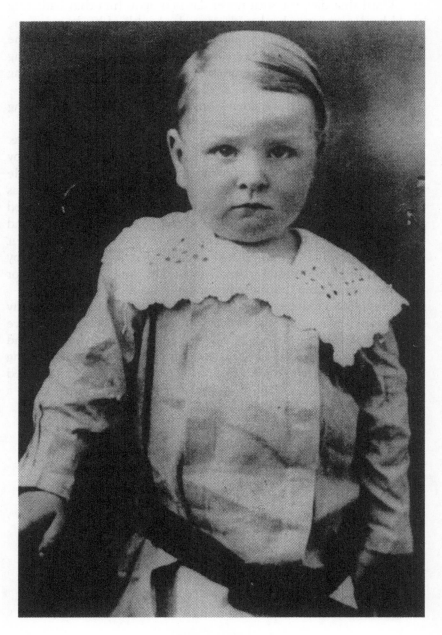

Young Willie Amos Criswell, Jr.

2

Our New Home
Texline: 1915

*"Train up a child in the way he should go:
and when he is old, he will not depart from it."*
Proverbs 22:6

WITH AN ANGRY HISS OF STEAM, THE GREAT IRON LOCO-
motive lurched to a stop. The conductor's voice echoed from some
distant place. "Texline!" he shouted. "End of the line!"

I remember clinging to the rail as I climbed down the rough,
metal steps that led to the platform of Texline's depot. I was a curious
five year old, awestruck by the journey and fascinated by every new
surprise along the way. As I hung suspended from the railing, my foot
not quite reaching to the ground, a black porter held out his hand to
assist me. He smiled. That porter was the first black man I had ever
seen. I accepted his offer of help with not a little curiosity.

Homesteading the Land

A tall, thin man walked across the gravel yard holding out his hand to greet my father. Wallie Amos Criswell looked surprised. The stranger put his arm around my father and began to speak rapidly as he tried to guide our family toward a large horse-drawn buggy parked nearby. For a moment my father hesitated, questioning the stranger earnestly. Finally, he nodded in assent. We climbed into that black leather buggy pulled by a matched team. The moment we were loaded, the stranger snapped a long-handled whip and we began the final stage of our journey into Texline.

This stranger was called a "land locator." He spent his time waiting at the depot and then offered his services to those who planned to homestead the endless, arid countryside that stretched from Texline toward the distant horizons. He would show my father the land that had not been filed on and charge us ten dollars for his trouble. If we didn't file, we didn't pay.

We turned left onto Texline's main street, past the feedstore and flour mill, the First State Bank, the Ward Howe Rooming House, the dry goods store, and the little lumber yard. The streets were not paved. A passing Model-T Ford with spoke wheels and white tires stirred up the dust and momentarily spooked the horses. The stranger pointed out the post office, the all-grade schoolhouse, and the wonderful little Southern Baptist church that would comfort, strengthen, and direct our family's life together. We unloaded at Texline's only hotel, while my father and the stranger drove away together.

Old-timers like to say that Texline sits "on the edge of nowhere." In fact, that little railroad town where I grew up lies in the very northwest corner of the Texas Panhandle, one-half mile east of the New Mexico state line and five miles south of the Oklahoma border. The hospital we visited during family emergencies was in Trinidad, Colorado, about eighty miles to the northwest, and our daily newspaper was the Denver Post. The great cities of Texas—Dallas, Fort Worth, Austin, San Antonio—seemed far away in some distant country.

By nightfall, Father returned. He would file with government agents for a half section of land just four miles west of Texline and six miles south of Clayton, New Mexico. The homestead law was clear. You must live on your land six months per year, make certain improvements on it, and pay roughly a dollar-twenty-five per acre to the government for the privilege.

Seeing Our New Homestead for the First Time

I clearly remember that next day. My father rented a horse and wagon from the wagon yard to drive Mother and us children for a tour of our new homesite. From the wagon I could look in any direction and see the horizon, shimmering in the hot summer sun. An occasional windmill stood silhouetted against the bright sky. Though flat as a table top, Texline is almost a mile high. The heat was dry and the land was brown and parched.

"We'll build our house there on that little rise," Father said quietly, "with rooms enough for everybody. And a barn over there with a corral for the stock . . . and a windmill."

My mother was silent. She clutched my hand and smiled gamely.

"We'll graze a small herd of cattle," Dad continued. "And we'll buy a team of horses and a mule to pull the plow."

He leaned over and tried to dig up a handful of earth from the hard, dry ground.

"We'll grow corn and beans and sorghum," he said. "This land is rich, you know. It only takes a few good rains to bring a harvest."

Prairie soil is rich, but without the rains there was no way to irrigate the crops. There was water down there, somewhere, but in those days we had no electric pumps to draw it up from deep below the surface. There were no natural springs to tap, no great rivers to divert. We were totally dependent upon the rain.

And it did rain occasionally in Texline. But it never seemed to rain enough. The windmill my father erected drew enough surface water for our family to drink and to water the stock. And often there was rain enough to get a crop (and my father's hopes) growing once again. But seldom did enough rain fall to irrigate the crop or raise up a harvest. I was too young to understand the incredible sense of loss he and Mother must have felt during those early years of drought and erosion, or the amazing courage they showed to plow and plant again.

I was just five years old when I first learned to harness the mule, hook up the go-devil, and guide mule and plow together up and down those fragile rows. I so well remember the difficulty I had in turning the mules around so that I could hit the row coming back in the exact middle and not cut up the shoots of maize or pinto beans. Sometimes the harness lines would tangle or drag. Sometimes the mule would stop or wander in the wrong direction. Sometimes I would trip and fall or struggle to maintain my balance, yelling all the while for the mule to "Stop!" or "Go!" or "Turn!"

Life in Our Little House on the Prairie

The home my father built for us was made to stand forever. He had absolutely no experience as an architect or builder, but he had a vision of his prairie house and refused to conform or to compromise that vision. Instead of wood, the walls were made of poured concrete. I still remember him driving our wagon out across the countryside to collect discarded iron implements to reinforce those thick, concrete slabs. Rusty fragments of iron wheels, iron beams and axles stuck out of the walls. And once the slabs were poured, the whole family working together could hardly maneuver them into place.

My father covered the cement walls with stucco and painted over everything with bright, white paint. Instead of wooden pillars to hold up the corrugated iron roof of our front porch, he poured cement pyramids and hoisted them into place. When my father built it, I thought it the prettiest house in the world! Seventy years later, when I visited our homestead for the last time and saw our old house standing there abandoned and ghostly on that little rise four miles from Texline, I felt strangely moved by the memories of my father and our family building together that not-so-pretty house on the "edge of nowhere."

From 1915, when we first moved into our little cement house on the prairie, we filled the place with music—not all on key, you understand, but enthusiastic all the same. My mother loved to sing the old hymns and gospel songs: "All the Way My Savior Leads Me," "Amazing Grace," "In the Sweet Bye and Bye." She had no piano to accompany her singing; nevertheless, she sang those hymns over and over, and we happily joined in the singing.

My father was very shy, but he too loved to sing. Unlike my mother, who was a talented musician and sight reader, my father couldn't read a note of music. "All those little round fly specks on a page of music just confuse me," he would say. Then one day he discovered square notes. I don't know if that little Dallas publishing house that invented square notes so the not-so-musically-gifted could read is still in business, but what joy those square notes brought my father! The melody note was not round like the others. It was shaped in a little half square. My father could pick out those little half square notes and follow them easily. In the process, he discovered that he had been gifted with a beautiful tenor voice.

My father especially loved Stamps-Baxter gospel songs and barbershop quartets (of course). He would rush to buy every square-note songbook that was released, and he would sing those songs for countless hours. In those days there were singing conventions. People like my father who loved to sing would come on Sundays from all around the county, meet at a designated church, have dinner on the grounds, and sing all afternoon and well into the evening. Sometimes they would divide up into duets, trios, quartets, sextets, and little choirs to perform for each other. Sometimes they would start at the beginning of a Stamps-Baxter gospel songbook and sing as one large choir every verse of every song from cover to cover.

Thank God for the singing. There was nothing else to do during those desolate prairie years but listen to the wind blow and watch the clouds of topsoil blown away by the fierce blue northers. We never had a car. There was no running water, no indoor toilets, no fancy gadgets in the kitchen. There was no electricity to power a radio, no record player, no television set. No movie house or drive-in, no MacDonald's or Domino's Pizza, no video games, no swimming pool. When it got dark, we went to bed. And when the sun rose, we got up to work again.

Eating was one happy diversion. Though we were poor, we ate well and often. Mother was always up first, preparing breakfast in the kitchen. The smell of bacon frying in the iron skillet was better than any alarm clock. She fried eggs sunnyside up, dozens of them, fresh from the chicken house just outside the kitchen door. And her pancakes were classic, fresh cream and oat flour batter covered in freshly churned butter and pure cane syrup. And the seven of us children downed gallons of milk from our own cows. We ate boxes of Kellogg Corn Flakes or Grape Nuts and now and then an apple from Washington, an orange from California, and even an occasional banana imported by ship and trucked to the edge of nowhere from some distant tropical land.

I don't think we ever ate a meal that wasn't prayed over first. My father's prayers were short and to the point. He expressed his gratitude for life, health, and the food we were about to eat, but he often included a quiet plea for rain.

Mother's prayers were longer and more down to business. I will admit that sometimes she preached at us through her praying. "Help the children in their studies. Help the children learn to clean their rooms or do their chores without complaining. Help the children learn to love and honor You with all their heart, soul, mind, and strength."

We sat around the table in silence as a parent or another child prayed before each meal. It was a tradition that we bowed our heads, closed our eyes, and clasped our hands together. Sometimes we finished morning or evening prayers by praying the Lord's Prayer in unison. When the morning prayers ended, we children ate quickly and noisily, and then rushed out to do our chores before climbing up in the wagon for the four-mile trip across the prairie to the all-grade schoolhouse in Texline.

The All-Grade School in Texline

I entered the all-grade school in Texline as a second grader. We were clustered together by grades around our study tables. There were four large classrooms, each heated by an iron, pot-bellied, coal-burning stove. The teacher read stories to the little circle of first-grade students, while second graders learned their addition tables and third graders memorized their spelling lists. It was chaos, and I did my best learning at home.

During those first years in Texline, Currie and I were too small to do many chores. While the older children helped Father plow and plant, brand cattle, and run herd on them, while Mother and the younger girls cooked, cleaned, and sewed, I read. I don't know where all the books came from, but somehow there was always a fresh supply of Zane Grey novels, Horatio Alger stories, old copies of *Literary Digest, The Baptist Standard*, and always the King James Version of the Bible.

The Bible was at the center of our family's life together. In the evenings when Dad had the strength, he would gather us to read the Bible and to pray. Sometimes Mother would read a psalm or story from the Gospels and talk about them with us. I was only six when I first tried to read the whole King James Bible from cover to cover, Genesis to Revelation. It wasn't easy plowing through those Old Testament laws or the New Testament genealogies, but with the aid of our trusted Webster dictionary and with occasional explanations from Mother or Father, somehow I managed. I remember that the more I read, the hungrier I got to read even more.

Texline's Southern Baptist Church

On Sundays we packed a picnic lunch, rode the wagon into Texline for the Sunday morning worship service, and stayed for the evening service. We filled two pews in that tiny Southern Baptist church. I suppose the church had about sixty members then. It was a little white church, box-like, with cement stairs leading up to the double doors, topped by a cupola with a cast-iron bell. I loved to ring that bell. Sometimes the pastor would let me ring it for ten or fifteen minutes before the service began.

The pastor usually greeted every member of each family by name before and after the service. We filed up the aisle, sat together in our pews, picked up the little paperback hymnal from the pew rack, and squirmed and whispered until the service began. The old upright piano hadn't been tuned in a hundred years, and the round piano stool squeaked noisily when the pastor's wife adjusted it up or down before she played the introduction to the morning hymn. (Between services I would spin Currie round and round, up and down on that little stool until he grew dizzy and staggered away. No wonder she had to adjust the stool at every service!)

Our home life was built around the church. Being a follower of Christ was everything. Our Christian faith and the standards for living taught us by our Southern Baptist preachers shaped our lives completely. We attended church every time the doors were opened. We studied and memorized the Bible. We prayed. We gave regularly of our tithes and offerings. And we shared our faith with friends and neighbors, and even with strangers we met along the way. And our personal lives were strictly governed by Southern Baptist rules and traditions.

For example, my father would not allow a deck of cards inside the house. Gambling and dancing were unspeakable evils. "Beer joints" were strictly off-limits. And swearing, even slang, would not be tolerated. If there had been a movie house in Texline, we would not have been allowed inside it. And in those days, if there had been a television in the living room, I'm sure my mother or my father would have censored it with an iron hand.

And though we children practiced the Christian faith, we weren't really considered bona fide Christians until we had accepted Christ as Lord and Savior on our own. It was something our parents prayed and worked toward from the moment of our birth.

Conversion

"Do you love the Lord, son?" the young pastor from Dalhart asked me as we sat in the kitchen drinking fresh buttermilk and eating my mother's oatmeal-raisin cookies still warm from the oven.

"Yes, sir," I answered honestly.

Pastor John Hicks had come to Texline from Dalhart, the county seat, to hold our annual revival. It was an honor to have the evangelist stay with our family for the week-long duration of the meetings. There

were services every morning at 10:00 and every evening at 7:30. Pastor
Hicks was young. His sermons were exciting. They made me laugh and
cry. I was just ten years old, but I remember that he treated me like a
man, and I admired him like teenagers today admire movie stars and
singers.

"So you like Zane Gray stories, do you?" Pastor Hicks asked with a
grin. "Me too!" he said before I could even smile or nod in reply. "But
don't tell my deacons," he added. "They think Southern Baptist
preachers should stick to Matthew, Mark, Luke, and John."

He laughed heartily and poured another glass of buttermilk.

"Your mother tells me that you're going to be a doctor like your
grandfather," he said wiping the foamy white buttermilk from his
mustache.

"No, sir," I answered. "I'm going to be a preacher."

Pastor Hicks leaned over conspiratorially and whispered. "Why's
that, boy? Preaching means hard work and no pay. Doctors make loads
of money."

I was surprised by his reply until I realized by the gleam in his eyes
that he was teasing me.

"I don't care," I answered, "I want to be a preacher and that's that."

I'm sure that desire came directly from God, but just when it
started or exactly why I'm still not sure. I just know that even before I
was saved, the Lord planted it deep in my heart that I would be a
pastor—not an evangelist, not a missionary, but a pastor. My father
didn't want me to be a preacher. My mother didn't want me to be a
preacher. But somehow I knew that in spite of everything and everybody, a preacher I would be.

The Wednesday morning revival service was held in our little
Southern Baptist church at exactly the same time I was supposed to be
in school. But my mother was glad to write an excuse, which I delivered to our principal. I arrived at the revival service ten or fifteen
minutes late and sneaked into a pew directly behind my mother. Pastor
Hicks winked at me as he stood to preach.

I don't remember what he read from the Bible that day or what he
preached about. I was sitting there listening with all my heart when
slowly it dawned upon me that this was the day I would accept Christ
as my personal Lord and Savior. By the time the sermon ended, tears
were running down my cheeks. I was only ten. I hadn't murdered
anybody and I wasn't a hardened criminal, but I did have a growing
conviction that this was my day to enter Christ's glorious kingdom.

There is a fountain filled with blood,
Drawn from Emmanuel's veins.
And sinners plunged beneath that flood
Lose all their guilty stains.

The pastor's wife had adjusted that piano stool and was playing that great old hymn of invitation. The little congregation made up mostly of women and little children were singing heartily. Pastor Hicks was leaning against the pulpit, his head bowed and his eyes closed in prayer. Suddenly, my mother turned around in her pew and leaned down to speak to me.

"Son, today will you accept Christ as your Lord and Savior?"

I looked up at her. My heart was pounding with excitement. Today would mark the end of one life and the beginning of another.

"W. A." she whispered, "will you give your heart to Christ today?"

"Yes, Mother," I said. "I will."

She smiled and nodded as I left my seat and walked alone to the front of the church. Pastor Hicks came down from the pulpit to greet me, but I couldn't even see him through my tears. I was a child, but I was so deeply moved by that moment. I was being born again. I was being saved. I was inviting Christ into my heart to rule my life forever. I was entering His kingdom, the kingdom of God. I was becoming a Christian. It felt wonderful. I was happy, but I was crying like a baby. And Mother told me later that everybody in the church was crying with me.

The next thing I knew, the pastor of our church in Texline, Brother L. S. Hill, was standing beside me addressing the tiny congregation.

"Today, this young boy, W. A. Criswell, Jr., stands before you accepting the Lord Jesus as his Savior and requesting to be baptized into the fellowship of the church. All of you who are in favor of receiving him on his confession of faith as a candidate for baptism, please raise your hand."

Every hand in the place shot up. Pastor Hill smiled and closed the service with a benediction. And every man, woman, and child in that little Texline Southern Baptist church lined up to shake my hand, to pat my head, to tell me how happy I had made them, and to welcome me officially into the body of Christ.

When the service was over I returned to school. My mother rushed home to find my father. That evening I noticed the excitement in his eyes when he looked at me.

"Come here, son," he said. "Let me see you."

For a moment he stood staring down at me awkwardly, his rugged, calloused hands at his side, his sunburned face wrinkled in a happy smile, and his eyes damp with tears. Then, overcoming his shyness, my father knelt down in front of me and held me in his arms.

"I love you, son," was all he said.

On that special day more than seventy years ago, my father's arms around me felt like the arms of Jesus.

Baptism

I was baptized that next Sunday in a galvanized tank that most of the year lay hidden beneath the wooden floor that held up the pulpit in our little Southern Baptist church. In order to hold the baptismal service, the deacons and the pastor had to move the pulpit, take up the floorboards and fill the galvanized baptistry with ice-cold water from a nearby well.

The service was at 2:00 on a Sunday afternoon in spring. There were only five or six rows of pews in our church, but they were jammed with people. The deacons had stretched curtains on each side of the baptistry. The women and girls would dress behind one curtain and the men and boys behind the other. We were instructed to wade into the water when our names were called and immediately after being baptized to change into dry clothing. It would be a shame to be baptized and on the same day to die of hypothermia or pneumonia. But that water was cold enough to do it.

Brother Hill was a tall, heavy man. His deep voice demanded immediate attention. I imagine that he read an appropriate scripture from the book of Acts that special day. And while the congregation was singing a rousing rendition of a baptismal hymn such as "Shall We Gather at the River," Pastor Hill waded down into the water and motioned for me to follow.

After a few words about the meaning of baptism, he put his right hand on my shoulder, and his left hand he lifted above me in benediction.

"In obedience to the command of our Lord Jesus Christ," he began somberly, "and upon your confession of faith, I baptize you, my little brother, W. A. Criswell, Jr., in the name of the Father, and of the Son, and of the Holy Spirit."

Then he gripped me firmly with both hands, lowered me quickly into the water, and pulled me out again. "Today, you are buried with the Lord in the likeness of His death and then raised in the likeness of His resurrection. Amen."

I remember the cold water, the beautiful words that flowed around me, and the excitement of rushing up out of the freezing tub into warm, dry clothing. But I remember more than that. Something actually happened to me that day. Baptism is not just a rite of passage. It is an act of wonder and mystery.

That day I was participating in a dramatic presentation of the gospel that is now almost two thousand years old. Anybody who has read 1 Corinthians 15 knows that baptism is testimony to another more ancient event, a demonstration to the world of what Christ has done to save us: He died. He was buried. He rose again.

Even though I was just ten years old, when bald Brother Hill lowered me into the icy water of that galvanized tank, I was dying and being buried just as Jesus had been. "You see," I was saying to my friends and neighbors in Texline, "Jesus paid with His death and burial for my sins and yours. And today I am remembering what He has done for me."

And when I came up out of that freezing water, I was saying to the people in that little Southern Baptist church, "You see, I too will rise up from the dead because of what Jesus has done for me. Now, through belief in His life, death and resurrection, I am a new person. Old things are passed away; behold, all things are become new."

To this day I remember every syllable of that exciting baptismal service except for one thing: I don't remember when it happened. I have forgotten the exact date. That is why I ask children to be baptized on a special holiday, a birthday or anniversary, the Fourth of July, or Thanksgiving Day. Then, unlike me, they will have the joy of remembering the exact date when they heard those precious words, "I baptize you in the name of the Father, and of the Son , and of the Holy Spirit. Amen."

I do remember that just seconds after I was changed into dry clothing, Mother and Father rushed to embrace me. Currie shook my hand and beamed. And the pastor and our little congregation pressed in to offer their prayers and congratulations. I had become a man, a new man in Jesus Christ. And baptism was my way of confessing it to the whole world.

3

The Elementary School Years

Texline: 1916-1923

*"Thy Word is a lamp unto my feet,
and a light unto my path."*

Psalm 119:105

"HOW COLD IS IT?" I ASKED MY FATHER AS HE BUNDLED
Currie and me into the open buggy behind our pony, Trixie.

"Ten degrees below zero," he answered. "Stay under the blankets.
They'll keep you warm. And when you get to school be sure to tether
Trixie in a sheltered place, out of the wind."

All night the blizzard had raged. At 6:30 that morning the snow
stopped falling. The sky cleared. And though the dirt road into Texline
was buried in drifts, Trixie knew the way to school and back with her
eyes closed, her lashes frozen.

"Trixie could die of the cold out here," I said, my teeth chattering,
my trembling hands struggling to hold the reins.

"Her winter mane will keep her warm, boys," Father assured us.
"Now, go! You'll be fine."

That third winter in Texline was a nightmare. The temperature fell well below zero and stayed there. With the wind chill factor figured in, the temperature dropped to a bitter forty or fifty below. We had to ride an hour or more each way in that kind of weather in an open buggy. Dressed in every piece of winter clothing that we owned, Currie and I huddled on the floor of the buggy beneath old quilts and trusted Trixie to get us to school and back again.

I could easily out-write and out-read almost everybody in my class, but I was cold and afraid and miserable so much of the time that I couldn't keep up with my studies. It was a terrible shock to my parents when I carried home the note from the teacher informing them that I had failed the grade.

Eventually, my mother decided that it was necessary to rent a little house in Texline in the winter so that Currie and I wouldn't have to make the long commute to school by horse and buggy. While my father struggled to save our homestead, Mother worked in town, baking occasional pies and pastries for extra funds, doing odd jobs about town, and caring for Currie and me. She was determined that we would get the best education possible, even if it meant being separated temporarily from my father.

The World of Books

Living in Texline during the school year made it possible for me to concentrate entirely on my reading. I borrowed books from the school library and from the personal library of our Southern Baptist pastor. I was especially fascinated with biographies.

Through books, I conquered Persia and India 323 years before Christ with Alexander the Great, the Macedonian general who laid the foundations for the Hellenistic world. I rode across the Italian Alps in 219 B.C.. with the North Africa's General Hannibal, his soldiers, and his elephants to ambush the Roman legions. I was an eyewitness at the assassination of Julius Gaius Caesar by his friend Marcus Brutus on the Ides of March, 44 B.C., and I was present at the coronation of Napoleon I, the "Little Corporal," in 1804.

But with the story of every great prince or king that I read, I became more and more fascinated with the story of Jesus, the Prince of Peace and King of kings. I read about the patriarchs—Abraham, Isaac, Jacob—who went before Him to found His people; about the prophets—Isaiah, Jeremiah, Ezekiel—who foretold His coming; about the kings of Israel—Saul, David, Solomon—who were His forefathers. I read the eyewitness accounts of those who followed Him—Matthew,

Mark, Luke, and John. I read about the great women of the faith—Sarah, Rachel, Esther, Deborah, Ruth, Lydia, Mary and Martha, Mary Magdelene, and Mary, His mother. I read the letters of Paul and the other apostles who helped Him plant and grow His church.

I heard the story of Jesus and the stories of those who believed in Him told over and over again during my young years in my home by my mother and my father, in church services, prayer meetings, revivals, and encampments. I attended the Baptist Young People's Union every Sunday and heard the stories again and again until they were written on my heart forever.

My fascination with God's Word did not go unnoticed. It was fun for me to read and memorize the Bible, but there were children in Texline who thought I was going too far, and they let me know it in no uncertain terms.

My First Sermon

"Here comes the little Bible Reader," George Abbott said with a sarcastic sneer as Currie and I walked past his front yard.

George lived one block away from the little house we rented in Texline. He was in my class at school and sat across from me in Training Union at our church. I thought he was my friend.

"Bible Reader!" he taunted. "Little old Bible Reader!"

I didn't say anything. I closed the distance between us in one quick step and hit him with a straight shot to the jaw. He sat down hard, scrambled to regain his footing, and charged at me headfirst like a wounded buffalo.

It was my first and last street fight. I don't think either one of us won the match. We punched and jabbed and swung at each other until an adult broke up the brawl and sent us home to our parents.

Poor George Abbott just couldn't understand why I was so eager to study the Bible. He must have grown tired of my jumping up in class to answer the teacher's questions and to quote long verses that I had learned. Even my father told me one day that I had "gone to seed on seriousness." I wasn't trying to impress or overshadow anyone. I just had a hunger to read the Bible from my earliest childhood. I don't remember when it began and I'm sure, now, that it will never end. Seventy years later, my hunger for God's Word still grows and grows.

The Bible has always been an endless source of comfort, guidance, and insight. I am happiest when I am reading and underlining in my Bible. I get restless when a day passes that I haven't had a chance to open and study the Word. I love to teach it and to proclaim it. In those childhood days, I suppose I seemed like a freak to other children like George Abbott, but there was nothing I could do but be true to the hunger for the Word that I felt deep inside of me.

And at least once, when I was still a little boy, having the Word hidden in my heart proved helpful even to poor George Abbott. It was upon the occasion of my first sermon. I was ten years old. For twenty-four hours my dog, Span, had been missing. George Abbott had joined in the search.

"Span!" we shouted across the empty prairie. "Span? Where are you, Span?"

For three hours we searched. Currie and I took turns calling out the name of our lively black cocker spaniel. He had disappeared the night before and we had walked for miles around Texline searching for him.

"Span!" I shouted again and again, my hands cupped against my lips, my ears tuned sharply for the slightest hint of Span's bark or cry, and my eyes searching the horizon for any sign of our missing pet.

We scoured the earth and couldn't find him. Finally, in a pasture east of Texline, we discovered Span's lifeless body. Someone had poisoned him. Currie cradled Span in his arms and wept angry, bitter tears.

"We'll get them," he said promising revenge. "Whoever did this will pay."

At the corner of the pasture was a tin shed. Cows rested beneath its shade during the heat of the day. A pile of boards and old planks lay nearby. We lay Span on a piece of wood and carried him home for burial. George and a handful of neighborhood boys and girls joined in that sad and solemn procession. When everyone was in place, the children, including George, looked to me.

"We're here to remember Span," I said, beginning the first sermon I ever preached. "It was a hateful thing to kill our little dog. But Jesus taught us that we must not hate the person who did it. Love your enemies," I said quietly, quoting Matthew 5:44.

The children nodded in agreement. Currie bit his lip and tried to forgive. We all stared down into the hole we had dug in the hard, dry earth. One little girl was crying.

"We all loved Span," I said, "and we thank God for him. We're going to miss our dog, but he's with Jesus now and one day we'll see him again."

We lifted Span's body from the little improvised stretcher and placed him in the ground. We covered him with buffalo grass and sunflowers. As each young mourner passed by Span's open grave, he or she dropped in a flower, a piece of wood, or a handful of soil.

"This is Span," the sign said that we tacked above his grave. "He was our dog and we loved him."

"Amen," I said.

"Amen," the children echoed.

"Amen," George Abbott chimed in and I could tell by the look in his eyes that he would never call me "Little Bible Reader" again.

"God Will Take Care of Us . . ."

I was ten years old. My brother, Currie, was eight. It was our first funeral, but it wasn't our first experience at saying good-bye. Our half-brother, Theo, and our half-sisters, Leona and Gladys Criswell and Edith and Ruth Glynn Criswell, had grown up, moved away, and were starting families of their own. We missed them.

It had all happened so fast. It seemed that one day we were one big happy family, and then suddenly only Currie and I were left. Joining three families into one hadn't been easy or painless. We had argued and fought, cried and made up. Currie and I had felt bullied, and though we were the smallest, we had exercised our own muscles against the crowd. But in Texline, we had become a family, united against the forces of nature that seemed determined to do us in.

The summers in Texline were as dry and deadly as the winters were cold and merciless. From the time we arrived in the Texas Panhandle, almost no rain had fallen. Every year we planted rows of beans and corn and sorghum. Every year the tiny sprouts fought their way up through the hard, dry ground. And every year they died in the merciless sun and strong, hot wind.

There were dust storms so fierce that we would awaken with dust in our mouths and half an inch or more covering our sheets and pillowcases. The worst dust storms were unforgettable. The wind would blow hard for days. Wherever a farmer had plowed or planted, the loose topsoil would lift up into the air, joining billowing clouds of dust that swept across the prairie, growing higher and higher like giant tidal waves until they towered thousands of feet into the sky.

One afternoon just after my father had finished planting the summer crops, a powerful northwestern wind struck without warning. As my father and I watched from the window of our cement house, the hundreds of little mounds of earth that he had so carefully shaped to cradle the seeds and to nourish them into life just disintegrated and disappeared, the clouds carrying the seeds and the land with them. When the wind stopped, I walked behind him out into the fields. He stood staring at the devastation. He was coughing up the dust and seemed to be having trouble with his breathing. I began to cry.

My father hadn't noticed that I was standing there until he heard my sniffles. Quickly, he knelt down beside me and put one arm around my shoulders. For a moment he didn't speak.

"Why does God do this to us?" I asked. "Why can't we have a good rain instead of all this wind and dust and disaster? Doesn't God care?"

My father never rushed to answer my questions. He was wise enough to leave them hanging there in the air just long enough for me to know how seriously he took them. And when he spoke, he chose his words carefully, afraid that my fresh faith might be blown away like his newly planted seeds.

"I don't know why, son," he answered. "I just trust God to take care of us."

Looking back now, with all my theological degrees and pastoral experience, I still don't think that I could improve upon his answer.

Texline Proved to Be God's Place

After bruising my father's body and soul for a few more years, the land he had homesteaded went back to the government. He lost everything but his faith that God would take care of us. I realize now that God not only took care of us, but that He also used those years in Texline to build into me a very hardy constitution that has served me well these sixty-plus years of ministry. We were poor. We lived through many mean seasons. But we survived and grew strong. And I have those long hot summers and desperately cold winters to thank.

Actually, little old Texline proved to be a wonderful place to spend my childhood. Those days on the northern prairies of the Texas Panhandle were exciting, growing times for me. I loved to ride bareback across the prairie, hanging on for dear life to my little pony. I loved to round up cattle with my father or even work alongside my mother in the kitchen, rolling out dough for pies or mixing batter for her hot, sugary cinnamon rolls. I liked to sneak away into the wilderness near our home to read the Bible, to think about my life, and to pray. And it was in Texline that I first fell in love with preaching.

My mother discovered that the wife of Mr. Sells, the man who ran the hardware store, had been an elocution teacher before she met her husband. Mother convinced her to teach me the "art of public speaking." We called it "declaiming" in those days, and from the time I was a little boy, I memorized poetry and prose, passages from Shakespeare and the Bible, and "declaimed" my heart out to my teacher, Mrs. Sells, with my mother a beaming audience of one.

"Louder, young man," Mrs. Sells would command from the back of a large empty room where we practiced. "Remember the lady in the back row who is half-deaf and the old man beside her who is sleeping."

"E-nun-ci-ate, Mr. Criswell," Mrs. Sells would interrupt again, jumping up from her seat and pacing about the room.

"Ev-e-ry syl-la-ble mussssttt be cle-ar!" she would demonstrate, twisting her face and lips into strange and wondrous forms.

"Breathe, boy, breathe," she commanded me. "Fill your lungs. Stand tall. Use your body to support each word. Pear-shaped tones, remember? Do you understand?"

"Yes ma'am," I answered quietly.

"Good boy," she would mumble returning to her seat. "Now, do it again!"

And I would take a deep breath, stand up tall, and start from the beginning. Finally, Mrs. Sells would relax, close her eyes, lean back, and listen as though I were singing an operatic aria or performing a piano concerto. And my mother, sitting next to Mrs. Sells, would glow with pride as the words flowed out of me and filled the room with their own special music.

It was also in Texline that I learned to play my beloved trombone. From earliest childhood I wanted to play an instrument, but there was never any money to buy one or pay for the lessons. Then, when Mother, Currie, and I moved into Texline, I got a job sweeping out the post office every day after school. Part of the five dollars a month that I earned went to buy a slide trombone from the Sears & Roebuck catalogue. It wasn't very shiny and the slide stuck slightly as I moved it up and down the scales, but it was a good starter instrument and the book enclosed was all I needed to teach myself to play. In the evenings I practiced my slide trombone until my brother ran from our rented house holding his ears and screaming with mock pain.

After I learned to read music from the hymnbook, the pastor invited me to play my trombone in the church. I played for offertories and accompanied the congregational singing. The more I played my trombone the more I loved to play it. But I began to long for a real brass and chrome trombone. I found pictures of the very best trombone in all the world, the Conn trombone made in Elkhart, Indiana. They cost forty dollars in those days, and it took me more than a year to earn and save enough money. And when my new horn finally arrived at the post office, the whole family gathered to help me unwrap it. I oiled the slide carefully. I polished the brass, shined the mouthpiece, and began to play. I loved that trombone immediately and dreamed of playing it in a high school or university marching band.

Texline, Texas, that little last outpost on the "edge of nowhere," proved to be God's perfect place for my growing-up years. It was in Texline that I found Christ as my Lord and Savior. It was in the Texline Southern Baptist church where I was baptized into a new life in Christ. It was in Texline that I preached my first sermon. And it was beneath a great, open-sided tent in the heart of town where I first dedicated myself to be a preacher.

The Call to Preach

"Good morning," said the charismatic young song leader as he bounded up on the platform. "My name is John R. Rice, and we've come to Texline for a good old-fashioned revival meeting."

I was twelve years old. I sat in the front row of a large tent that had been erected in an open lot near our house in Texline. I was fascinated by both the song leader and the silver-plated belt buckle that he wore inscribed with the image of a bear and a single word: Baylor.

"I'm from Baylor University," John R. Rice said proudly, "where the best Baptist preachers in the world are trained."

I can't describe the excitement I felt that day when Brother Whaley, pastor of the First Baptist Church in Memphis, Texas, began his two week revival in Texline, assisted by his energetic music man, the young John R. Rice. I felt like a minor league baseball player watching Ty Cobb or a movie fan in the presence of Charlie Chaplain or a young soldier meeting Black Jack Pershing face to face.

"Let's stand and sing 'Onward, Christian Soldiers,'" Rice exclaimed. The pianist played a short, enthusiastic introduction and John R. Rice lifted his arms to lead us in a rousing song.

I couldn't take my eyes off of Rice and his shiny silver buckle. One day I would go to that Baylor, "where the best Baptist preachers in the world are trained." One day I would stand behind a great pulpit and proclaim God's Word. One day . . . .

At the close of the first service, I rushed to the platform.

"Hey, kid, what's your name?" John R. Rice shouted, shaking my hand and leading me to the group of leaders standing around Brother Whaley.

"My name's W. A. Criswell, Jr.," I answered, "and I want to be a preacher, too, one day."

Rice walked right through the crowd of older men in animated conversation with Brother Whaley.

"This is W. A. Criswell, Jr.," Rice said, introducing me to our guest preacher, "and one day he's going to be a preacher, too."

"Sit down," Rice said, straddling a rough wooden bench and gesturing for me to join him. "You really want to be a preacher?"

"Yes, sir," I answered, "more than anything in the world."

"Are you sure?" he asked, leaning down toward me to effect a moment of confidence between us.

"Yes, sir, I am sure."

"Then you must come to Baylor," he said.

I couldn't take my eyes off that Baylor buckle. I decided then and there that one day I would have one exactly like it. And when I enrolled in Baylor just five years later, I did just that. I marched straight to the campus store, plunked down my money, and bought a Baylor buckle that I wore for many years.

John R. Rice spent at least an hour with me that day talking about Baylor and training for the ministry, about Bible classes and summer preaching missions, about being called, licensed, and ordained. It was all so new and exciting to me. I had never been to a large church or heard a great preacher. I had never seen a congregation with more than sixty or so people in it, and my mind whirled with the possibilities.

"Well, let's just turn this over to the Lord," John R. Rice said at the close of our conversation. Then he surprised me by kneeling beside that rough wooden bench and closing his eyes to pray.

"Father," Rice began, "this is W. A. Criswell, Jr., and he feels called to preach. Bless him, Lord. Guide his steps. Go before him a cloud by day and a pillar of fire by night. Make sure his call is true and use him in building Your kingdom. Amen."

Nobody had ever prayed for me like that. I was trembling.

"Do you have a Bible, Brother Criswell?" Rice asked as he got up from his knees and placed one hand on my shoulder.

"Yes, sir," I said showing him the well-worn Bible that I carried.

"It's the sword of the Lord," he said. "Keep it sharp. Keep it swinging."

"Yes, sir," I answered, realizing for the first time that there were other young people like me who hungered for the Word.

"Praise the Lord," Rice said, leaving me in that empty tent. "See you tomorrow."

The following morning I was right there again, fourth row center, wide-eyed in wonder, waiting for the next miracle in my young life.

"I'm going to invite everyone of you who feels called to full-time service to come forward this morning," Brother Whaley said at the close of his message. "Give God your life right here, right now."

The music played. The people sang. And suddenly, I was moving out into the aisle, walking down to the platform, and standing directly in front of John R. Rice and Pastor Whaley. I don't know exactly what I thought might happen that day as I answered the call to the ministry. Trumpet fanfares? Angel choirs? People cheering?

As I stood alone at the end of that sawdust trail, what did happen was disappointing to say the least. No one even looked in my direction. Not even John R. Rice noticed that I had come forward to present my life for full-time Christian service. Brother Whaley had jumped down from the platform and was rushing to embrace another man who had responded to the invitation.

"My dear brother," Whaley said, and the two men wept in each other's arms.

Our guest preacher's blood brother was a hard dirt farmer who lived in New Mexico not many miles from Texline.

"All my life I have run from God's call," the elder Whaley said as tears streamed down his weather-beaten face. "But today I'm going to quit running. Pray for me."

I stood near the platform alone and feeling really quite awkward. I was twelve. The elder Whaley must have been close to seventy. He was thin and haggard. His skin was wrinkled and burned from too many years of following the plow beneath the open sky. He walked with a severe limp, and his arms and hands trembled.

Brother Whaley was telling his brother's story in bits and pieces. The congregation was weeping and praising the Lord. John R. Rice led the people in a praise chorus. I slinked back to my seat wondering if God hadn't noticed me either.

That Sunday morning, everybody gathered to hear the preacher's brother, elder Whaley, preach his first and probably his last sermon.

Willie Amos and Anna Currie Criswell

He stood before us creaky and rheumatic. His voice was weak. His body bent. Never once did he look up at us. It was impossible to hear him past the front row, but the congregation strained to listen. It was moving and at the same time it was tragic.

Pastor Whaley and John R. Rice praised the elder Whaley for his courage. The congregation was polite and loving. It was a lesson that I will never forget. If you're going to serve the Lord, you sure better do it now, because when the day of grace passes, your opportunity is gone forever. If you're called to a ministry, large or small, answer the call! Don't postpone! Don't put off! Don't hesitate or make excuses! Don't wait another day, or you'll end up like that poor old farmer looking back at what might have been but now can never be.

The next morning, the tent was packed away, the benches disassembled, and the sawdust swept up and discarded.

"Good-bye, W. A. Criswell, Jr.," John R. Rice shouted at me from the Pullman door. "See you at Baylor," he added as the Fort Worth and Denver headed south.

I smiled and waved, but inside I felt a terrible sense of loss. The great meeting had ended. I had pledged my life to full-time Christian service and nobody had even noticed. Worse, when I told my parents I had been called to be a preacher, they just smiled politely and looked away. Plainly, they didn't like my decision. My mother wanted me to be a doctor like her father. My father had seen what congregations often do to preachers, and he didn't want it to happen to me.

The Pastor's Plight

Even as a child, I, too, had seen our local pastors suffer at the hands of their congregations. Almost always, the salary that the people paid their minister was not enough to live on. The pastor was regularly paid late, if at all. And more often than not, when there wasn't enough money in the treasury to pay the pastor, he was blamed for the dilemma. "The offerings have been low, Pastor. Times are hard, Pastor. You don't need that much anyway, Pastor."

To make matters worse, there were seldom any other benefits or allowances, no full- or part-time staff, no equipment or supplies, no office, and no vacation pay. And even worse, in those days, a congregation could fire a pastor on the spot, even in the middle of a Sunday morning service. Those confrontations were always heartbreaking and sometimes vicious.

I remember visiting a nearby congregation one Sunday morning when I was just a teenager. As the pastor stood to preach, a deacon who represented a majority of the congregation interrupted. The pastor sat back down near the pulpit in embarrassment, shock, and surprise. They made him sit there and listen while one by one the people said all kinds of terrible things about him. I could see the pastor's wife and son sitting in the front row of pews. The pastor's wife was crying. Her young son was trying to comfort her.

When I told my father what I had seen he grew silent. When he finally spoke, I understood better why he didn't want me to enter the Christian ministry. "I was chairman of the committee that had to fire Pastor Wilson," Father explained. Brother Wilson had succeeded Pastor Hill in our church in Texline. "It was horrible and I will never, never, never be a part of anything like it again."

"You'll be a doctor, like your grampa," Mother urged.

"Anything but a preacher," Father exclaimed. "I don't want to see you starved and cheated and embarrassed like so many pastors have been."

"Do It All in the Name of Jesus!"

Then Pastor Campbell came to pastor our church in Texline. He had fought with our British and French allies on the western front against Kaiser Wilhelm's forces in 1918. He was gassed by German shells while fighting in France under General Pershing. The gas had crippled Pastor Campbell, but he refused to be daunted by his handicap. His body stooped slightly and his gestures were stilted and strange. But he loved the Word and he preached it powerfully.

Pastor Campbell invited me to spend time with him in his little library in the parsonage. Books were piled everywhere. Besides the Bible and Bible commentaries, he read history, philosophy, and science. He loved Aristotle and Aquinas. He read Darwin, Freud, and even Marx. It was in his library that I read the stories of Hannibal, Alexander the Great, Caesar, and Napoleon. I also read the newspaper stories he had collected chronicling World War I battles and the stories of the fighting men and the politicians who won or lost the battles. He worried about the growth of communism in Russia and China and told me the story of Rasputin, the evil chaplain to Czar Nicholas II, and of the abdication and eventual assassination of Nicholas and the murder of his beautiful young family.

Brother Campbell brought the world to Texline. I often visited his library to borrow books or to discuss with him the books that I had read. He had an exciting mind. His thoughts tumbled out one on top of the other. He stood and paced when he got excited, words pouring out of him. He dreamed great dreams for Christ's church. And he admitted that pastors sometimes get "eaten by the sheep," but he praised my decision to be a preacher, and he encouraged me to pursue it with all my heart, soul, mind, and strength.

"Don't do anything halfway, Criswell," he said. "What you start, finish!"

He saw our Christian faith as warfare against the Evil One.

"World War I was nothing," he said, "by comparison to the battles that we Christians must fight and win for Christ's sake."

He saw laymen as foot soldiers and pastors as officers who led their troops into battle.

"In front of them, Criswell," he said, "not behind them. We are leaders, not followers. If we take the risks, the people follow and the battle is won. If we cower in the trenches, we lose the battle and the people die."

"In the name of Jesus, Criswell," he would say. "Do it all in the name of Jesus. And leave the rest of it in His hands!"

How often I've wondered if people like Brother Campbell who make so much difference in our lives ever really know it. In Texline there was the black porter who reached out his hands to help a young boy down off the Pullman steps. There was the generous grocer, Brother Downing; my elocution teacher, Mrs. Sells; my principal, Mr. Keith; the pastor from Memphis, Brother Whaley; and the enthusiastic song leader with the silver belt buckle from Baylor, John R. Rice.

There were my pastors, Brother Hill, Brother Wilson, and Brother Campbell, the workers in my Baptist Young People's Union, my teachers at the Texline all-grade school, and, of course, my mother and father, my half-brother and sisters, and my little brother, Currie. Each in his or her own way made a lasting difference in my life. I wonder if they ever really knew the difference they had made?

Fifty years after I moved away from Texline, Dr. Wallace Bassett, pastor of Cliff Temple Baptist Church in Dallas, and I were talking about my childhood conversion. "I was saved when I was ten in a revival meeting held by a Brother John Hicks," I told him.

"Johnny Hicks?" Dr. Bassett asked incredulously. "The pastor from up in the Texas Panhandle?"

"That's right," I answered, "from Dalhart, the county seat. He came to Texline to hold a week of meetings and he stayed in our home.

Of an evening, he would sit in my mother's kitchen, drink fresh buttermilk, and talk to me about Jesus."

"Johnny Hicks," Dr. Bassett said, shaking his head sadly. Then he told me a story that almost broke my heart.

"Just a few years ago," he said, "I visited my friend Johnny Hicks at Baylor Hospital here in Dallas. He was dying. And on his deathbed he said to me, 'Wallace, my preaching days are finished and I haven't done anything for Jesus.'

"I tried to comfort him," Dr. Bassett said, remembering that dark day. "But he would not be comforted."

For a moment we sat looking at each other in silence. Johnny Hicks pastored small churches in faraway towns. He never stood before great congregations or administered budgets in the millions. He probably never wrote a book, preached on a radio program, or had a television ministry. Nobody ever named a building in his honor or held a party to celebrate his life and ministry. And on his deathbed when he looked back on all those years, he felt as if he had been a failure.

"And you say that you were converted in John Hick's revival?"

"Yes," I answered softly, "I and so many others."

"Isn't that something," Dr. Bassett said to himself. "And the dear old man died thinking he had failed."

"In the name of Jesus, Criswell," Brother Campbell told me those many years ago. "Do it all in the name of Jesus. And leave the rest of it in His hands!"

4

The High School Years

Texline and Amarillo: 1923-1927

"Remember now thy Creator in the days of thy youth, while the evil days come not, nor the years draw nigh, when thou shalt say, I have no pleasure in them . . ."
Ecclesiastes 12:1

"OF COURSE YOU CAN'T GO SWIMMING," MY MOTHER said firmly.

I was a freshman in Texline High School in 1923. My fellow students were clinging to the last days of summer before the northwesters began to blow cold again, icing over swimming holes and blocking country roads with drifts of snow. Indian summer had struck with a vengeance that Saturday morning in September. A rancher's son had invited me to cool off with a swim in a man-made lake his father had built to water his cattle. I wanted desperately to swim with my friends and enjoy one last fling that summer.

"You might drown," my mother added in the quiet whisper that signaled the matter closed.

45

I didn't slam the door—though I felt like slamming it—and I didn't whine or protest. It wasn't my way. I just swallowed hard, walked to the room I shared with my little brother, and began to read.

My mother was tough. Let's face it. And because of her toughness, I led a rather sheltered childhood. I couldn't swim, play football, or wrestle because my mother didn't want me hurt. I couldn't go hunting, either. "You might get shot," she exclaimed. And I couldn't hang around with the boys from school. "You might pick up bad words," she warned, "and bad habits grow like weeds once they get their roots in."

My father was easier to convince, but he was four long miles away still trying to coax a crop from our homestead while my mother, my little brother, and I were living in a rented house in Texline, closer to the Southern Baptist church and our little high school.

I couldn't fight my mother's strict standards. It just wasn't in my nature to argue with her. Besides, she worked so hard to provide for us, I felt any kind of confrontation would have seemed like ingratitude. And at the bottom of it all, I loved her, and I didn't want to cause her any pain.

Texline High

Besides, there was plenty else to do those first two years in high school. On September 18, 1923, I was elected president of the freshman class. With classmates, I worked on freshman projects and benefits. I was often called to sing or to recite in school assemblies and to lead the little student body in our team's fight song, to the tune of "Barney Google."

> Texline High School is a school that can't be beat.
> Texline High School to the students is a treat.
> We bar no com-pe-ti-tion—
> We out-class them all and one.
> Texline High School is a school that can't be beat!

We didn't win any prizes with our anthem, but we sang with fervor and conviction. I also studied hard to earn a place each month on the high school scholastic honor roll. I played my trombone in the Texline High School orchestra and accompanied a three-act original comedy, "The Poor Married Man," to help raise money to send our girls' basketball team to the district championships in Tucumcari, New Mexico.

During my freshman year, I played forward on the boys' basketball team, in spite of mother's protest. Because physical education was required, basketball seemed "the lesser of the other evils." As a sophomore I won the regional "declaiming" meet in Canyon, Texas, and went on to capture the silver "declaiming" trophy in 1924 at the state meet in Austin. I also served as assistant business manager and then editor of the Texline High School news journal, "The Soapweed."

I hated the name, "Soapweed," and argued for its change. Actually it was a pseudonym for the beautiful yucca plant, common to that part of Texas. And though the yucca was tough and resilient and used for making rope, sandals, mats, and baskets, I was of the opinion that its nickname didn't lend itself to a strong newspaper masthead.

"A weed is a plant which persists in growing where it is not wanted," I said in the full debate that flared up around the change. "And though we have a strong constitution and can thrive in any atmosphere in which we are placed, we do not like to be classed as unwanted material."

Championing a new name for our little paper, I used my debating skills to see it adopted by my fellow students.

"The Nor'wester," I urged, leaning heavily on the school's team spirit, "is a strong wind which cannot be stopped." The students cheered. "Like our athletic and our declaiming teams, we will blow away the competition and bring honor to our school and to those who have gone before us."

And though I won that battle to rename our high school paper, I am still somewhat embarrassed by it. After all, it was those same nor'westers that blew away my father's dreams. During my freshman year, my father watched his last crop blown heavenward in a duststorm that roared through the countryside leaving devastation and heartbreak in its wake.

The Criswell Barbershop

"But we are together again," my father said the day our homestead was repossessed by government agents. "That is something!"

He hugged my mother, Currie, and me in the living room of our little rented house in Texline and urged us not to cry.

"I'll have a thriving barbershop in this town before the winter," he promised, and my father always kept his promises.

He had been cutting cowboys' hair every evening and on Saturdays to keep bread on his family's table. Country folk around Texline liked my father and were eager to see his barbershop established. Money was borrowed. A vacant building was rented and supplied, complete with brass spittoons and a red-and-white-striped barber pole. It wasn't long until my father's barbershop was once again at the center of a community's life.

Some late afternoons while I waited to sweep the post office and almost every Saturday, I was in my father's barbershop. How quickly it became the rendezvous point for farmers, ranchers, railroad men, shopkeepers, and traveling salesmen. The men would sit and talk for hours. They would listen to the news on my father's radio and then sit and argue while they smoked their cigarettes, chewed their tobacco, and stood to spit in the brass spittoon. My father swept and sharpened, cut hair, and shaved. He was quiet and really rather shy, but he knew just the right thing to say when the shop went silent or when a loud argument was moving toward a fistfight or a riot.

Our nation prospered. The stock market boomed. Calvin Coolidge was re-elected. But in Europe and America, the seeds for the Great Depression and World War II were already springing into life. Black Monday was just a few years away. Hitler's Nazis and Mussolini's Fascists would soon consolidate their evil hold on Germany and Italy. Once again, the world was drifting toward chaos. And once again, my father's barbershop was the most exciting place to be in Texline. Talk! Argue! Sit! Smoke! Chew! Spit! And day after day, I watched and listened and wondered where it all would end.

The Cimarron Canyon Encampment

My pastor in Texline, Brother Campbell, was one of the first people in memory who took seriously my call to preach. When I was barely in my teens, he took me to a Baptist encampment in the panhandle of Oklahoma, north of Boise City up there under the Black Mesa in Cimarron Canyon.

Southern Baptists came to Cimarron Canyon from Oklahoma, Texas, Colorado and New Mexico for a week of spiritual renewal. A few cabins dotted that rugged canyon landscape. Tents were pitched everywhere. People cooked their own meals on open fires and gathered in the open air to hear sermons, to study the Bible, to discuss issues of importance to the church, and to pray for revival and renewal.

In the afternoons, the people would divide into interest groups while the preachers met to talk church business. Brother Campbell assumed that I would meet with the young people to play horseshoes or hike down into the canyon. Instead, I followed him into the circle of preachers. No one seemed to notice me. The discussions about the Book of Genesis and the Scopes Trial, about J. Frank Norris and biblical interpretation got hotter and hotter. It felt like home.

"Isn't Norris right to raise the question about interpreting Genesis as an allegory?" I asked without even raising my hand. "Doesn't the Bible say what it means and mean what it says about Creation?"

My voice sounded a bit squeaky. The pastors all turned in my direction. Brother Campbell smiled.

"Meet Brother W. A. Criswell, Jr." he said. "It won't be the last time you hear from him."

Though I was just fourteen years old, the preachers accepted me as one of their own. I can't remember the name of the distinguished old pastor who was acting as convener during my first encampment in Cimarron Canyon. Brother Campbell told me that the man had been a very gifted preacher himself, but a stroke had left him partially paralyzed and unable to preach. Instead of becoming angry with grief and disappointment, that wonderful man spent his full time studying the Bible. His fellow pastors asked him to chair their discussions because he was so well grounded in biblical exegesis, Old and New Testament theology.

"Good work, young fellow," he said to me at the close of the encampment. "Brought back lots of memories," he added softly.

Then he paused for a moment, unable to continue. His left arm hung lifeless at his side as evidence of his stroke. With his right hand he pulled out a large white handkerchief and wiped his face. His eyes were damp with tears.

"Keep studying the Word," he said softly. "Don't let anybody keep you from it. You have the brains and the heart to be a good preacher. But don't be satisfied with skimming and scanning the Bible. The people are hungry for real food. Go all the way with your studies. Learn Hebrew and Greek. Give your life to the Word, and God will bless your preaching and give you a mighty harvest."

He paused again. Then he smiled, touched his right hand to my shoulder, and turned to go. I watched him as he made his way painstakingly down the rugged canyon pathway. Years ago when he was young and full of dreams, he, too, had answered God's call to ministry. The battles he fought for Christ had left him bruised and somewhat bewildered—but he had been faithful, and in his faithfulness, he had found joy. That day in the Cimarron Canyon I discovered again that God sends people into our lives just when we need them, to say the right word, His Word, just when we need it.

In those encampments of my youth, I learned so much from those dear preachers and evangelists who were often poor, always over-worked, often persecuted by their people and ridiculed or ignored by their community. These men of faith left upon me the impression of the reality of God, the glory of Christ, the truth of the Bible, the genuineness of our experience with the Lord, and the power of trusting in Him and in His Word.

Amarillo: 1925-1927

"We're moving to Amarillo," my mother announced upon my return from the encampment.

Somehow she had learned that Texline High School was not fully accredited. She was afraid that graduating from an unaccredited high school might keep me out of medical school. To my mother, nothing was worth that risk. She was determined that I was going to be a doctor like her father, and she would overcome any barrier that stood in the way.

"Your father will go on barbering and make plans to join us when he can," she announced firmly. "And I will move your brother and you immediately to Amarillo to enroll in Amarillo High."

It would be our second separation from my father. Amarillo was a hundred and twenty-five miles south of Texline, but that distance from the northwestern tip of the state to the heart of the Panhandle seemed a million miles between us. I could see that my father was trying hard not to weep as mother boarded the train for Amarillo and motioned us to follow.

Mother rented a large, two-story house in the heart of downtown Amarillo on the corner of Tenth and Polk. Immediately, she put a sign in our front window: "Room to Let." Then she walked to the nearby grocery store of Mr. Abe Saxtine where she bought apples, berries, and rhubarb and returned to our new home to bake three perfect fruit pies.

"Don't you touch them, boy," she said with mock ferocity. "I'm going to put you through your schooling with those three pies."

And she did. From that day on, Mother's Amarillo kitchen was always fragrant with the sweet smell of peeled apples, sliced peaches, and fresh berries topped by crusts of cinnamon, sugar, flour, and butter, baking and cooling and waiting for delivery. Still in their glass pie plates and covered lightly with a fresh cloth, those pies were delivered bubbling hot by Currie or me to a drug store just a few blocks away where they were served to grateful customers at a long counter by a pretty young woman dressed in a starched white uniform with a huge, pink handkerchief in her apron pocket.

With the money my father sent to her every month, with the income from her two second-story boarders, with the extra sewing and alteration work she took in, and with twenty-five cents a pie from the hundreds of pies she baked and sold, my mother had just enough money for her tithes and offerings, our rent and utility bills, and to send Currie and me through Amarillo High School.

Public Speaking and Debate

On our first Sunday in Amarillo, we joined the First Baptist Church on Ninth and Polk. Dr. G. L. Yates was the pastor there. On a good Sunday, attendance reached nine hundred souls. The excitement I felt sitting with my mother and Currie in the front rows of that great church cannot be described. When the organ played and the choir stood to sing, I felt an electric charge that started in my toes and set my hair on end. When Dr. Yates stood to preach, I opened my Bible to his text. I wrote down his every point. And at the close of each service when he gave the invitation to come forward to confess faith and join the church, my heart beat with the anticipation of what might happen.

Mother urged Currie and me to join the Baptist Youth Training Union the Sunday we arrived in Amarillo. It was 1925. I was fifteen years old, called to preach, trained in public speaking, and dying to try my wings. On July 21 that same summer, the Scopes "Monkey" trial had ended. John Scopes was found guilty for teaching Darwinian evolution. Five days later, William Jennings Bryan, the man who had defended a literal interpretation of Genesis with eloquence and power, died of a cerebral hemorrhage. I felt the loss personally, and when it came my turn to stand up before the Training Union class and deliver the message, I opened up both guns on "modernism" and "evil-lution," quoting Old and New Testament passages from memory, defending with all my powers the literal interpretation of Scripture.

I didn't notice that the door was open just a crack. And I didn't hear until years later that the educational director and a visiting preacher were listening in.

My ability to stand before a crowd and speak passionately gave me a wonderful open door. Almost immediately after enrolling in Amarillo High School, I was accepted on the debating team. A fellow named Donald Honey was my partner, and we specialized in such esoteric subjects as child labor laws and prohibition. Donald and I represented Amarillo High School successfully in debating convocations in Abilene, Wichita Falls, and Lubbock. Several clubs in

Amarillo invited me to speak at their meetings. One by one, other trophies were added to my mother's shelf to stand beside the silver Loving Cup I won in declaiming at West Texas College while I was still a student in Texline.

"You are a gifted speaker, young man. We could use you in my office."

I had just finished a Rotary Club address in Amarillo. The meeting had ended with a song and the clanging of a brass bell. Everyone applauded and headed for the exits of the hotel ballroom. I was about to step down from the platform when a tall, distinguished gentlemen reached up to shake my hand.

"Thank you, sir," I answered, looking first into his eyes and then at the Rotary name badge he wore on his lapel.

He was the senior partner in a very prestigious law firm.

"How about a little chat?" he added, pulling out a chair and motioning for me to join him.

He introduced himself quite cordially, complimented me again on my speech, and told me about his law firm. I didn't know where the conversation was going, but the man was persuasive and I listened with growing interest.

"I want you to think seriously about becoming a lawyer," he said finally. "My firm will send you to law school and pay your room, board, and tuition. All you have to do in exchange is to spend your summers as one of our law clerks and seriously consider joining our firm when you graduate."

I was surprised and taken aback by his generous offer. He was obviously sincere and taking a real risk on a sixteen-year-old high school kid still wet behind the ears. I thanked him for his confidence in me.

"But God has called me to be a preacher," I said proudly. "I am grateful for your offer and flattered by it, but there's no way under heaven that I could even think about accepting it."

For a moment it was his turn to be surprised. But it turned out that he, too, was a Christian, a good man and devout in his beliefs.

"Well, well," he said, speaking slowly and looking directly into my eyes. "I think I've been turned down."

"Yes, sir," I said, "but...."

"That's all right," he interrupted. "I think I understand. You are giving your life to a greater calling than the law, young man. May God bless you in it!"

John Philip Sousa and Will Rogers

After public speaking, my second love in Amarillo was playing my shiny brass Conn trombone. In spite of my mother's gentle objections and her nightly nudge to concentrate on my English and literature major, I played in three bands at the same time: the Amarillo Municipal Band, the YMCA Hi-Y Band, and the Amarillo High School Marching and Concert Band.

One of the greatest moments of my two years in Amarillo came the night I joined the massed bands of Central Texas in the Amarillo Civic Auditorium to play first trombone in a concert conducted by the March King himself, Mr. John Philip Sousa. Our own directors rehearsed us for hours the day before, and again when we assembled before the concert. Then, just before the auditorium doors were opened, John Philip Sousa marched into the room wearing an all-white uniform complete with gold braid and bright red trim.

The moment the maestro walked out onto the stage, every member of the massed bands stood as one and began to shout and applaud, whistle and cheer. Sousa was seventy-five years old, already a legend as America's greatest bandmaster and composer of military marches. He was trim as a young athlete and stood before us ramrod straight. He had pure white hair and a bushy white mustache. He bowed as a Prussian general might bow, tolerated our applause only briefly, and then tapped his long white baton against the lead clarinetist's music stand.

We jumped back into our chairs, tuned our instruments carefully, and sat at attention waiting for his command.

"Tonight," he said, "we celebrate the music! Play with all your heart. Hold nothing back! Nothing!"

For a moment he looked at us rather sternly through his rimless glasses. I felt shivers run up and down my spine. This was the composer of the greatest military marches in U. S. history—"Semper Fidelis," "The Washington Post," "Stars and Stripes Forever." His music had mobilized a nation during World War I and set a million feet marching against the kaiser and his forces. This was one of the last concerts he would conduct before his death in 1932, and there was both the joy and the sadness in the old man's face. I was afraid that I couldn't see the music through the tears of excitement that were forming in my eyes.

Suddenly, the maestro mounted the little conductor's platform. Quickly he scanned the face of every young man and woman in that massed concert band, tapped his baton, raised both hands above us, and with a twist of his wrist, almost two hundred young musicians were filling that huge auditorium with the martial sounds of "Stars and Stripes Forever." In the concert that night, when the last fanfare sounded, more than a thousand parents and friends leaped to their feet in a grand applause. The musicians joined in the standing ovation. Somewhere out beyond the footlights, my mother was standing with the crowd. And when I found her later, her eyes were still rimmed with tears.

During my senior year at Amarillo High School in that same auditorium, my classmates and I were privileged to attend a special performance by Will Rogers, America's "Cowboy Philosopher." Rogers was another of this nation's living legends. When I was sixteen, I had read his syndicated weekly column in the Amarillo newspaper, and over the years I had enjoyed all three of his witty, sometimes off-color, but always pointed and perceptive books, *Rogerisms: The Cowboy Philosopher on Prohibition* (1919), *Illiterate Digest* (1924), and *There's Not a Bathing Suit in Russia* (1927). I sat in the front row of that auditorium with my notepad in hand, studying his classic style.

"So, you've come to hear some jokes," Will Rogers said to us, standing on the stage in his battered boots, leather chaps, crisp white shirt, bright red bow tie, and beat-up cowboy hat.

"I'm sorry to disappoint you," he continued after the applause died down, speaking in his quiet drawl, twirling his old rope and preparing to unleash his new stories as he blinked out at us over the bright lights.

"I don't make jokes," he explained. "I just watch the government and report the facts."

The Speakers and the Preachers in My Life

Just a few years after his performance in Amarillo, Will Rogers was killed with the famous pilot Wiley Post in a plane crash in Alaska enroute to the Orient. Rogers was just one of the dynamic public figures who may have influenced my speaking style during those formative high school years. Over the radio I had listened with fascination to the measured, low-key cadence of Woodrow Wilson; the brilliant and impassioned rhetoric of William Jennings Bryan; the angry, sullen strength of Clarence Darrow; the witty, winsome, sometimes wicked Will Rogers. But in fact, all my real heroes were Texas preachers, and while a student in Amarillo I got to hear the best of them.

Almost every Sunday I sat in a pew near the front of the First Baptist Church in Amarillo to hear my pastor, Dr. G. L. Yates, a very fine biblical exegete and expositor. His sweet spirit, his broken heart, his loving commitment to me and to my ministry was one of God's great gifts.

The preaching of Dr. L. R. Scarborough, the president of South-western Baptist Seminary, also made a deep and lasting impression. He was a guest preacher in Amarillo several times during my two years in high school there. Scarborough was a distinguished scholar and at the same time brought the ancient Word to life for me. I was always surprised that a man with such academic achievement could also preach with passion and even a sense of humor. Unlike Dr. Yates, who never moved from behind the pulpit, Dr. Scarborough paced back and forth, holding his Bible in one hand and gesturing with the other.

At the Palo Duro encampment near Amarillo, I heard Wallace Bassett preach for the first time just after our move from Texline. He was the biggest, most handsome, and most moving preacher I had ever seen in my young life, and I loved to listen to him. I was fifteen that first summer in Amarillo, but I remember to this day Brother Bassett's sermon from Ecclesiastes. The wisest man in the world, old King Solomon, sets out to find happiness. He tries this. He tries that. And he tries the other. Finally, Solomon comes to this conclusion: the best thing in life is to love God and to keep His commandments. What a sermon! I felt like applauding when it ended. Solomon came to life for me. For that whole encampment, I was a Wallace Bassett groupie, following that dynamic preacher around from event to event, questioning him like a reporter, writing down every word he said.

During the next summer in Amarillo, a Hi-Y band tour to the state YMCA convention in Fort Worth gave me the chance of my young lifetime to hear the preacher my mother had "roasted" at many a family supper. Our band was chosen to lead the Sunday afternoon parade of young delegates through the streets of Fort Worth. It had been one of my life dreams to visit the Fort Worth Baptist Church to hear the controversial J. Frank Norris in his own pulpit before his own people. And though my mother found it difficult to believe that I would go to all that trouble to hear "the devil incarnate" preach to his "poor, misled people," she wrote a note to our bandmaster granting me permission for the Sunday morning excursion.

The First Baptist Church in Forth Worth was packed with people, young and old, rich and poor. The excitement was electric, filling the room. I had to sit near the back, and I can still remember the pipe organ playing the prelude and the great massed choir singing a call to worship. As the anthem's "amen" echoed through the church, Norris walked dramatically onto the platform and stood silently beside the pulpit. He was wearing a beautiful double-breasted suit, but the jacket was unbuttoned, the suit unpressed. He looked casual, even sloppy, but he commanded attention, and immediately upon his entrance, the people grew silent. No one moved.

Norris spoke softly at first. Everyone leaned forward in the pews, straining to hear his words. Sixty-three years later, I can still remember that sermon. Norris was preaching on the evils of sin. Before the message ended, I could smell the acrid smoke and feel the burning coals of hell. I could see sinners who had rejected God's love twisting in agony and I could hear them moaning in pain and desolation. When Dr. Norris gave the invitation, the aisles filled instantly with men and women, boys and girls, all weeping, all moving forward to pledge their lives to Christ.

During those days, J. Frank Norris was alienating the leadership of almost the entire Texas Baptist Convention, but he could preach with such power that even his critics were momentarily stunned into silence. I was sixteen. I didn't cry in public in those days, at least not very often, but after J. Frank Norris preached, as the organ played and the choir sang the invitation, I stood there and cried like a baby.

Of all the great Texas Baptist preachers, no one influenced my life any more than the great George W. Truett, pastor of First Baptist Church of Dallas. I heard him preach for the first time when I was just thirteen years old and my family still lived in Texline. That summer of 1922, my mother took Currie and me to Amarillo to visit her eldest daughter, Edith Guthrie, a pianist at First Baptist Church in Amarillo.

Already, Dr. Truett was one of my childhood heroes. I had read with schoolboy excitement of the great man's recent preaching tour of Europe, where he had been invited to proclaim God's Word to thousands of American soldiers in mass services under the open skies and to the people of occupied Germany in their great Lutheran churches and cathedrals. Dr. Truett was widely known and respected throughout Texas and the nation for his work at First Baptist, for his revival meetings around the world, for his unique ministry since 1902 at the annual Cowboy Roundup in West Texas, preaching every year to thousands of cowboys, wealthy ranchers and farmers, and for his preaching at the great pre-Easter noonday services before thousands of people in the Palace Theater in Dallas.

I remember passing Dr. Truett in the corridors of the church in Amarillo when I was thirteen. My heart raced with excitement when he shook my hand and said, "God bless you, son." The next summer I saw him again at the Texas State Convention in Amarillo. My sister Edith had a new baby. Again, Dr. Truett was walking through the hallway, surrounded by an entourage of denominational officials, when he spotted my newborn niece, put his hands upon the child, and said quite sincerely, "What a precious baby!"

The third time I saw Dr. Truett was during my senior year at Amarillo High School. He was making a dramatic appeal to the Texas Baptist Convention on behalf of Baylor University. By the time the pledges were made and the offering taken, I was more convinced than ever that one day I would be a Baylor student preacher just like George W. Truett. Even as he spoke, I thought again about Baylor student John R. Rice and the silver buckle he had worn in that tent meeting in Texline, and about the excitement I had felt during my own call to ministry.

High School Commencement

My elementary and high school years were shaped almost entirely by my family and the Southern Baptist churches in which I grew up. During those years I thought the nation was divided into two main groups: Baptists and all others. And I was convinced that Southern Baptists were the only Baptists in the world. Southern Baptist churches, schools, seminaries, retreats, encampments, and denominational gatherings were my universe. Southern Baptist preachers were my heroes, my models, my teachers, and my friends.

I didn't see my father much during my junior or senior years. I had school for nine months, and I worked summers first as a delivery boy for Abe Saxtine, my mother's wonderful Jewish grocer, then in the wholesale department of the J. I. Case Threshing Machine Company, and finally as a soda jerk at the Green and Green Drug Store near our home on Polk and Tenth. Currie and I both traveled with the Hi-Y and high school bands. Currie played the clarinet and had become a skillful declaimer himself. Mother had her pie business to maintain, her boarders to care for, and her sewing and alteration business on the side. Currie had an early morning paper route with more than a hundred and fifty newspapers to deliver. There just wasn't time or money to make the trip to Texline.

Finally, in 1927, my father closed his barbershop in Texline and moved to Amarillo. He began the third barbershop of his career, after Eldorado and Texline, in the San Jacinto district of Amarillo. It was good to have him home again, just in time for my high school graduation.

What a year that was! Babe Ruth broke all records with his sixtieth home run in one baseball season. Gene Tunney defended his world heavyweight crown against Jack Dempsey in a fight that almost caused a riot in my father's new barbershop. Henry Ford produced his fifteen millionth "Tin Lizzie," the indomitable Model-T. Cecil B. de Mille released his biblical spectacle, the motion picture *King of Kings*. (It would not have crossed my mind to see it then. It was the same year that Al Jolson's *The Jazz Singer* introduced the "talkies," and movies of every kind were strictly off limits to Southern Baptist boys, even seniors in high school.) On May 21, 1927, Charles Lindbergh completed the first solo airplane flight from New York to Paris in his plucky little monoplane, "The Spirit of Saint Louis." Just days later, wearing a dark blue cap and gown, I joined two hundred of my classmates in the Amarillo Civic Auditorium for our high school commencement exercises.

The four of us walked home from graduation together as a family. My father seemed especially proud of my academic accomplishments. My mother was pleased, but determined that in college I would do even better. I had not graduated with special honors. I had not delivered the commencement address. I had not won a major scholarship to college. But my grades were high and my accomplishments in music, debate, journalism, and public speaking had to count for something.

"I'm proud of you son," my father said as we walked up the stairs and across the porch into our little living room.

My mother didn't say anything. She just walked into her sewing room, rummaged in her closet, and returned with a shiny black Remington typewriter cradled in her arms. Suddenly, that little sewing and alteration business that my mother had maintained "on the side" made perfect sense. The Great Depression was just months away. Our family was dirt poor, but my mother had toiled late at night and early in the morning to buy me a brand new typewriter for the coming years of study at Baylor in preparation for my coming work.

"You're going to need it, son," she said. "Pre-med studies require a lot of writing and research."

I hugged my mother gratefully, knowing even then that one day soon she would have to give up her plans for me to become a doctor like her father. She knew of my plans but refused to take them seriously. And she was working so hard to see her dreams for me come true. I didn't know how I would ever have the courage to disappoint her. At the same time, I knew that God had called me to preach, and I was determined to answer God's call.

5

The Freshman Year at Baylor University

Waco: 1927-1928

"Yea, though I walk through the valley
of the shadow of death, I will fear no evil:
for thou art with me . . ."
                                    Psalm 23:4

LICENSED TO PREACH

My mother had scouted all the major Texas colleges and universities on my behalf. She had written, telephoned, and even visited campuses, including Baylor, trying to determine which school offered the best pre-med training programs. She had read through dozens of letters, catalogues, and brochures. What a relief it was when Baylor University was included on her final list. ·

My mother was an unusual woman. During my childhood and youth, she was totally committed to my education. Had Mother decided that I should go to any of those other schools that she investigated, I suppose I would have done it, even though I was determined to go to Baylor and lobbied days without end to get my mother to agree.

Finally, she threw up her hands and smiled with mock surrender. I hugged her and thanked her for agreeing on Baylor. In fact, she had returned from her trip to Waco as committed to Baylor as I had been.

"Why not?" she said smiling. "They have the best pre-med training in the whole country."

I nodded enthusiastically.

"And their preaching program isn't bad either," she said under her breath, "not that I know about such things."

My mother hoped with all her heart that I would follow in the footsteps of her doctor father. She did everything she could to pass her dream on to me, but in the end she gave me freedom to decide for myself.

The pre-registration papers were mailed. I was accepted as a Baylor freshman early in the summer of 1927. In July, Pastor Yates and a committee of deacons interviewed me. Two weeks later, the pastor called me to his office.

"Brother Criswell," he said, "I have good news. The deacons and I have decided to license you for ministry."

For two years the pastor had been watching me. Through a half-open door, he had heard me speak to the Youth Training Union. Businessmen in our congregation had told him about my speeches to the Rotary and Kiwanis clubs. A teacher at Amarillo High School informed him about my debate team victories. Earlier, Pastor Yates had questioned me at length about my call to preach. Finally, just before I enrolled in Baylor, he was ready to honor that call.

"To be a student preacher you must preach," the pastor said, leaning forward in his chair and smiling broadly. "And to preach you must have a license from your local church." He reached for an envelope on his desk and handed it to me. "It is with great confidence, W. A. Criswell, Jr., that I have the honor of awarding you that license on this very day."

"Thank you, sir," I replied, taking the envelope in my hand and holding it tightly.

We had prayer together and then I bolted from the room. Just outside the pastor's office on Polk Street in the shade of a clump of elm trees, I tore open the envelope, unfolded the single sheet enclosed, and read the thirteen lines typed on that First Baptist Church of Amarillo stationery.

"This certifies that Brother W. A. Criswell is a member of the First Baptist Church of Amarillo in good and regular standing and is held by us in high esteem. We believe him to have been called of God

W. A. Criswell as a young pastor in Texas

to the work of the gospel ministry, and do hereby give him our entire and cordial approbation in the improvement of his gifts by preaching the gospel, as providence may afford him opportunity. And we pray the great Head of the Church to endow him with all needful grace and crown his labors with abundant success. Done by the order of the church in conference this the 27th day of July 1927."

At the top of the single sheet in bold letters was the word LI-CENSE. At the bottom were the signatures of the pastor, G. L. Yates, and the congregation's clerk, J. M. Cook.

I ran up the stairs of our home in Amarillo waving that priceless document and shouting with delight. I was seventeen years old and I was officially licensed to preach. My parents smiled politely and then looked away. They loved me very much, but they couldn't understand this "preoccupation with preaching."

"You've gone to seed on seriousness," my father said, patting me on the back, urging me to enjoy my youth while I had it. It wasn't the first time he had said it.

There was nothing I could do about it, really. I was born serious. I never joked. In fact, I was slow to recognize a joke when somebody told one, and the puzzled look on my face often made the others laugh even harder. People liked me, but they never saw me as a good ol' boy or a hail fellow well met.

My father may have been right. I may have "gone to seed on seriousness" from a very early age. It was certainly true that I didn't have a gift for "wasting time." Occasionally I went to a Sunday school class party, and when it seemed absolutely necessary I played a game of "flinch" or "bunko" with my friends. But mainly I went to school. I participated in class discussions. I played my trombone in the band or orchestra. I helped edit the school paper and was a member of the debate and public speaking teams.

At home, I studied and did my chores. I practiced my trombone. I read and underlined in my Bible and I prayed. Every time the doors were open, I went to church. My life was shaped almost entirely by the church. I hardly remember a day in my childhood or my youth when I didn't feel called to preach, and I don't remember a day when I wasn't determined to be faithful to that call.

Baylor University

I was still seventeen that summer of 1927 when my mother, Currie, and I moved to Waco. My mother was determined to stay with me during my first year at the university. She was hoping to point my academic career "in the right direction." My father stayed on in Amarillo, supporting us with earnings from his barbershop. Currie was a third-year student at Waco High School. He continued playing his clarinet in the high school band.

When we arrived in Waco that afternoon late in August, it was hot enough to fry toast on the asphalt roadways. Undaunted by the heat or the humidity, my determined mother marched from the train station to a large, two-story house that she had arranged to rent on Waco's main street just up from the Brazos River. Once again, she placed a "Rooms to Let" sign in our front window, and within a day or two she had rented out every extra room in the house to boarders, sparing only a small bedroom above the kitchen for herself and a larger bedroom with a study area for Currie and me.

We rode a horse-drawn trolley out past Sand Town on the Brazos River to the Baylor campus on Fifth Street and Speight Avenue. The university campus was composed of just four main buildings then, clustered in a quadrangle around the old Burleson statue, surrounded by a neighborhood of homes, a school, and several churches. My mother and I stood side by side in silence in the shade of a large pecan tree. Squirrels chased each other noisily up and down the trunk and the widely spreading branches. A few Baylor students wandered by carrying new books and registration forms.

"That must be Carroll Science Hall," my mother said pointing to her right at a three-story, yellow brick building on the corner of Fifth Street and Speight Avenue. "The college of medicine is in Dallas," she said, "but I think the pre-med studies are taught in the Carroll Science Hall."

Mother was looking at a simple map on the back of Baylor's thin catalogue. The school had been chartered in 1845 by the Republic of Texas. By 1927 there were nine hundred students enrolled on the Waco campus.

"That building with the flat-topped dome must be the library," she said, looking to her left across the Baylor Quadrangle.

In the center of the campus, Old Main loomed four stories above us, elegant, stern, professorial, a yellow-bricked, white-towered edifice with arched doors and windows, pillared garrets, watchtowers, and pointy roofs topped with crosses and lightning rods.

We picked up my registration papers, walked past Georgia Burleson Residence Hall, and stood before the large, white, wood-framed chapel where several thousand people had gathered just a few months earlier to remember the "Immortal Ten," members of Baylor's basketball team who had been killed when their bus collided with a train near Austin. The doors were closed. But we could hear the sound of a piano playing a hymn and a quartet of student voices practicing for the opening chapel service.

In the library bookstore, we bought used textbooks for my courses in English, literature, history, science, and Bible. I think I had most of them read and underlined in that next week, before the fall term even began.

I still remember how my heart raced with anticipation as we walked back across the campus. I thought Baylor was the most glorious place I had ever visited. The entire quadrangle couldn't have covered more than four or five blocks in the heart of that quiet residential neighborhood in Waco, but I knew that over the next four years God was going to do something wonderful in my life in that exciting place. I couldn't wait for classes to begin.

On Sunday, mother and I walked forward at the close of the service to join the Baptist church on Seventh and James Streets. Soon after, the pastor appointed me the leader of Training Union class for seventeen-year-old boys.

"Shall we pray!"

On Monday, September 5, 1927, in Baylor's wooden chapel, I heard the booming voice of Dr. Samuel Palmer Brooks for the very first time.

"Oh, Lord, we are Your children," he prayed. "We are here because You have called us to be here and to do Your work in this place."

Dr. Brooks was the president of Baylor. He was a big man, heavyset and balding, with a thick brown mustache. He wore double-breasted suits with starched, breakaway collars and wide silk ties. His gold wire-rimmed glasses sometimes slid precariously close to the end of his nose when he began to sweat. His demeanor was stern and professional, but I thought him saintly.

"Lord, thank You for the comfort of Your presence during these last tragic days. Now, fill this place and these students with Your joy. In Jesus' name, amen."

Every morning, Dr. Samuel Brooks conducted chapel services for the entire Baylor family. He announced the hymns. He prayed the prayers and read the Scriptures. There were guest preachers and evangelists invited to address us from time to time, but it was usually Dr. Brooks who led us in our morning meditation. He was not a preacher. But he was a scholar, thoughtful and devout, and a Christian layman who knew his Bible better than most preachers. His words in chapel made my heart beat fast and my spirit soar. He spoke with prophetic urgency. Dr. Brooks was a magnificent Christian leader and an example to us all.

Dr. J. Henry Trantham was another inspiration to me. He taught history and Greek at Baylor. He was a brilliant man who walked into class just as the bells would ring, and without any wasted words he would begin his lecture on the fall of Rome or the origins of the industrial revolution, quoting from memory hundreds of names, dates, and places, never glancing at an outline or a text. History was his story and he knew it age by age, exactly as he knew his own life and times.

Although I can't remember all my teachers' names from that first year at Baylor, I do remember the excitement I felt entering their classrooms and sitting at their feet. But I was called to preach, and you don't learn preaching out of books or in the classroom. You learn to preach by preaching. So, I joined the Baylor Volunteer Band that first week of school and got involved in ministry.

Actually, the Volunteer Band was organized by students who were studying to be missionaries. They met once a week to hear guest missionaries speak or to visit with students from other nations. The

Volunteer Band prayed for missionaries. They raised money to provide missionaries with travel and support funds. They read and discussed letters, reports, books, and journals from missionaries around the world. I met many of my closest friends in those Volunteer Band meetings: Baker James Cauthen, Eloise and Lois Glass, and perhaps my best friend, Christy Poole. The times we spent together were informative and inspiring, but they didn't offer me a chance to preach, and I longed for that day.

Sand Town on the Brazos

One afternoon I was walking on a pathway near the Brazos River, just north of the Baylor campus. I was thinking about preaching and wondering if I would ever get a pulpit of my own.

Suddenly, I found myself on the edge of Sand Town, Waco's largest slum built on an alluvial plain along the shores of the Brazos. Most students skirted Sand Town, a large collection of shanties, shacks and old, dilapidated houses built on damp, marshy, mosquito-ridden ground. The once-paved streets of Sand Town lay rutted, pot-holed, and precarious. Most of the little paths and alleys were made of dirt packed down by horses, wagons, and the feet of a thousand poor people, black, white, and brown.

Guinea hens screeched and ran away clucking as I entered the area. Shotgun houses, approximately fourteen by twenty-four feet, were crammed together side by side. Built of used planks for walls and rusty tin for roofs, the long, narrow houses were partitioned inside for three rooms, each holding at least one family. They were called shotgun houses because with the front and back doors open, a 12-gauge shotgun could be fired down the long hallway without hitting anything.

People wearing torn overalls and feedsack dresses sat on front porch steps or on abandoned furniture in the street and stared up at me blankly. Little children, knee-deep in mud, faces splashed and dirty, stopped playing to watch me pass. I smiled eagerly. No one smiled back.

Inside a broken-down storefront, young black men sat around a bright red Coca-Cola icebox, savoring the cool rush from the melting ice. They watched warily as I passed, their animated conversation cut short by my accidental visit. From a building just off the main street, I heard a muffled shout. Then the loud groans of several men filled the air, followed by the sound of fists banging on a table and loud, raucous laughter. Then the street grew silent once again. I later learned that the little outburst came from a row house that doubled as a gambling joint. The men must have been playing cards. Someone drew a winning hand.

An old white woman sat in a rocking chair on the edge of Sand Town cooling herself with a large white paper fan printed with the advertisement of a local mortuary. She smiled at me.

"Good afternoon," I said.

"Praise the Lord," she replied. I was not surprised. The woman had an old King James Bible in her lap. She was leaning forward and staring at the Bible in my hand.

"Well, I'll be," she said quietly. "The Lord gives and the Lord takes away."

The little gate to her picket fence was broken and hung on one rusty hinge.

"Come in, child," she said. "Come in and sit by me."

I remember thinking that old woman must have been at least a hundred years old. Her skin was dark brown from the hot Texas sun and deeply wrinkled. Her eyes sparkled as she watched me approach.

"You've come to talk about Jesus, haven't you," she said.

"Why, yes," I answered. "I'm a Baylor student. Gonna be a preacher one day."

"Well, well," she said, "why not today?"

"I don't have a church yet," I replied quickly, sitting down beside her on the porch. "Don't have a pulpit to pound."

She grinned. I was amazed at myself. Maybe my father was wrong. Maybe I hadn't "gone to seed on seriousness." I had told a kind of joke and it had made the old woman smile.

"Son," she said, not smiling any longer. "You've got no time to wait for a church or for a pulpit. These people need Jesus now."

She stared at me, her eyes brimming with tears, her hands trembling.

"I'm going to die one of these days soon," she said and her voice was no more than a crackling whisper. "But I've prayed and prayed that the Lord would let me live until a preacher came to take up my burden for this place."

The old woman took my right hand in her hands and began to pray.

"O Lord, Jesus," she said. "Thank You for this young man and for his ministry among us. Bless him, Jesus. Bless him!"

She lay back against her rocker and smiled at me through her tears. I thought she might speak again, but she just lay there patting my hand and smiling. Finally, I thanked her for her prayers and promised that I would visit her again.

"The Lord gives and the Lord takes away," she had said. And I remembered ten young athletes on the Baylor bus and a craggy old woman sitting in her rocking chair on the edge of Sand Town and Brother Hicks who led me to the Lord and then died thinking he had never made a difference.

From that day, almost every afternoon between the time my classes ended and sunset, I walked up and down the streets of Sand Town, knocking on doors, introducing myself and asking if the person who answered would like to talk about Jesus. When I stumbled on a little crowd, young men around the Coke machine, women watching their children near the Brazos, workers eating cold fried chicken and chitlins under the pecan trees, I just opened my Bible and preached the Word. And so many people, young and old, men and women, black, white, and tan, gave their lives to Jesus as we talked. Never once was I rejected. Never once did anyone threaten or belittle me.

After a few weeks, the old woman just disappeared.

"She up and died," a young neighbor girl told me one afternoon that winter. "And her people done took her away."

"The Lord gives and the Lord takes away," she had said.

When I was just seventeen in Sand Town, that slum on the Brazos River, I discovered again that nobody needs a church to preach. Nobody needs a pulpit to stand behind. The world is waiting to hear the Good News of the gospel. And what a glorious thing it is to share that Good News wherever God may place us!

Old Deacon Stovall

During my freshman year at Baylor, Ralph Cooley, a senior preaching student, took me under his wing. He served a tiny, little church out in Bell County not far from Temple, Texas, and he invited me to lead the singing and occasionally to even take his place in the pulpit. I led the singing for Ralph's first revival meeting in his little church. Other student preachers came to support Ralph's meetings, saw me leading the singing, and then weeks or months later would ask me to lead the singing in their revival meetings. Suddenly, I was afraid that my career was heading away from preaching and toward sacred music. So I quit leading the singing altogether. I was called to preach. Nothing else would do.

In November, 1927, the rather prosperous Southern Baptist church in Mount Calm, Texas, was searching for a full-time pastor. Kermit Melugin, a senior student and Baylor's shining star preacher, had been called to fill the pulpit until a permanent pastor was found. One weekend, Kermit woke up too sick to travel. At the last moment I was called to take the train to Mount Calm and preach in his stead.

Deacon Stovall, a wonderful old pillar of the Mount Calm church, had been sent to pick up the replacement preacher. I was the only one standing on the depot platform, but Deacon Stovall walked by me several times, looking at his watch and pacing in and out of the depot's little waiting room. I was seventeen years old. Apparently, he couldn't imagine that this young boy could be the pinch-hitting preacher from Baylor. Finally, he stopped.

"Don't know a W. A. Criswell, do you son?" he said staring doubtfully down at me.

"Yes, sir, I'm afraid so," I replied, "and you're looking at him."

He drove me to the church in his shiny black Hudson without saying a word. Poor Deacon Stovall just sat there looking disappointed. The sadder he looked the harder I prayed that God would help me preach the Word with power and might.

"This is our preacher for today," he announced to the congregation almost apologetically. "I'm sorry he's still wet behind the ears," he might have added by the look on his face.

Eagerly, I strode to the pulpit, opened the Word, lowered my voice to its lowest range, and preached my heart out. When I gave the invitation, a young man stood and walked forward to give his life to Christian ministry. The congregation was all smiles. Deacon Stovall was weeping. I could hardly hold back my own tears. It was the first time that someone had come forward at the invitation under my preaching in a church. Of course, the man turned out to be a Presbyterian, called to minister within that great denomination. But it didn't matter. God had spoken to that young Presbyterian through my preaching, and I trembled with excitement.

That same evening, in Deacon Stovall's home, he thanked me one last time and handed me a ten dollar bill. I wouldn't take it.

"I don't preach for money," I told him.

The deacon didn't argue. He just smiled and led me to his Hudson for the short drive to the depot. When I sat down in the train, I found that same ten dollar bill stuck into the brim of my hat.

"Mother," I said when I arrived in Waco that night, "what shall I do with this ten dollar bill? Deacon Stovall gave it to me for preaching the gospel, and I don't preach for money."

My mother didn't hesitate. She knew how much an education cost. She knew what my father and she had sacrificed on my behalf through all those early years. We were half-starving at the time, living in those rental rooms, surviving off what my father sent to us from his barbershop.

"We'll give it to the Lord," she said, and that next Sunday at the Baptist church on Seventh and James, I put Deacon Stovall's ten dollar bill into the offering basket.

My Mother's Dream

From the beginning, I lived to preach. During my first year at Baylor, I spent every spare moment preaching. And though my mother tried to understand, there were times when she got very concerned about my "preoccupation" with preaching. I was at Baylor "to study." I was a "student, not a preacher . . . at least not a preacher yet!" At the end of my first semester, when I received four A's and one B+, my mother seemed unnerved by that sign of academic imperfection.

"But Mother," I replied to her remonstrance, "a B+ is still a passing grade, you know."

"It isn't easy getting into medical school," she replied sternly, "and we need a scholarship besides. Every B+ is a mark against us."

Mother didn't like anything that threatened my studies, but she was proud that I played in the Baylor band. On Friday evenings she stood on the front porch like a drill sergeant to give me one last inspection before I headed for the campus in my green and gold uniform with the white plumed hat. Occasionally, she would attend a band concert or even stay at a football game long enough to watch our band perform at halftime.

We trombone players got the front row in a marching band. I suppose we made the other musicians somewhat nervous marching behind us, moving rapidly up and down the scale with the trombone slide held loosely between our thumb and forefinger. Band members know that if that slide gets away just once, it will sail through the air nailing someone painfully in the lower back. So in the Baylor band the trombones led the way, and I marched in the front right guard position. I was the pivot point. If I ever wavered a step, the whole band would follow like drunken sailors. I think the bandmaster put me in that position knowing how determined I was in real life, as well as on the football field, not to waver from the line of march.

The Philomathian Debating Society was the other extra-curricular passion that my mother supported during that first year at Baylor. At the public debates, she sat in the front row cheering me on.

I remember once as our team entered the auditorium, I leaned over to greet my mother.

"I don't like him," she whispered, nodding toward the captain of the University of Texas debate team. He was tall, handsome, and obviously intelligent. Worse, he looked very confident.

"Why don't you like him?" I asked her, knowing full well the reason why.

"He looks smart," she said, "too smart."

My mother hated for me to lose. Anybody that posed a threat was her enemy. She smiled and applauded politely when the University of Texas captain and his debate teammates were introduced, but I could tell she wasn't smiling inside. In fact, in all my high school and college debates, I could see my mother scowling in the front row, looking over the opposition, her hands trembling slightly, praying for me to win.

On my eighteenth birthday, December 19, 1927, my mother invited a handful of my classmates to our rented home for a turkey dinner and a birthday cake. Instead of a room filled with pre-med students as my mother had hoped, my friends were all preparing for full-time Christian ministry as either preachers or missionaries. My friends and I spent our afternoons together preaching around Waco. When I wasn't making my "pastoral rounds" through the dirty streets and dilapidated houses of Sand Town, my classmates and I were together, singing and preaching in the Waco town square, in the jail, or in the poorhouse.

Instead of animated conversations about bone structure and cadavers, my mother heard endless talk of street meetings and people who had given their lives to Jesus. Instead of sharing information from the latest medical journals or scientific textbooks, we were memorizing Scriptures and outlining the sermons we would preach. Instead of volunteering our extra time in a local hospital or medical clinic, we were praying and fasting for the lost.

My mother was a deeply committed Christian. She loved the church and was committed to it, but until that first year at Baylor she continued to hope that I would outgrow my calling to the ministry.

"Son," she would say to me, "God can use you as a doctor, too. Imagine the good that you could do. You would be a fine preacher," she would add, "but what a great doctor you will make!"

From my childhood, my mother had dreamed that dream for me.

"What a doctor you will make!" she exclaimed over and over again as she sacrificed her own life to guarantee my proper education.

Exactly when my mother first saw her dream begin to die, I do not know. I'm not even sure why she was so committed to that dream or so unwilling to let it go. Sometimes I think it was Anna Currie Criswell who wanted to be a doctor just like her father. She was qualified mentally and physically for the job, but she was a woman and the times were against her. Women in America couldn't even vote until seven years before, let alone be educated and licensed in the field of their choosing. In fact, there was not one woman present on August 26, 1920, when the Secretary of State signed the papers certifying ratification of the Nineteenth Amendment to the United States Constitution granting women their right to vote.

On the other hand, sometimes I think my mother was still trying to please her father, Dr. David Currie, who had served the Confederacy with distinction during the Civil War. If she could bring home a grandson who was destined to someday take over his medical practice on that great ranch near San Angelo, maybe daughter and father could be truly reconciled again.

Then again, she might have dreamed the dream just for me. Mother had seen our own family struggle financially during those difficult years in Texline. And she had witnessed the impoverished conditions in which so many ministers and their families were forced to live. She had also seen too many preachers mistreated by their congregations. In the Texas frontier, a family doctor was revered. If I entered medicine, my future and the future of my family would have been secure.

At the close of my first year at Baylor, my mother and I returned to our home in Amarillo. I spent that long, hot summer of 1928 working again in the wholesale department of the J. I. Case Threshing Machine Company. In the evenings when Currie, my parents, and I gathered for supper, my mother would occasionally raise the subject of my studying to be a doctor.

"There's plenty of time to choose a pre-med major," she would say quietly, ladling me a second helping of her very special vegetable soup or cutting me an extra piece of pecan pie still hot from the oven. "And you could preach on the side. A doctor with a gift for preaching would be quite unique, you know."

I smiled and nodded as I looked into her eyes and slowly, painfully, watched her dreams for me die that summer.

"I love you, Mother," I would say, hugging her awkwardly and trying to ease her pain. "But God has called me to preach and I have to answer that call."

Ordination

That same summer, on August 28, 1928, I was ordained for ministry by First Baptist Church and San Jacinto Baptist Church in Amarillo. The six Baptist leaders who made up my ordaining council examined me in the home of my pastor, Dr. G. L. Yates of First Baptist Church. After assuring themselves of my "genuine conversion and unmistakable call to the ministry" and after finding me "unusually sound and well posted in all the Baptist doctrines," we adjourned to meet at San Jacinto Baptist Church on August 29 at 8:00 in the evening.

The church was packed. I sat on the platform between D. D. Sumrall, pastor of the San Jacinto church, and G. L. Yates. I searched for the faces of my mother and father in the crowd. Dr. Yates gave an impressive charge from 2 Timothy. Using those ancient words from Paul to his own young apprentice, Dr. Yates' voice echoed across the large sanctuary: "Study to shew thyself approved unto God, a workman that needed not to be ashamed, rightly dividing the Word of truth."

Then pastors and deacons from churches across Central Texas gathered in a circle around me for the laying on of hands. Reverend Sumrall prayed the prayer of dedication and the congregation echoed their "Amen!" Finally, I saw my mother smiling up at me through her tears. My father was standing at her side looking pleased and proud.

That next Monday I boarded the train for Baylor all alone. My mother had left my father the first time to move with Currie and me into Texline when those long, freezing buggy rides threatened to interfere with our education. She had left my father a second time to move with me to Amarillo to be sure that I graduated from an accredited high school. And she left him yet again to move with me to Baylor to see for herself that I would get the finest education available. Driven by her dream for me, my mother had dedicated thirteen years of her life to my education. But at that ordination service, my mother's dream must have died forever. She knew that God's call had been more powerful than her dream. Suddenly, she realized that it was time for her to step aside and let me answer that call.

"Good-bye, son," she said as we embraced one last time on the platform of the Amarillo depot.

"We love you, boy," my father said shaking my hand. "Don't you forget that."

As the train began to move, my father turned to leave. But my mother just couldn't seem to tear herself away. She removed a large white handkerchief from her pocket, dabbed her eyes, and strained to see me through the clouds of smoke and steam. Suddenly, Mother spotted me as I waved through the open Pullman window. She smiled and waved back. As we drew farther and farther apart, she stood on her tiptoes and waved faster, almost frantically. I knew what she wanted to say and I knew, too, why she couldn't find the words to say it.

"I did my best to shape your life," she might have said. "I wanted you to be a doctor, but God had other ideas. Now it's time for me to let you go."

After pausing to dry her tears she might have added, "I may be staying home this time, but remember, son, you are not going back to Baylor all alone. God goes with you. He has a dream for your life. Trust Him to see that dream come true."

6

The Sophomore Year at Baylor University

Waco: 1928-1929

"Be careful for nothing; but in every thing
by prayer and supplication with thanksgiving
let your requests be made known unto God.
And the peace of God, which passeth all understanding,
shall keep your hearts and minds through Christ Jesus."
Philippians 4:6-7

HERBERT CLARK HOOVER ACCEPTED THE REPUBLICAN Party's nomination for President of the United States just five days before I returned alone to Waco in 1928 to begin my sophomore year at Baylor University.

"A chicken in every pot, a car in every garage," was Hoover's platform slogan.

"We in America today," he told a cheering crowd in the Stanford University stadium, "are nearer the final triumph over poverty than ever before in the history of the land."

"Sure could fool me," my friend Christy Poole replied, looking up from the Waco daily paper's coverage of that event.

Christy was one of my dearest friends at Baylor. He grew up on his parent's vegetable farm in Grapevine, Texas, somewhere between Dallas and Denton. Christy was working his way through the university as a janitor. Every day, without fail, I could see Christy making his way across the campus with a sharp stick poking trash into a large canvas bag that trailed behind him or with an oversized rake piling up the leaves and burning them.

"I can get you a job on the sanitation gang," Christy offered generously the day I arrived to begin the fall term.

"I'm going to wait awhile, Christy," I replied. "I've saved some money from the J. I. Case Threshing Machine job and I'm hoping to find a little church that can help me pay for the rest of my schooling."

I wanted to preach my way through college more than anything I had ever wanted in the world.

"I'm not ashamed to be a janitor," I cried out to the Lord that same morning, as I sat in the shadow of a large pecan tree near the Burleson statue on Fifth Street, "but, dear God, could I please make my way through Baylor pastoring a country church that needs a part-time pastor? Surely there's some little congregation out there who could use me."

During the summer, my father had heard my story about that ten dollar bill from Deacon Stovall.

"Son," he said trying not to laugh, "when God gives you a gift, just say thanks and take it. You don't have to give it back."

In my ordination interview, Pastor Yates responded to the same story with a Bible verse. "The workman is worthy of his hire, W. A. Even preachers need to pay their bills."

Fortunately, pre-ministerial students at Baylor had their tuition paid by the Baptist Convention of Texas. Those wonderful Baptist brothers and sisters, farmers and ranchers, merchants, housewives, and retirees, reached down into their pockets and gave generously to support the young men who would one day be their pastors. But there was still board and room to pay, along with books, clothing, travel, and incidentals. It didn't amount to much by today's standards, but to a teenager in 1928, it seemed a small fortune.

I stored my suitcase and a duffle bag in Christy's room while I walked around the neighborhood looking for a place of my own. Just south of the Baylor campus I found a familiar "Room to Let" sign in the front window of a home at 1001 Speight Street. The stately, two-story residence had belonged to Dr. R. E. Rogers, a Waco physician. When he died, Mrs. Rogers opened up her home to Baylor students. I still remember that gracious, rather fragile old woman standing at the open door, smiling at me.

I'm sure I blushed and looked away as I stammered out my answers to her pointed questions about my habits with liquor, tobacco, and "women from the town." But apparently, they satisfied the wary Widow Rogers, and after eyeing me carefully one last time, she patted me on the arm and motioned for me to follow. "Young man," she said, "you'll do just fine."

The living room was rich with polished wood floors, plush Persian carpets with intricate woven patterns, windows draped in dark velvet, high ceilings with carved moldings, decorative tin medallions and an impressive crystal chandelier. It was barely fall, but a fire in the huge brick fireplace filled the room with light and moving shadows. Family photos in ornate silver frames covered the imported marble mantelpiece, the old grand piano top, and every lacquered table in the room. The dark velvet sofa and matching chairs were covered with delicate lace doilies.

I followed Mrs. Rogers through the living room and into a short hall with walls covered with daguerreotype photos in round, polished wooden frames chronicling the ancestry of Dr. and Mrs. R. E. Rogers and their people.

"This will be your room, Mr. Criswell," she said as we entered into a large, oblong, rather Spartan bedroom with a double feather bed, one large desk, a Tiffany lamp that made stained glass patterns on the walls, and a high-backed wooden chair. "It is rather simple," she said, "but you have a private bath and plenty of room for your books. I hope it is to your liking."

Well do I remember returning to that wonderful room with my suitcase, my duffle bag, and a pile of brand new textbooks that I had just purchased with my meager summer earnings. I sat at the desk and opened each book, folding down the right cover to crease the binding, then the left. It has been a lifelong habit to break in each new book with gentle, loving care, folding down the covers one at a time, then the first few pages, then the last, bending, creasing, back and forth until the book feels comfortable and relaxed, ready, waiting, eager to be read.

Samuel Palmer Brooks

Monday morning at the university's chapel service, President Brooks welcomed us back to Baylor.

"Did you have a good summer, Mr. Criswell?" he asked me as I stood in line to greet him at the close of the chapel service.

I was surprised that he called me by name. Dr. Brooks had been president of Baylor since 1902. During that quarter century of leadership, he had seen Baylor grow from a small college with no endowment and a few hundred students to a great university, well endowed, with several thousand students; yet he seemed to know each one of us personally.

"Yes, sir," I answered shaking his hand, "a good summer."

In just a few seconds, with a touch of his hand, a brief greeting, and a warm smile, Dr. Brooks could make a student feel like a member of the University's Board of Trustees. Now, looking back, I realize that God used that man to shape my life in so many ways.

Above all things, Samuel Palmer Brooks was a Christian. Converted as a young man, Dr. Brooks often shared his testimony with the Baylor students. I remember that massive man standing before us with tears in his eyes talking about the sacred day when he went alone into the woods, got down on his knees, confessed his sins, trusted Christ as Lord and Savior, and experienced the forgiveness and love of God. That conversion experience was for Samuel Palmer Brooks a "fixed stake" that he could cling to.

I can still hear Dr. Brooks' voice booming out from the chapel pulpit: "My faith in God's Word is unshaken by any fact of philosophy or science. Trust the Lord, dear students," he would say. "Hide His Word in your heart and it will become your source of strength and wisdom, comfort and courage."

Dr. Brooks wasn't a preacher, but his beloved Bible was dog-eared and worn. He carried it proudly about the campus. He placed it lovingly on the pulpit in Baylor Chapel when he stood to lead us. He quoted great passages to us by memory and taught us the Word on every possible occasion. With God's Word as his guide, President Brooks led the university neither to the right nor to the left, but straight to the heart of God. He was a soul winner, and when he prayed in the Baylor Chapel, the mountains moved and faith stirred to life in every student's breast.

He was sixty-five years old when I returned to Baylor to begin my sophomore year. His voice was still strong and his handshake firm, but I was surprised to see how pale and worn he looked. The president was energetic and forceful in his manner, but there were already signs of the still unknown malady that would rob him of his robust health, cripple him, and, sooner than anyone could imagine, take him from us.

The Church at Marlow

It was good to return to the old routine. I spent those first busy weeks in daily chapel services, in my classes in history, math, science, literature, English, and Bible, in the library, at band practice, at the debate society, with my friends of the Volunteer Band, renewing friendships in Sand Town, and in my room reading textbooks, cramming for exams, writing papers, and preparing outlines for sermons I would preach in Sand Town or, hopefully, in that little country church that God would give me.

Then, suddenly, the call came. Can you believe it? Just weeks into that fall term God answered my prayers.

"Come over to Marlow and help us!"

Marlow? I rushed to find a map.

"Marlow?" the librarian echoed, squinting through her glasses at the reference map of Texas laid out on the reading table in Old Main. "I can't find it on the map."

Oh, Lord, don't mock me. I've just gotten called to preach in a little church in a town that doesn't exist.

"Here it is," the librarian said finally, interrupting my panicked prayer, pointing at a hand-drawn map of Milam County. "Marlow is just across the Little River from Cameron, the county seat. No population reading. Must be real Texas country," she added with a grin. "Good luck in finding it."

At 5:00 that next Sunday morning, I was driving a borrowed old clunker down the farm road south of Waco fifty miles into Milam County. The sun was just rising over Sugar Loaf Mountain.

I turned left at Cameron's gray stone courthouse and headed out across the marshlands of the Little River. White cranes grazed on spindly legs, and frogs leaped narrowly out of harm's way.

"Don't cross the railroad tracks," a friend had warned me. "Take the first farm road after the bridge. You'll wind around through mesquite trees, bull nettles, and an occasional farmhouse for about a mile. Then suddenly, Marlow Baptist Church will appear nestled in a cluster of oak trees just to the right of the cemetery."

My watch read 8:30. I was at least an hour early. The little wooden church was freshly painted white and locked up tighter than a jail. I could see through a window the eight or ten rows of pews facing the brown pulpit on a slightly raised platform. With the little all-grade Marlow school next door, the church and the cemetery made up the Marlow Civic Center. There wasn't another building in sight, not even a farmhouse or a barn.

I could smell horsemint, primrose, and freshly mowed grass as I walked into the cemetery, trembling with excitement, waiting for my first parishioner to arrive. Somewhere a mockingbird sang her unlikely song. Tree crickets chirped. A fly buzzed me several times and then retreated from my flailing hand. I was alone in the wilderness waiting for God's people to gather.

I risk telling you this, but at that moment I knew a little of what Abraham must have felt gathering God's children in Ur of the Chaldees, or Moses assembling God's enslaved people under the noses of the Egyptians, or Joshua lining up God's armies to march around Jericho. The people of Marlow were about to assemble in that little white box-like church to hear the Word of God. And for that moment, I was chosen to be His spokesman. Who can tell, let alone explain, the thrill of it?

The first man to arrive was old, slightly stooped, and certainly short sighted. He stared down at the brass ring in his hand searching for the right key to open the church door. He must have walked to the church from a nearby farmhouse. Soon, I could see clouds of dust up and down the winding road. A family with six stair-step children arrived in a hay wagon pulled by an old white mare. A young couple rode up in a shiny black buggy. They teased each other and laughed openly as they dismounted and tied their horse to the iron fence that circled the cemetery. Old couples and whole families walked slowly up the road together. Young children raced through the meadow behind the church, playing tag and shouting happily at each other. I learned later that the average morning attendance was no more than eighteen or twenty, but on my first Sunday morning, nearly fifty people crowded into the church to hear their new, part-time, teenaged preacher.

Except for my borrowed Model-A, there were no other cars in front of the church when I walked across the gravel yard and into the sanctuary where God's people had gathered. A deacon announced the hymn. A pump organ played the introduction. The people sang and prayed and listened to the reading of God's Word. Each member of the congregation in his or her turn stole a glance in my direction. The children stirred, grinned, pointed, and poked each other. The old man squinted up at me and then turned away. The young couple held hands in the front row smiling at each other and once or twice at me.

A deacon made the introduction. He seemed most impressed that I played the trombone in the Baylor marching band. I smiled and stood to speak. I was wearing my good suit. Actually, it was my only suit, dark blue worsted wool, cuffed and double-breasted, with a matching blue vest, a dark blue tie, black suspenders, black shoes and socks.

It isn't difficult to remember what I wore to preach that day. I wore that suit almost every Sunday for the next three years. In fact, that suit in all its variations has been my pulpit uniform now for more than sixty-three years. Even when the temperature went well over a hundred degrees inside the sanctuary and the air was so warm and damp that you could eat it with a spoon, I wore my suit, vest, and tie. There's something about standing up to speak God's Word that requires the very best we have to offer in what we say and in what we wear when saying it.

I preached my heart out. The people listened. Even the old short-sighted man seemed moved by my sermon. Every time he cupped his hand to his ear, I spoke louder. By the time the sermon ended, I was shouting. The people gathered around me at the close of the service. I got at least ten invitations for Sunday supper. It was a good sign. These gentle, country people had opened their hearts and homes to me. From that moment, I determined not to fail them in rightly dividing God's truth. And they responded generously with their promise to pay me seventy-five dollars to preach three Sundays every month in their little church in Marlow. It was the most they had ever promised to a preacher and they smiled proudly with their offer. They had accepted me. I drove back to Waco a most happy fellow, singing hymns of praise at the top of my lungs and trying to see that little country road while blinking back my tears.

The Church at Pecan Grove

"What exactly is a 'quarter time' church?" I shouted over the noisy rattles and loud backfires of Brother Lemon's rather overused 1924 Dodge as we lurched through beautiful Coryell County.

"You have three Sundays at Marlow, don't you, boy?" Brother Lemon shouted back.

I turned to him and nodded, afraid my voice would give up the ghost before I even started to preach that first Sunday morning in Pecan Grove.

"Well, that means you have one Sunday left over for a 'quarter time' church," he explained. "The people of Pecan Grove have been holding revival meetings every summer. Now they want to start a church. They can afford to pay a pastor for just one Sunday a month. That's a 'quarter time.' Don't you see?"

"Yes, sir," I yelled, appreciating his confidence but wondering how I could be a full-time student and still pastor two churches, each more than fifty miles away from Waco in two different directions.

"Don't worry about it, Criswell," Brother Lemon answered loudly. "Pecan Grove Baptist Church is just getting started. They'll be glad to get whatever you and the Lord can give them."

A half-dozen miles south of Gatesville, the countryside began to change. Brother Lemon grew silent. The road twisted through white, sandy bluffs spotted with scrawny pine trees and colorful button bushes. Scarlet paintbrushes and bright yellow foxgloves flourished along the roadside. As we rumbled past, a white-tailed doe and her round-eyed fawn looked up nervously from their grazing. Suddenly, we were down off the bluff and riding through a pristine valley where cattle grazed knee-deep in green meadows bordered by pecan groves and shaded by great white clouds piled up in perfect, azure skies.

"Welcome to Pecan Grove," Brother Lemon said as we turned into a little clearing alongside Coryell Creek, an idyllic stream that wound its way across the entire county toward Belton Lake and the Leon River.

The silence closed in as I stepped down from Brother Lemon's old Dodge and began to walk along the creek toward the arbor where the people of the Baptist church in Pecan Grove were already beginning to gather.

"Something about this place makes me think of the River Jordan," Brother Lemon whispered looking down at the clear green water flowing gently past a white pebbled beach shaded by pecan trees that dipped their branches in the stream. The early morning sun streaked through the trees and dappled the water. Somewhere, a mockingbird sang.

I could almost see John, clothed in camel's hair and dried skins, standing in Coryell Creek, blinking back the shock of recognition as Jesus waded toward him in the sparkling water moving in and out of the bright light and hazy shadows.

"Baptize me," He said.

"I am not worthy," the Baptist answered, his heart pounding wildly, his voice just a whisper.

"Suffer it to be so now, John, that all might be fulfilled."

A brief prayer? A strong embrace? Buried in the water and raised back to life again?

And suddenly in the skies above Pecan Grove, I could visualize the heavens open and the Spirit of God descending like a dove and a voice saying, "This is my beloved Son, in whom I am well pleased."

"I've never been to the River Jordan, son," Brother Lemon admitted as he walked beside me along the silent, moving stream, "but if the

Jordan doesn't look like Coryell Creek, it sure enough ought to look exactly like it."

There was no church at Pecan Grove when we arrived that day, but the people had built a wonderful tabernacle. Thick, sturdy branches of old pecan trees held up a kind of thatched roof over a hard-packed dirt floor. Pews built of pine planks were lined up facing a pulpit made of flat stones piled up and mortared together. A Bible lay open on the flat limestone top that finished the pulpit like an ancient sacrificial altar. Only a handful of people were there, but even as Brother Lemon and I approached the arbor, they stopped their conversations and rushed to greet us.

I don't remember all those early sermons at Marlow and Pecan Grove, but I do remember how my friends in the Volunteer Band were affected by them. One Sunday morning they reserved an old Baylor bus, packed a picnic lunch, and drove to Pecan Grove to hear me preach.

"Open your Bibles and turn with me to Matthew 3, verse 10."

I paused dramatically and looked down over that stone pulpit as my new parishioners and my friends turned to my Sunday morning text.

"And now also the axe is laid unto the root of the trees," I read, my voice booming out across that open arbor. "Therefore every tree which bringeth not forth good fruit is hewn down and cast into the fire."

I held my Bible in my left hand and gestured enthusiastically with my right. I paced up and down the front of the tabernacle. My voice rose and fell. My gestures grew more expansive as the text came to life within me. And my friends, who had never heard me preach in a church setting, sat in the back rows with their eyes unblinking and their mouths open wide.

"You can't preach like that, Criswell," one boy admonished on the bus as we returned to Waco late that Sunday afternoon. "That style is okay for the poorhouse and the jail, but there's not a church in the world of any consequence that will call you."

"You're so loud, W. A.," a girl chimed in.

"And you move like a caged animal," criticized a third. "I couldn't even concentrate on what you were saying for worrying that you would step off that platform or run into a post. . . ."

". . . and knock down the whole church like Samson," Christy Poole added with a wink. "You have potential, Criswell," he said, moving to sit beside me on the little Model-T bus, "but you need work, lots of it."

I was crushed. I had preached my heart out and they had been offended. I couldn't even pretend to laugh it off or take it in good humor. I felt like crying.

"Don't worry, W. A.," Christy said when he saw that I was taking their criticism rather seriously. "I have the solution."

Martha Folks Hawn

During the first thirty years of this century, Martha Folks Hawn was the only expression teacher in Waco, Texas. She was known for her great love for the spoken word. She had taught generations of private students the fine art of public speaking, and she had produced and directed some of the greatest theatrical events in Waco's history. The people of the community loved Martha Hawn so much that they had built her a little theater just behind her home to use in teaching elocution and to present the plays of William Shakespeare, George Bernard Shaw, and William Butler Yeats, the Irish poet and playwright.

"Miss Hawn?" I said hesitantly, standing at her door with my hat in hand.

"Yes, young man?" she replied. "May I help you?"

"My name is W. A. Criswell," I began.

For a moment Miss Hawn looked puzzled. Obviously, she had heard my name, but she couldn't recall exactly the context or the reason for hearing it. Then she nodded.

"Holy Roller . . ." she said quietly.

I blinked. When my close friends wanted to torment me, they called me Baylor's "Holy Roller preacher with an A-plus average." One of them, probably Christy Poole, must have warned her that I was coming.

"What exactly is a Holy Roller?" she asked, looking me right in the eye without a flicker of humor or contempt.

"I guess it's people who preach too enthusiastically," I explained. "I know God wants me to preach," I added, "and I preach all over the place. But my friends say that if I don't change my style, there is no full-time pastorate in the country that will call me."

"And what would you like from me?" she asked.

"I need you to reshape me," I answered. "Calm me down and show me how to preach."

Miss Hawn paused to speak. Then, suddenly, she changed her mind.

"Follow me," she ordered.

Miss Hawn led me down the stairs, through her rose garden and into the small courtyard that faced her little theater. As we passed through the double doors carved with cherubs and gilded in gold paint, we entered another world. The little lobby was lined with posters from past performances and pictures, many of them autographed, of great actors and dancers—including Anna Pavlova, the Russian ballerina, Giacomo Puccini, the composer of "La Boheme" and "Tosca," stars of the silent screen, little Jackie Coogan and Charlie Chaplain, British playwright and Nobel Prize honoree George Bernard Shaw, Dame Ellen Terry, the queen of British theater, and young Helen Hayes, Broadway's newest sensation, dressed in her costume from Shaw's "Caesar and Cleopatra."

She didn't pause to introduce her heroes or to explain the history of that fascinating little place. She just marched into the darkened theater, disappeared momentarily behind bright red curtains, and with a flick of the master switch flooded the stage with light.

"On stage, Mr. Criswell," Miss Hawn said firmly as she settled into a front row seat.

I stood awkwardly beneath the gold proscenium arch. Miss Hawn looked up at me.

"Preach, Mr. Criswell," she said quietly.

"A whole sermon?" I answered in disbelief.

"Absolutely," she replied. "As you would preach in any church."

I bowed my head for a moment and asked for God's guidance.

"In the book of John," I began, "there is a story about a rich and powerful man who came to Jesus by night to ask the Master one simple question: 'What must I do to inherit eternal life?'

"'Verily, verily, I say unto thee,' Jesus answered, 'except a man be born again, he cannot see the kingdom of God.'"

For thirty or forty minutes I preached to a congregation of one gracious old lady who sat staring up at me without moving a muscle or saying a word. I quoted verses from the third chapter of John describing that exciting moment when the Pharisee named Nicodemus, a ruler of the Jews, came to Jesus by night to question Him.

"'How can a man be born when he is old,' Nicodemus asked, his voice mirroring the confusion growing in his mind.

"'Except a man be born of water and of the Spirit,' Jesus answered, 'he cannot enter into the kingdom of God.'"

My voice grew louder and stronger as the excitement of that secret, nighttime encounter grasped my imagination once again.

"'How can these things be?' Nicodemus asked.

"'If I have told you earthly things, and ye believe not,' Jesus answered, 'how shall ye believe, if I tell you of heavenly things?'"

By the time I reached that incredible, historic moment when Jesus raised His voice to announce the greatest news of all time, I was moving up and down the stage, gesturing and speaking passionately with the music of the text.

"For God so loved the world," I said, tears streaming from my eyes, "that He gave His only begotten Son, that whosoever believeth in Him should not perish, but have everlasting life.

"For God sent not His Son into the world to condemn the world; but that the world through Him might be saved."

By the time I gave the invitation to accept Christ as Lord and Savior, Miss Hawn was staring up at me blinking back tears of her own. I finished the invitation and stood waiting for her response. She just looked at me in silence. When she finally spoke, her voice literally echoed with authority.

"Mr. Criswell," she began, "I'm going to tell you something now I want you never to forget."

I felt my knees tremble.

"From now on," she said, "and for the rest of your life, when you stand up there in your pulpit, you do exactly as you feel like doing."

Miss Hawn stood and walked to the edge of the stage.

"If you feel like doubling up your fist," she said, "then double it.

"If you feel like stomping on the floor, then stomp the floor.

"If you feel like pounding the pulpit," she added as her voice began to rise, "then pound the pulpit."

She walked up the stairs and stood beside me on the stage without missing a beat.

"Always do exactly what you feel like doing," she said. "I'm not promising that people will like it, but I am telling you this: They will always listen to what you have to say."

She took my hands in her hands.

"Now, you go out the door," she ordered. "This is your first and last lesson. Don't let anybody tell you how or what to preach. You be yourself. You preach just exactly as you want to preach, and God will bless you!"

For a moment Miss Hawn just stood there clasping my hands. She didn't pray, but her words fell like a blessing on my heart. To this day I don't know anything about her religious beliefs, but God used her strong words and the loving look in her eyes to wipe away forever any doubt I might have had about preaching the Word in the only way I knew to preach it.

I turned from Miss Hawn, walked up the aisle, and then paused one last time to thank her. She was sitting again in the front row seat of her little theater looking up at the empty stage. I still remember her sitting there thinking about God's Word among the echoes of all the great words that had been spoken in that place. "For God so loved the world that He gave His only begotten Son. . . ." Whether we have great or small gifts at proclaiming it, God's Word will triumph. God's Word will be heard. And whether we feel gifted or unable, we can trust Him for that.

The Marlow Meetings

That whole year I preached every Sunday in either Marlow or Pecan Grove. In fact, it was my preaching during one special meeting in Marlow that still causes me no little embarrassment when I think about it. The Baptist church was down by the river. Up on the hill stood a Presbyterian church, and somewhere in between there was a community church where all three churches joined together for a communal Sunday school.

"But without our own Sunday school," I warned the deacons in the lowest, most mature voice I could muster, "there's no way our church can grow."

My first few weeks in Marlow I had started a Training Union class for the young people. Within two or three months, most of the teenagers who lived around Marlow were attending. But without having our own Sunday school, there was no way to attract new children to our church. Get the children and you'll get their families. Forget the children and your church is doomed.

"Brother Criswell?"

A tall, thin, angular man stood before me one Sunday afternoon on the porch of our church in Marlow.

"I was hoping I would find you here," he said. "I'm the pastor of the Presbyterian church up on the hill, and I've been wanting to meet you."

We sat on the steps and talked until the evening. The kindly Presbyterian minister had come to suggest that we hold a revival together.

"I was thinking of a two-week meeting," he explained. "You preach one morning and the same evening. I preach the next."

We agreed. He had such a sweet spirit that I loved him right away. But he couldn't preach. He read each long sermon from a manuscript. He seldom gestured or even looked up from the pulpit. I was young. I paced and shouted and told exciting stories from the Old and New Testament. I quoted long passages from the Word. I even made people laugh now and then. The young people loved to hear me preach and brought their families every other morning and night to the joint revival meeting. Almost no one came to hear my Presbyterian brother.

It was sad. When I gave the invitation, half the countryside lined up to join our church. When my Presbyterian brother gave the invitation, he stood beside the pulpit pretty much alone. I don't think he got a single member. Not one. I felt awful about what had happened.

In a very short time, the Presbyterian church closed down. The pastor made one last visit to see me before he moved away.

"Keep on preaching the Word, son," he said. "He is blessing you for that."

I have never met a more gracious or understanding man. Soon the Presbyterian church and the little community church closed their doors forever as the children and youth of Marlow came to the Baptist church with their mothers and fathers close behind.

The Correspondence

My mother wrote at least two letters a week from our home in Amarillo to "encourage" me, she said, and to make sure that I was "still open to whatever God might have in mind." Somewhere down inside, my mother still held some small hope that I might change my mind about preaching and follow her father's example in medicine. She didn't pressure me, really. She seemed proud that I was on my own and she left me free to make my own decisions, but through her letters that year and the next, she tried diligently to keep the option alive that one day I would be a doctor like her father.

Alvin V. Daves was my other regular correspondent during my sophomore year. Alvin was one of those special friends who comes into your life, touches you deeply, and then just disappears forever. I don't remember exactly how or when we met, but during my sophomore year at Baylor, I received a letter every two or three weeks from Alvin, and I've saved those letters for sixty-two years.

During our freshman year, Alvin and I had walked the streets of Sand Town, sharing our faith with Waco's "down and outers." Alvin didn't feel called to preach, but he joined heartily in the singing during our street meetings at the Waco City Square, at the town jail, and in the poorhouse. Then, during our freshman summer, Alvin left Waco, found a job as a wildcatter with an oil crew in Seminole, Oklahoma, and went off to make his fortune.

Just weeks after we exchanged letters one last time, I heard that Alvin V. Daves had drowned while swimming in Lake Oakmulgee, just north and a little east of his worksite in Seminole, Oklahoma. I sat alone in my room staring down at the pile of Alvin's letters that I had saved in my desk drawer. Each bore one bright red two-cent stamp and the address scrawled in green ink to Mr. W. A. Criswell, Jr., 1001 Speight Avenue, Waco, Texas.

Alvin was just nineteen when he drowned, his head full of dreams about serving Christ. He loved the Southern Baptist work. He loved Baylor University. And he loved me. We don't find many such friends along the way who confront us, who speak their minds freely and clearly, and yet love us all the while. I opened the first letter Alvin wrote that year. "My dear buddy . . . " it began. Suddenly, I was sobbing. Tears blurred my eyes as one last time I read that twenty-three-letter history of one short but dedicated life.

Later that night I lay on my bed, staring at the stained-glass patterns on my walls and ceiling, thinking about my friend, grieving that never again would a letter appear in my mailbox that began "Hey, old chum . . . " or ended with "Just your friend, Alvin." I felt lonely. And I have to confess I felt angry, too. Why does God allow good friends to die? I didn't know the answer then. I don't know the answer now. But the Word is clear. "Trust in the Lord with all your heart and lean not unto thine own understanding; in all thy ways acknowledge Him and He will direct thy paths."

Sometimes the journey of faith is joyful and bathed in light. Other times the cold, dark shadows of mystery and doubt cloud the way and threaten to extinguish the little flame of faith we have to guide and to sustain us. God's Word is that flame. Without it we will perish. Early in my life I learned that in those times when the darkness threatens, we pause in our journey just long enough to focus on the flame and feel its warmth while we wait for the morning light.

7

The Junior Year at Baylor University

Waco: 1929-1930

"Humble yourselves therefore
under the mighty hand of God,
that He may exalt you in due time:
Casting all your care upon Him;
for He careth for you."
1 Peter 5:6-7

"NATIONAL DEATH TOLL MOUNTS FROM DRINKING POISON LIQUOR!"

"AL 'SCARFACE' CAPONE INVESTIGATED FOR VALENTINE'S DAY MASSACRE!"

"MAJOR SLUMP NOTICED IN VALUE OF AMERICAN STOCKS!"

"REVIVAL PREACHER BILLY SUNDAY PACKS 'EM IN FOR JESUS!"

My nineteenth summer fell during a year of bold, disturbing newspaper headlines. Chaos and calamity lay just around the corner for our nation and the world. Looking back upon all that excitement, I realize how far removed it all seemed then. Although I am embarrassed to admit it, one of the personal traumas that touched me most that third summer in Waco was quitting the Baylor marching band.

"I'm sorry, sir," I told Baylor's bandmaster, "but I must resign."

I placed a bundle on his desk, including my green-striped pants, the green and gold jacket with the gold buttons and matching gold braid, and the tall green hat with the white feathered plume.

"I can't play at weekend games and still pastor my two little churches," I explained. "And those churches mean everything to me."

"I understand, Criswell, or at least I'm trying to," he said, shaking his head and frowning. "I sure hope you're not making a mistake. There are lots of preachers around this place but not many 'bone players with your gifts. Who will I get to fill your right guard position? We'll end up marching in circles without you, W. A. You sure you want to give up the band for those country churches?"

"I love the band, sir," I answered honestly, "and I love playing my trombone, but God has called me to those little churches, and when God calls, you just don't have a choice."

I believed it then with all my heart and I believe it now. God has plans for the life of every believer. And you are never too young or too old to give your life without reservation to those plans. But sometimes it means trading the good or the better for the best.

Even when I was a student, I spent time every day on my knees with my Bible open before me seeking God's guidance for my life. And even though my parents, several of my teachers, and many of my friends thought I was crazy to spend every weekend driving into the countryside to pastor my little flocks, I knew that those tiny churches and their people were at the heart of God's plans for me. I love books and libraries and classrooms, but the best place to learn about life is on the front lines, where people live and where people die.

The Blue Chevrolet Coupe

On Friday afternoons after spending five days in classrooms and the library, I jumped into my blue Chevrolet coupe and drove those dusty Texas farm roads into Milam and Coryell counties to pastor the churches at Marlow and Pecan Grove. That slightly used dark blue Chevy coupe with running boards, white-walled tires, and shiny chrome stripes was one of God's great gifts to me. Fred Shepherd, a big-hearted layman in the Pecan Grove church, made it possible for me to own the car, and I drove it for almost five years while I was a student at Baylor and even during my first years of graduate study at Southern Seminary in Louisville, Kentucky.

Actually, that blue Chevrolet coupe was my second car. I shared ownership in my very first automobile with a friend from Amarillo High School, Drew Crossett, a master mechanic who could tinker up a miracle. Drew and I bought an old, castoff, junked Model-T Ford for nineteen dollars during our high school senior summer. He reworked and remade that Model-T while I handed him tools and lay beside him underneath the carriage, staring up at the maze of rusted, greasy parts that needed to be repaired or replaced. But what fun we had together bringing that old dead Ford back to life!

"Let's name her," Drew said the day our own "Tin Lizzie" was ready for its baptism and road trial.

"What about J. P.," I said, pronouncing each letter slowly, hoping Drew would get the joke.

At first he didn't respond. He just stood there staring proudly at his handiwork. Remember, cars were treasures in those days. Henry Ford had established his first Model-T assembly line in Highland Park, Michigan, in 1913, just sixteen years earlier. In 1927, the year I entered Baylor, the last of fifteen million "Tin Lizzies" rolled off the assembly line. For a teenager to own his own car in those days was some kind of miracle. And for two poor boys from the country to scrape together enough to buy and rebuild an auto, even one they had discovered rusting in a wrecking yard, was quite an accomplishment.

After endless patching and pounding, puttering and painting, she stood before us as beautiful as the Amarillo High School homecoming queen. Suddenly, my friend Drew got the message. He yelled with delight and pounded me on the back.

"J. P." he screamed in sudden recognition. "Janet and Pauline!"

Drew repeated the names two or three times with delicious sarcasm in his voice.

"Perfect, Criswell," he added turning to me with a malevolent grin. "You are a genius!"

Janet and Pauline were the reigning queens of Amarillo High School society. Their fathers were wealthy businessmen. Pauline rode proudly behind a chauffeur in her father's Duesenberg while Janet had her own bright yellow Franklin Sport Coupe with a black leather top, the first six-cylinder auto that Drew or I had ever seen. Those two campus beauties didn't have the time or the energy to even smile at us poor country boys, so we took matters into our own hands and named our car in their honor. Before long the wonderful irony had spread across the campus. Smiling students winked and waved enthusiastically as we chugged and rattled by in old "J. P." Needless to say, Janet and Pauline weren't sure how to feel about the "honor."

Drew Crossett and I entered Baylor together. I had no use for a car during my freshman year, so Drew drove it those last good miles around Waco before "J. P." finally gave up the ghost and returned to the dump, laden with new glory and still shining from Drew's daily wash and polish. Then, just as our car reached retirement, the church in Marlow called me to be their weekend pastor.

At first, I hitched rides from Baylor down to Cameron, Milam's county seat. Then I waited in the shadow of the yellow brick court-house until somebody from Marlow would pick me up and drive me to the church in a buggy, a wagon, or on lucky days in a Model-T or an old Buick coupe.

During my sophomore year, it became just too complicated to hitch rides southeast to Marlow three weekends a month, and on every fourth Friday southwest through Coryell County to Pecan Grove. There was no train or bus route to these out-of-the-way places. Friends grew tired of transporting me. The few students with cars would hide when they saw me coming toward them on Friday afternoons.

"Lord, I need a car," I prayed, and even then the prayer seemed selfish. Texas was suffering another drought. Crops were dying in the fields. The rolling countryside had turned brown. Clouds of dust boiled heavenward. Bales of hay were being trucked in to feed the cattle. Farmers and ranchers were struggling to survive. The stock market's Black Thursday and the world's Great Depression were just months away; still, I prayed for a car.

"I don't care, Lord, how old or how ugly it is. Just let it get me there."

Through the generosity of Fred Sheperd, a layman from Pecan Grove, God answered my prayers with the most beautiful blue Chevrolet Coupe that ever led a dust cloud across the country roads of Central Texas.

White Mound Baptist Church

Even with my slightly dented but irresistibly beautiful blue Chevy, pastoring two congregations more than fifty miles apart be-came impossible. In the spring of my sophomore year, the Baptist church at White Mound, just four miles from Pecan Grove, asked me to be their part-time pastor. That decision would end the long commute in two different directions. I prayed and fasted and asked for

God's guidance. Thankfully, the people of Marlow understood. They hugged me and wished me God's blessings.

On my last Sunday in Marlow, I said good-bye to the old deacon with the ring of keys, to the young couple whose wedding I had performed, and to the superintendent of Marlow's First Baptist Sunday School, an inadvertent and unplanned "gift" from a big-hearted Presbyterian pastor who had no idea where our joint revival meeting might lead. And I began my third year in Baylor as the pastor of two beautiful little churches in Coryell County.

"Shall we gather at the river, the beautiful, beautiful river?"

The pianist was playing that old gospel song as crowds of country folk gathered for my first revival meeting in White Mound. A long, hand-painted banner announcing the meeting dates hung from the eaves of the tabernacle, an open-air meeting place with a shingled roof held up by wooden pillars, a cement floor, and chairs formed into rows. Brother Fred Swank stood beside me singing softly to himself the words to the hymn. As we stood in the shadow of the little white church, an amazing scene began to unfold before our unbelieving eyes. We thought fifty, maybe sixty people would gather that first night. But as we watched, the large churchyard filled to overflowing with buggies and wagons, with farmers, ranchers and townsfolk, their wives and children.

"I've never seen so many people gather for a meeting in these parts," Brother Swank said. "God's going to do a wonderful work here. Just wait and see."

I nodded in agreement, but frankly, I was growing more terrified by the minute. I didn't know exactly why. I had been preaching for almost two years. I had held one revival meeting in Pecan Grove and though it was small by comparison, I should not have been afraid. But something about that huge crowd gathering from White Mound and the neighboring communities left me trembling.

"Will you look at that," Brother Swank whispered as an impressive Buick sedan pulled to a stop, raising a cloud of dust and scaring the tethered horses with one last backfire. "That man owns land all over Texas," my friend reported. "He hasn't darkened the church doors for years. He's a real hellion, I can tell you."

Brother Swank was just a few years older than I. He was a student at Hardin-Simmons University, getting ready to be a pastor himself. And he had a real gift for song-leading. Fred knew the people of Coryell County and was much beloved by them. Suddenly, he quit looking at the crowds and turned in my direction.

"What is it, man?" he asked. "You look pale. Your hands are trembling. Why, Brother Criswell, I do think you're suffering a bit of fright."

I managed a weak smile and a nod.

"Don't worry about it, W. A." he said, placing his hands on my shoulders. "Come over here. I want to show you something."

I followed young Brother Swank to the little parsonage just west of the church. He sat down on the cement steps leading up to the kitchen door.

"Sit beside me," he said, patting the cool cement and grinning at me.

I was nineteen years old and wet behind the ears for certain. I had no great experience of life. I wasn't married. I didn't have a family. I hadn't fought in the trenches of a world war or struggled to keep a crop alive after months of drought and dust. The recent, troubling decline in the New York Stock Exchange hadn't eaten up my life savings. But the people gathering in that tabernacle had been through it all. They needed to hear God's Word preached powerfully by a wise and experienced prophet. I was just a kid from Baylor and suddenly I was afraid.

"I can't do it," I said to my friend as we sat side by side on the steps. "When I saw that great throng arriving from the ends of the earth, my heart just sank."

Swank listened patiently. I poured out my heart to him and not once did he interrupt with false or easy words of comfort or try to scold me for my lack of faith.

"Are you through, Mr. Criswell?" he said finally, reaching over to take the Bible from my hand.

"I'm going to read you something from the Word," he said, turning the pages rapidly to 1 Peter 5, verses 6 and 7. "Are you ready for this?"

I didn't reply. There was no time. My friend just stood up before me and began to read. His voice was strong and clear. The verses he read from God's Word went straight to my heart.

"Humble yourselves therefore under the mighty hand of God," he read, "that He may exalt you in due time: Casting all your care upon Him; for He careth for you."

Then he stopped, closed the Bible, and handed it back to me.

"Casting all your care upon Him," he quoted again, "for He careth for you."

I smiled feebly.

"I want you to get down here on your knees," he ordered, "right here by my side. I'm going to pray for you Brother Criswell," he added. "And you are going to stand up from this holy place, walk up to that pulpit, and be God's voice to these people."

I knelt beside my songleader. He placed his left hand on my shoulder and his right hand in the air above my head.

"Be with Brother Criswell, Lord," he said. "Help him mightily. Drive away all fear. Give him Your peace as You have promised. And let him rise up from his knees to proclaim Thy Word boldly to these people."

To this day, I can still remember kneeling in the shadows of that little parsonage, feeling Fred's hand on my shoulder. At that moment, it was the hand of God. I felt God's strength pour into me. I jumped up to my feet. I hugged Fred and led him through the throng of people to the platform. I stood before that huge crowd that flooded the tabernacle and overflowed in all directions. People were sitting in buggies and in open cars. They were standing under the pecan trees and in the grassy areas and in plowed fields around the churchyard.

Standing before them, I took a deep breath, prayed one last silent prayer, and then began to preach. People told me later that they could hear my voice clear across the town. One of my deacons who stayed home from the meeting too ill to attend said he heard me through his bedroom window five miles away!

We had a glorious meeting in White Mound those next two weeks because Fred Swank knew the power of God's Word and turned to it in my time of crisis. "Casting all your care upon Him," he read that night, "for He careth for you." Fred reminded me to take God at His Word. And when I cast my fears upon God, He took them away exactly as He had promised. How many times in the years ahead I would remember kneeling at that little church with Fred's hand on my shoulder and the Word of God echoing in my heart and mind.

To this day when I feel unsure or afraid, I open my Bible to 1 Peter 5:6-7 and I read those words again.

The Stock Market Crash and the Great Depression

Isn't it amazing how quickly storm clouds can blow in to darken the sky and block out the sun? I had never been afraid to preach before that night in White Mound. Then suddenly, fear swept over me like a valley fog, dense, dark, disorienting. How glad I was to have a friend present who knew the tricks of the devil. And even better, that friend knew the one power that the devil cannot stand, God's Holy Word, and with the Word we fought and conquered him.

What happened to me in the shadow of the tabernacle in White Mound—a sudden rush of fear and helplessness—happened just weeks later to the entire nation. On the third day of September, just days after our revival meeting's successful completion, the New York Stock Exchange reached 381, an all-time high. And though the market began to slide soon after, every immediate sign pointed to prosperity. There was no real reason to worry about the financial state of the nation. The people of Central Texas had been struggling through a drought, but no one dreamed that the clock in the courthouse at the county seat was ticking toward doomsday.

Then suddenly, on October 23, stock prices plummeted in massive liquidations. Twenty-four hours later, on "Black Thursday," October 24, 1929, the market crashed, plunging the nation and the world into the Great Depression. During the long, erratic slide between September and November of 1929, and especially during those two frantic "black" days of trading in October, the four million Americans who owned stock in our nation's businesses lost between twenty-four and seventy-five billion dollars in personal and corporate worth, three times as much money as the United States spent in fighting World War I.

During those depression years, five thousand banks would fail, three-quarters of a million farmers and at least a million businesses would go bankrupt, and nearly seventeen million Americans would lose their jobs. One historian reported, "The machinery of government was impotent. The banking system was paralyzed. Panic, misery, rebellion, and despair were convulsing the people and destroying confidence in the promise of American life."

Quickly, the suffering spread to Texas' farmers, ranchers, and business folk. The people of White Mound and Pecan Grove watched their life savings disappear in failed banks and plunging prices. Local stores boarded up for lack of business. Cotton crops died unharvested in the fields. Tenant workers drifted away toward California. People were broke and hungry, but I was nineteen and a child of the King. After that joyful experience on my knees behind the parsonage in White Mound, I was more confident than ever that God would take care of us. Of course my family had always been poor. I might not have even noticed the Great Depression but for the terrible suffering of the people I served.

"Morning, Brother Criswell. Praise the Lord."

Every Saturday afternoon in the little country store in White Mound, I stopped to drink an ice-cold Coca-Cola and to pay my pastoral call on Brother Johnson. The "Amen, brother," was my traditional response to his cheerful greeting. But on that morning in December, just days before my twentieth birthday, the old man's voice sounded tired. His "Praise the Lord" didn't have a very convincing ring. He didn't rush forward to shake my hand or to pound me on the back. My usually high-spirited deacon just kept on sweeping his empty store, looking up at me occasionally with sad, discouraged eyes.

"Where's all your customers, today?" I asked him as I reached down into the tub of chipped ice for my cold drink and held out a nickel to Brother Johnson.

"They're gone, Pastor," he said, once again refusing my nickel, "and this time I'm afraid I'm going with them."

It was my first real introduction to the terrible impact of the depression on local people. Brother Johnson's general store and White Mound Baptist Church were at the heart of country life in that part of Coryell County. It was unthinkable that either institution could be boarded up or abandoned.

"When people don't have money," Brother Johnson said quietly, "they can't buy. And when the buying stops, the stores close down."

Just then, Ray Childres, a molasses salesman from Gatesville, the Coryell County seat, drove up in a cloud of dust, parked his car and entered the store. For a moment, the salesman paused in the open doorway, took off his sweat-stained hat, and wiped his forehead with a large white handkerchief. Brother Johnson leaned on his broom and just looked at the salesman, shaking his head sadly. For a while neither man spoke.

"Sorry, Ray," Brother Johnson said, breaking the awkward silence. "I don't need any molasses today, or next week or the next, I'm afraid."

Ray Childres was a portly, good-natured man who usually filled the store with laughter on his Saturday visits. "Close your ears to this one, preacher," Ray would mutter loudly just before he told another of his traveling salesmen jokes. "This is for the poor box," he would whisper, peeling off a few dollars from the roll of bills he carried. Ray always laughed and backed away when I tried to share the gospel with him, but this time the poor man wasn't even smiling. He stood at the open door, hat in hand, and looked long and dolefully at Brother Johnson and then at me.

"Well, that does it then," he said. "I'm finished."

No one spoke. After a long, rather tragic silence, I walked to the ice chest, fished out a Coca-Cola, and offered it to the molasses salesman.

"No thanks, son," he said, walking down the steps and toward his battered Buick. "Charity isn't good for the soul."

"I'm sorry to see old Ray end up bankrupt like the rest of them," Brother Johnson said, taking off his leather apron and sitting down beside me on a covered pickle barrel. "But there just isn't any business.

The people of these parts have been giving away their cotton at five cents a pound. They've been buying their supplies from me on credit hoping to pay in the fall. Soon, the credit will run out and we grocers, dry goods salesmen, and molasses salesmen will end up in the apple lines."

The times were tragic, heartbreaking. Country folk ended up in the city waiting in long lines with other hungry, unemployed workers just to get a free apple, a sandwich, or a cup of coffee. My how the people suffered! But somehow Brother Johnson managed to keep his store open. And the good people of White Mound continued to pay me fifty dollars a month to be their three-quarter-time pastor, and the church in Pecan Grove never missed their twenty-five dollar monthly payment for the one-quarter time I gave to them.

Seventy-five dollars a month wasn't much even in those days, but with a little stretching, it was plenty for me. I never allowed myself more than ten cents for breakfast, twelve cents for lunch, and eighteen cents for dinner. I could buy a glass of milk for five cents and a bowl of cereal to put it on for just another nickel. I could buy a vegetable for three cents, and often I had three fresh vegetables for my noon meal. And in the evenings for less than a quarter I could get meat, potatoes, and even a piece of fresh-baked pecan pie.

After tithing to my churches and helping to support the cause of world missions through Baylor's Volunteer Band, what money was left went to pay college bills and to buy gasoline, tires, and maintenance for those long weekly commutes from Waco to Coryell County. I didn't know then that the professors, staff, and administration of Baylor were suffering. When the money ran out, the professors were paid in script, promissory notes that they could save, trade for products, or sell at a loss for cash. Times were hard, but I don't recall ever hearing any professor complaining about the hardships of those depression years. I still have great regard for those underpaid and overworked Baylor professors, but one man especially, Doctor A. J. Armstrong, Baylor's distinguished professor of English literature, passed on to me a love for the written word that shaped my life forever.

Dr. A. J. Armstrong

"Criswell?"

"Yes, sir?"

"Did you memorize the Browning verses as you drove mad-dash across Texas to minister to your little flock?"

It was a typical, windy, not so tongue-in-cheek greeting from Professor Armstrong as I entered his Monday morning class in English literature. He was an imposing man who filled the classroom with his gigantic intellect and his passion for poetry. He assigned long poetic passages, especially the works of Robert and Elizabeth Barrett Browning, to be "unearthed lovingly as a archaeologist might uncover a priceless artifact" and to be memorized on the weekends while, he said mockingly, we students were "at ease in Zion."

"Sorry, sir," I replied, knowing exactly what would follow.

Although Professor Armstrong was large of girth and rather sedentary, he moved quickly from his desk to stand towering over me.

"Was it a psalm you memorized, then, a shepherd poet's idyll, or another trenchant list from Leviticus that you hid away in your heart as your blue chariot carried you southward into the rolling hills and verdant pastures of Coryell County?"

Armstrong was merciless, prodding us toward perfection, begging, bribing, bossing us to behold and be moved by his beloved poetry. I looked up from my desk. His voice was stern but his eyes twinkled behind the wire-rimmed spectacles that he somehow managed to pinch to his nose.

"No time, sir," I mumbled, trying not to laugh.

Of course, I had memorized the verses. But the professor loved a good war of words, and he was in fine fettle that morning, feisty and fishing for a fight.

"No time, Criswell?" he said and his *basso profundo* voice echoed through the classroom and under the doorway into the hallways beyond.

"Ah," I answered, beginning rather melodramatically a quote from Robert Browning's 'Andrea del Sarto,' "but a man's reach should exceed his grasp, Professor, or what's a Heaven for?"

It was one of the poems he had assigned for that weekend's study and memorization. The class laughed. For a moment we thought the good professor had been thrown off guard. But without missing a beat he replied:

> There's a great text in Galatians,
> Once you trip on it, entails
> Twenty-nine distinct damnations,
> One sure, if another fails.

The skirmish was over. The battle had been won. I joined in the applause as the professor thrust out his chest, re-pinched his glasses, and grinning to himself walked majestically back to his desk at the front of the classroom.

Don't misunderstand. Dr. Armstrong was seldom frivolous. Nor did he usually quote the Brownings out of context or in jest. He was a man of excellence who saw poetry as the one sure proof that God loved humankind above all the other animals. And to read and memorize a poem, or better yet, to write one, was for Professor Armstrong the most humanizing of our tasks.

There were those who criticized Dr. Armstrong for "elevating the works of Robert and Elizabeth Barrett Browning above the works of Scripture." In fact, the Professor loved and honored God's Holy Word above all literature, including the poetry of his beloved Brownings.

"God Himself is the best Poet," he answered his critics, quoting Elizabeth Barrett Browning. "And the real poem is His song."

"I love the works of Robert and Elizabeth," he would tell us time and time again, "but God's Word is in a class by itself.

"Imagine the miracle of it. Dozens of authors over a period of no less than one thousand years, inspired by God and superintended by God's Holy Spirit, wrote His story once for all times to all the peoples of the earth."

And though he urged us to study the Word carefully, he also encouraged us take some time "to listen to its music without pausing to critique each note or phrase.

"The Word is made up of words," the professor reminded us. "And each word in it is inspired by a loving God who wanted His story told cor-rect-ly." He pronounced each syllable so that we would know how important it was to "rightly divide the Word of truth."

"But never forget," he added, "that the words are also beautiful. Hear them. Feel them. Be inspired and transformed by their power.

"When you study the Bible," he reminded us, "work hard to understand exactly what it means. Learn Hebrew and Greek. Immerse yourself in the history and culture of those ancient biblical times. Translate each word carefully, prayerfully, but when you've cracked open the secrets and exegeted the truth of God's holy inspired Word, then sit back quietly and read the words again. Only this time let their exquisite beauty wash over you like cooling rain on a hot summer day."

Professor Armstrong suspected that his critics were more anxious to criticize his view of the Bible than they were to read either it or the Brownings. After a particular scathing editorial against him in a local paper, Dr. Armstrong called his critics "blueberry pickers." It didn't take long to find the source of his retort in Book VII, line 821 of Elizabeth Barrett Browning's 'Aurora Leigh.'

> Earth's crammed with heaven,
> And every common bush afire with God.
> And only he who sees takes off his shoes,
> The rest sit round and pluck blueberries.

During my junior year, Dr. Armstrong inducted me into Sigma Tau Delta, a small group of Baylor students whom the Professor determined would distinguish themselves through the written or the spoken word. One evening in Dr. Armstrong's home as the students gathered to discuss the spiritual quest of Robert Browning, I shared with him my experience in White Mound that night when Fred Swank ordered me to my knees and read those words from 1 Peter. When I told Dr. Armstrong how suddenly my fear disappeared and my heart filled with peace, the usually dour professor took my hand and seemed overcome with emotion. After a pause to collect himself, he quoted these memorable lines from Robert Browning:

> All outside is lone field, moon and such peace,
> Flowing in, filling up, as with a sea,
> Whereupon comes Someone, walks fast on the white,
> Jesus Christ's self. . .
> To meet me and calm all things back again.

More than sixty years later, in my library alongside my Bible, my Greek and Hebrew dictionaries, and the commentaries I have used almost daily these past years are the collected works of Robert and Elizabeth Barrett Browning. Sometimes, sitting alone in my study I can still see A. J. Armstrong towering over me, his glasses sliding down his nose, his eyes twinkling. "Did you memorize the poem, Criswell? Did you hide it in your heart right alongside God's Word?"

One day I will thank him for demanding that I stretch my memory to include those poems. They have brought me endless joy and inspiration through the years.

The Tenant Farmer and His Wife

One Sunday, following the morning service in White Mound's little wood-framed church, a thin, young, red-faced farmer approached me nervously.

"Pastor," he mumbled, "would you come pray for our baby?"

The young man standing before me was only nineteen or twenty, about my age, but his face was already deeply lined and burnt red from the sun. His eyes were bloodshot, his shoulders slightly stooped. The young man was a tenant farmer, struggling through the drought. He clutched an old baseball cap in both hands and looked down at his worn shoes for just a moment, searching for the right words or for the courage to say them.

"I think the baby's dying," he said finally. "Maybe you could help us?"

Holding the young man's trembling arm, I guided him through the little crowd of parishioners standing at the rear of the church, down the three cement steps, across the gravel lot, and into my blue Chevrolet coupe. He didn't talk much. He just pointed the way and mumbled occasionally to himself.

"She got sick first," he said referring to his wife. "Couldn't nurse the baby. No milk. Then the baby got sick."

I asked about a doctor.

"No money," he mumbled. "And we thought the baby was getting better. Then just yesterday she began to cry all the time. Couldn't stop her crying."

I asked the tenant farmer about his wife.

"She's fine now, but the baby just gets worse. She's quiet all the time. Just looks straight up, breathes hard, won't eat."

"There," he said, rising up in his seat and pointing toward a ramshackle old cottage in a clump of black oak trees on the edge of an endless field. The earth was bone dry. A cloud of dust rolled over us as we stopped the car and walked toward the tenant farmer's cabin. I could see the crops that he had planted standing dead and gray in perfect rows stretching toward the distant horizon.

"Come in, please," he said holding open the torn screen door and motioning me into the semi-darkness.

The room was silent except for the squeaking sound of a rocking chair moving slowly back and forth and the voice of a young woman humming quietly. That young mother, maybe sixteen years old, sat in the shadows holding a baby. She didn't look up as we approached. She just kept rocking and humming and looking down at the little child lying dead in her arms.

"Baby?"

The young farmer knelt down beside his wife. He looked for a moment at his lifeless daughter. Then he looked back over his shoulder at me.

"The baby's gone, sir," he said. "There's nothing we can do now, is there?"

Then, without waiting for my reply, he turned back to his little wife.

"Baby's gone," he told her gently. "Baby's gone."

Everything happened so quickly. I had raced into the room hoping that I could help. Instead, death was waiting. The young father took the child, covered her with a thin blanket, and laid her on the bed. Then he took his wife in his arms and held her. I wrapped my arms around both of them and began to quote words of consolation from the Psalms.

"Though I walk through the valley of the shadow of death, I will fear no evil. For Thou art with me."

The psalmist's ancient words filled that little shack with comfort. Then I began to pray.

"God, we don't understand why babies die, but we do understand how much You love the children. Take this beautiful infant in Your arms, Jesus. Hold her close. And let this little mother and father feel Your peace, knowing that their beloved baby is in Your loving care forever."

Suddenly, the young farmer and his wife were both crying hard, hugging each other and hugging me. For a moment, I continued quoting words of comfort from the Psalms. Then the three of us just stood in the middle of that little cottage holding each other and crying together.

"Will you bury our baby?" the young man asked me later, after we had talked and prayed together.

It was my first funeral service. Only a handful of people gathered to remember the child's passing.

I stood before them with the Bible in my hand.

"In the book of Mark," I said, "there is a wonderful story about a ruler of the synagogue named Jairus who fell at Jesus feet begging the Master to heal his daughter.

"'She lies at the point of death,' he said. 'I pray thee, come and lay thy hands on her, that she may be healed; and she shall live.'"

The young tenant farmer sat in the front pew with his wife. They were holding hands and looking up at me. On a table in front of the pulpit, a rough wooden box held the body of their infant daughter. The mother had placed a bunch of wildflowers on the box before the service began. There were scarlet paintbrush, bluebonnets, and white prickly poppies in her little bouquet. The eyes of everyone present were filled with tears as I told the ancient story of another little girl who died while help was on the way.

"'Thy daughter is dead,' someone came running with the news. 'Why troublest thou the Master any further?'"

The story seemed so powerfully familiar. Jesus had rushed to bring help and healing, but He too had found death waiting. The room had already filled with mourners weeping loudly and tearing their garments in grief.

"'Why do you weep?' Jesus asked them. 'This damsel is not dead, but sleepeth.'"

"And the Bible says in Mark 5, 'They laughed him to scorn.'"

"Jesus didn't hesitate. He put the mourners out of the room, asked the parents to gather by the child's bed, and spoke quietly to her.

"'Damsel,' He said, 'I say unto thee, arise.'

"And the Bible says clearly that 'straightway the damsel arose and walked. And the people were astonished with a great astonishment.'"

I looked down at the little couple in the front row. I wondered if they might be asking themselves why I hadn't brought their baby back to life in Jesus' name. How often I, too, have wondered why God answers some prayers with miracles and other prayers with silence.

"But this one thing we know for certain," I told them. "Jesus was not afraid of death. He knew that dying is just a step from this world into a better place where God is waiting to welcome us home. Jesus brought that little girl to life because He wanted all of us to know that He has power over death and that when we trust Him, death has no power over us. Death is not the end for those who believe. It is just the beginning. And though we weep now for those who go before us, one day soon we will be reunited and together again we will live with Him forever."

I had never preached a funeral sermon. I had never stood behind a casket looking down into the eyes of those who mourn. Until that day, I wasn't sure that speaking God's Word would be enough to comfort people walking through the valley of death. But as I read from the Word of God in the little Baptist church in White Mound, as I told the story of Jesus' love to those dear tenant farmers who had lost their only child, I discovered again that God's Word has incredible power. In times of suffering and death, we can trust God to use His Word to wipe away tears and bring hope and healing to those who weep.

We sang a hymn and prayed a closing prayer. Two deacons placed the child's casket on the back of a flatbed truck. The young couple sat beside me in my little blue Chevrolet coupe. The mother clutched the bouquet of wildflowers and tried hard not to cry. The truck led us down the dusty road to White Mound's pre-Civil War cemetery on the edge of town. While we were riding together, the girl began to sob quietly. Awkwardly, her husband placed his arm around her and began to comfort her. As he spoke, I realized again what a difference the Word of God can make even in times of death and separation.

"There, there sweetheart," he said, "our little baby is in heaven. Don't you remember what the pastor said? God will take care of her. We don't need to worry anymore. God will be better to the baby than we could ever be. And one day when we die and go to heaven, God will have her waiting for us. Isn't that wonderful?"

The young woman nodded through her tears. I can still remember her clutching that little bunch of wildflowers to her breast and smiling as the deacons placed her baby's body in the ground.

That young but "awfully loud" preacher from Oklahoma

8

The Senior Year
at Baylor University
Waco: 1930-1931

*"Those things, which ye have both learned
and received, and heard, and seen in me, do:
and the God of peace shall be with you."*
Philippians 4:9

PECAN GROVE BAPTIST CHURCH BEGAN JUST AFTER THE
Civil War under an open-air tabernacle in a shady stand of pecan trees
on Coryell Creek. For more than half a century, farmers and ranchers
from as far north as Davidson and as far west as Lime City gathered in
that idyllic grove for their summer revival meetings. New converts
walked from the tabernacle down into the emerald-green waters of
Coryell Creek to be baptized, while the people gathered on those
pristine banks to celebrate the spiritual birth of each new man, woman,
or child who came up from the waters into a new life in Christ. The
grove echoed with their prayers and their songs of praise.

At the turn of the century, Christian believers in that area
formed Pecan Grove Baptist Church, and when they hired me as their

quarter-time pastor nearly thirty years later, they were still meeting for revival and Sunday services in their tabernacle in the grove, and for fall and winter worship services and Sunday school in a community school several miles away.

"I baptize you in the name of the Father, of the Son, and of the Holy Spirit. Amen."

The strapping young farmer struggled up out of the water not entirely confident that one so young and slight as I could handle the chore.

"Thank you, Pastor," he said, wiping water from his eyes and wading up out of the creek to his waiting family.

The little stream had seen six new believers plunged beneath its flood that day. The depression had wracked financial havoc through-out Coryell County. Cotton had dropped to five cents a pound. Mort-gage banks were foreclosing on our people, but as is often true, the church was growing in the midst of troubled times.

"We need to build a permanent place of worship," I told the deacons, and though the men nodded in agreement, no one, including their young pastor, had any idea where the money would come from.

Early one Saturday morning, I arrived at the little school house-community center where our congregation met. I was the Sunday school superintendent, the primary teacher, the worship leader, and the pastor all rolled into one. In fact, during my entire tenure at Pecan Grove, I couldn't find one man who would even volunteer to pray in public, and no one dared to ask a woman to lead in worship or to pray in those days. That morning I was moving desks into a corner and arranging chairs to face our makeshift pulpit. I arranged the Sunday school supplies in neat little piles and placed a stack of *Baptist Standard* newsletters on a table near the front door.

"We need to build a permanent place of worship," my own words echoed in my brain.

Suddenly, I found myself walking across the rolling pastureland toward the nearby home of Will Burt, our chief deacon. I could see him plowing his fields behind a team of mules. He waved when he saw me coming.

"Morning, Pastor," he called out to me. "Just hoping to get a crop of hay for the cattle before winter sets in," he said. "Not been weather for hay lately."

In fact, I knew for certain that Brother Burt, like most of the farmers in my congregation, had run out of cattle fodder during the drought. Now they were selling off what few head of cattle they still owned in hopes of getting enough cash to buy food for their families or to make one more mortgage payment on their farms before the banks foreclosed.

"Deacon Burt," I said as we sat on his rickety porch drinking lemonade and staring at the distant storm clouds, "we need to build a church."

Will Burt nodded slowly, placed his cool glass up against his face, and then settled back in the rocking chair.

"Sure do, Pastor," he consented. "Sure do."

"If the men would take the risk and work together," I suggested, "why we could build a church house here in Pecan Grove just as sure as you're sitting there."

Deacon Burt didn't say a word. He just took another drink of lemonade and rocked even faster back and forth in his squeaky porch chair. He didn't have any money. Nobody had any money in those days. But you can't stop building the church because the people have no money. Money or not, you have to trust God and build anyway.

Burt was a good man, devoted to his wife and family, hard-working, committed to his community and to the church. And he was flat broke. He hadn't made a mortgage payment in several months. The family was eating what they raised and the canned food, preserves, and slabs of pork and beef they got in trade for odd farm implements or pieces of furniture they could sacrifice.

"If I just had one man to stand beside me," I ventured, "we could build us a church."

Burt stopped rocking. He put his glass of lemonade on the porch rail, leaned toward me, and reached out to take my hand. I don't think I'll ever forget the look on his deeply lined, sunburned face as he said, "Pastor, I will be that man."

Sitting on Brother Burt's front porch, he and I drew plans for a simple but gracious little church house in the shape of a cross, topped by a steeple and a bell. We would build it a few steps from the old tabernacle on the quiet banks of Coryell Creek.

That afternoon we rode into Gatesville, the county seat, to show our crude plans to a lumberman who carefully estimated every foot of lumber, every sack of cement, and every bucket of white paint that we might need. Then he added up the figures and gave us one grand and overwhelming total of two hundred and forty dollars that we would need to raise.

Sunday afternoon, the deacons gathered in the school house. I was trembling with excitement as I stood to make my presentation.

Brother Burt sat nearby looking scared, but trying in his way to lend me encouragement.

"We men could build the church with our own hands," I explained. "We wouldn't need expensive labor. And the women and children would help paint and sand and decorate. The whole community could join in."

I was walking up and down the front of the classroom, gesturing and pointing at the plans and the list of materials tacked to the wall behind me.

"All we need are two hundred and forty dollars," I said. "We can do the rest."

Nobody even whispered when I finished. The men shifted restlessly in their chairs. They looked past me out the windows and waited for someone to break the awkward, painful silence.

I was exhausted. A wave of doubt swept over me. Had I pushed these poor farmers way too far? The Great Depression had seriously wounded every man in the room. Each was struggling to survive. That two hundred and forty dollars was a fortune. I might as well have asked for the moon. For a moment I stood before them feeling tired and overwhelmed. Suddenly, their blank looks and that awful silence knocked the props out from under me. I sat down in a student desk, put my head in my hands, and began to cry.

I don't know how many seconds passed. I just remember sitting there not knowing what to do or say next. Suddenly, I heard a desk move and the shuffling sounds of a man standing to his feet.

"Listen, son," a familiar voice said softly. "Don't cry. We'll build that church. You'll see."

Brother Burt was standing in the middle of the room before the other farmers.

"You just get your pencil and paper," he said to me, "and stand up there and write down what I tell you."

I opened my satchel, took out pencil and paper like a school boy before his final exam, and stood up beside Brother Burt.

"Now you brothers know my wife and I don't have a dollar to our names, but a long time ago God gave me a beautiful leather saddle. I was saving it for that day when I could buy a horse again. But sitting here just now I decided to give that saddle back to the Lord. I know a rancher who will give me fifteen dollars for it, and I want to pledge that saddle to our new church."

Brother Burt paused. He seemed surprised and pleased at his own daring act.

"Write it down, preacher. Burt: fifteen dollars."

Without a moment's hesitation, Brother Burt turned next to Alex Davidson and gripped the farmer's shoulders in his hands.

"Now, Alex, you tell the preacher what you're going to pledge to our new church."

Brother Davidson didn't even try to wiggle away.

"Pastor Criswell," he said, "if we sell a few more quilts and have any luck at all laying away the last of the cotton, I think we could manage ten or twenty dollars . . . over the next few weeks or months."

"Why that will buy the studs," I said, "and almost all the nails. Thank you, Brother Davidson."

Burt turned next to Pete Martin, but before he could grip him by the shoulders, Brother Porter made his pledge.

"Five dollars this month and seven dollars next, the Lord willing," he said quickly.

"That's twelve bags of cement," I exclaimed crossing that expensive item off my list. "Praise the Lord."

Brother Burt continued the process until every man in the room had pledged. The total came to just under two hundred and fifty-five dollars. When I added it up, the men cheered. I noticed that Brother Burt's eyes had filled with tears.

"I'll be that man," he had said to me, and with his example and his courage, the money was pledged and the church was built. It still stands today in that quiet pecan grove on Coryell Creek.

Baylor's Student Ministerial Association

Almost every Sunday night, after preaching and pastoring on the weekends, I drove back to Baylor feeling excited and inspired by what God was accomplishing in Pecan Grove and White Mound. Country folk were finding Christ as Lord and Savior. Our Sunday schools were growing and our worship services were filled with believers and new seekers, young and old alike.

"But are you getting your homework done?" one professor asked me rather sternly when I tried to share what God was doing. We were standing together in a coffee line during a break in his afternoon class on the Old Testament.

"Yes, sir," I answered, feeling angry and demeaned by his insinuation. "But grades aren't everything, you know."

I was a graduating senior. That professor in the Bible department knew fully well that in the past three and a half years at Baylor I hadn't earned less than an A grade in any class, including his. He had been a pastor himself. He should have also known that pre-ministerial students need more than just bookwork.

"You go to seminary for that," the professor answered when I tried to explain.

"By then it may be too late," I shot back.

During my four years at Baylor, I had seen young men come to study for the ministry, only to walk away from their calling and even lose their faith. I recalled the name of one young man we both knew well.

"He got straight A's," I told the professor, "but his spirit shriveled up and died. He not only left the ministry," I reminded him. "He left the faith."

"And if your story is true, and I'm not saying that it is," the professor goaded me, "what do you think caused the problem? Classes? Books? The library? You don't lose your calling in the library, do you, Criswell?"

"You can," I answered. "I've seen it happen. Book knowledge is important. I'm an English major and a philosophy minor. I know about books, but books are not enough. You can't wait until your intellectual training is finished to begin the training of your heart."

"Let Baylor train your heart, Criswell," he said. "You don't need to drive all over Texas for that."

A crowd of students was beginning to gather around us. The chance encounter was becoming a full-blown debate. Sides were being taken. Feelings were running high.

"Sir," I said intensely, "I believe that hand-in-hand with books, classes, and libraries, we students need to work with people who are struggling with the real problems of life. We need on-the-job opportunities where we can put our intellectual training into practice. It's too bad when your head outgrows your heart and it can be fatal spiritually!"

For a moment the professor just stood there staring at me. His hand was trembling. Coffee splashed from his cup.

"Look, Criswell," he said, "I'm not against your work in Coryell County. You know that. But you'll have the rest of your life to hold revivals and to build churches. You only have a few short years in the classroom and the library."

"I respect you for driving me to the library," I said, "but it's the people in my little churches in Pecan Grove and White Mound who drive me to my knees. I need professors and books and libraries to stimulate my brain, but I need those humble people of Coryell County to keep my heart warm and my eyes fixed on Jesus."

"Criswell," the professor said condescendingly, "you are still just a student. Students come and go. They bring their enthusiasm. They make their demands. And then they exit, leaving us to pick up the pieces. One day maybe you'll see the issue in a larger perspective."

The bell rang. The professor took one last sip from his coffee and headed back to class.

Maybe I had spoken out of place. Occasionally, even in those wonderful years at Baylor, my enthusiasm got the best of me. But when that professor called me "just a student," his words cut me like a knife.

I had worked hard for Baylor as president of the student's Ministerial Association, a hundred and twelve students who felt called to pastoral ministry. With very little backing from the faculty or administration, we had conducted preaching missions in the prison, in the poorhouse, and in Waco's City Plaza. We had organized prayer meetings and Bible study groups, special lectures and seminars on the pastoral ministry, and even found churches where those young men could serve part-time while they were still students. We did our classwork during the week and on weekends drove twenty thousand miles every month serving little churches in fifteen different counties.

We Baylor ministerial students were helping plant and grow Baptist churches in Texas and, at the same time, we were helping to plant and grow our own personal Christian faith. I expected Baylor's professors, especially in Bible and theology, to support our work. They didn't. Generally, they were in sympathy with our goals, but seldom did even one of them take time to help or to encourage us. They were preoccupied with lectures, books, and learned papers. They didn't seem to value practical, down-to-earth Christian ministry as a significant part of our training. And when we tried to tell them about the good it did in our lives, they smiled, nodded politely, and asked, "But did you get your homework done?"

The Great Baylor Campaign

On the first Sunday in our new church in Pecan Grove, I took an offering from those poor but deeply committed ranchers and farmers for Baylor University. The professors were practically starving. The script they received in lieu of salary had proven almost worthless. Students couldn't pay their tuitions or their fees. Businessmen who once supported Baylor with large donations had been wiped out by the stock market crash and by bank failures and foreclosures. Support for the university was drying up.

The Rockefeller Foundation, a benefactor of Christian causes with a unique, long-standing commitment to Christian colleges, seminaries, and their student bodies, heard of Baylor's plight and offered to donate five hundred thousand dollars to the university if the Baptists of Texas could match their gift by raising an equal amount. In response, the Great Baylor Campaign was launched at the height of the depression years. President Brooks appointed Carr Collins, the president of the Fidelity Union Life Insurance Company in Dallas and a dedicated Baptist lay leader, to head the campaign.

Even though I disagreed with many of Baylor's professors, I loved the university and was committed to her future. With all my heart I believed in President Samuel Palmer Brook's vision for a great Christian university where a love for God's Word was at the heart of the curriculum and an active, growing Christian faith was the goal for every student.

When the Great Depression threatened that vision, I immediately enlisted my two small churches to help the Baylor Campaign. I wrote to Mr. Collins thanking him for his work on Baylor's behalf and enclosed the offerings from the churches in Pecan Grove (twelve dollars) and White Mound (eighteen dollars). Mr. Collins seemed inspired by our quick and sacrificial response. He invited me to his Waco office.

After a brief conversation, Carr Collins asked me to present the Baylor campaign to other churches across Texas. Those brave Baptist people of the churches in Coryell, Milam, and Brazos counties loved Baylor and reached deep into their nearly empty pockets to help save the school. Mr. Collins was amazed.

"Brother Criswell," he said, "I want you to present the Baylor Campaign to the faculty, staff, and students of Southwestern Seminary."

Though stunned and terrified by his request, I agreed. I was a Baylor undergraduate and had just turned twenty. Southwestern Seminary was the center of Baptist life. Who was I to make such a major presentation?

"You'll do fine," Mr. Collins said, grinning at me from behind his massive oak desk. "Don't let those gray beards fool you. They put their pants on every morning just like you do."

Dr. L. R. Scarborough, the seminary's distinguished and acclaimed president, was shocked and obviously disappointed when I showed up in Carr Collins' stead.

"Son," President Scarborough said, rising up from his desk just before the great seminary convocation was scheduled to begin, "I don't know why on earth Carr Collins would send you to present the Great Baylor Campaign to the faculty and students of Southwestern. But anything Carr Collins wants, we will help him get. So you will speak in chapel as he has asked. And you can take up your collection—but remember, nobody gets blood from a turnip. These people are starving themselves. Don't be too disappointed if the baskets come back empty."

I prayed one last urgent prayer, swallowed hard, steadied my knocking knees, stepped up to that great pulpit with its roots in Baptist history, opened my Bible to Luke 6:28, read my text, and preached my heart out.

"Give, and it shall be given unto you; good measure, pressed down, shaken together and running over."

The baskets came back full. Dr. Scarborough was amazed, Carr Collins elated. The moment I got back to my little room at Baylor, I breathed a sigh of relief and dropped to my knees to pray a long, sincere prayer of thanks.

Two weeks later, I was summoned from my Tuesday class in medieval literature to the office of the university's president. I had no idea why his secretary would dare to interrupt Professor Armstrong's lecture on Dante's "Inferno" from the *Divine Comedy*, except that maybe I was about to feel the flames of hell myself. What had I done wrong? Was the world coming to an end? President Samuel Palmer Brooks has sent for me. Oh, my!

A secretary opened the door into the president's inner sanctum. President Brooks came around from his desk to greet me.

"So you're the red-headed student preacher that I've been hearing so much about," he said shaking my hand, leading me to a sofa, and sitting down beside me.

Just then I noticed Carr Collins sitting across the room in an oversized red leather chair. He winked at me conspiratorially, and his grin stretched from Brownsville to the Texas Panhandle.

"Morning, Criswell," he said, his voice hoarse and strained. I returned his greeting, looking puzzled and probably a bit comical. What was wrong? Why were we all sitting there?

"Laryngitis," he whispered in response to my first unasked question. "Can't talk."

"You represented Baylor well at Southwestern," President Brooks began, "and Mr. Carr here wants you to represent us one more time."

Besides the seminary presentation, I had spent six or seven Sundays traveling to little churches south of Waco to take collections for the Baylor Campaign. I was glad to volunteer for more.

"In chapel," the president explained, "Today!"

My face collapsed in shock. Mr. Collins got tickled by my obvious surprise. His good-hearted laughter ended in a fit of coughing. President Brooks looked concerned.

"Pardon me, sir?" I whispered, looking first at Dr. Brooks and then across the room at Mr. Collins.

"Mr. Collins can't speak above a whisper," the president replied. "He thinks that you are the one to make his presentation . . . ."

"To the university, man," Collins' raspy voice interrupted, "to Baylor, to the board of trustees, to the faculty and staff, and to the whole student body. I want you to stand up in that spanking new Waco Hall this morning and present the Great Baylor Campaign to the people whose lives are dependent on it."

For a moment, I was speechless. My heart was pounding and my throat was turning dry.

"Well," I said in a kind of stage whisper, my voice sounding more like Mr. Collins' voice than I intended, "I'll just do the best I can."

I will never forget that next moment as long as I shall live. My hero, President Samuel Palmer Brooks, stood up and hugged me. One of the spiritual giants in my life put his arms around me and said softly, "I'm grateful, lad."

"We both are," Carr Collins croaked enthusiastically, moving to shake my hand. "Now go get your Bible and meet us at the Hall."

Waco Hall was crammed to capacity. I sat between President Brooks and Carr Collins on the great platform beneath the proscenium arch. My friends sat down front, their eyes wide and their mouths open in shock.

"What are you doing up there?" one gestured silently.

"Pray for me," I signaled back.

President Brooks led a thousand student voices in the morning hymn. His prayer for Baylor that morning moves me still when I remember it. Then he turned to me and smiled bravely.

"Our speaker this morning has had exactly twenty-three minutes to prepare."

My friends in the Volunteer Band and the Ministerial Association looked up at me and then back and forth at each other in wonder and surprise. The Board of Trustees and the Baylor faculty sat staring straight ahead, their faces blank, wondering why the launching of the campaign upon which their futures might depend was left in my inexperienced hands.

The crowd grew silent as I opened my Bible to read from Paul's first letter to Timothy, chapter 4, verse 12:

"Let no man despise thy youth; but be thou an example of the believers . . . in charity," I exclaimed.

And for the next thirty minutes, I paced up and down that great platform preaching the Word and promoting the Baylor Campaign with every ounce of strength that I could muster. In those frightening moments before the service began, sitting on the platform, staring out at my fellow Baylorites, I had asked God to do His work with these good people through me. And as I began to speak, I could feel the Spirit of God speaking through me. His voice echoed through my voice off the balcony walls and filled the Hall with expectation.

"These may be the years of the Great Depression," I exclaimed, "but the kingdom of God is not depressed. God still reigns. His hand controls the sun by day and a billion stars by night. His angels and His saints still wait to do His bidding. How can we doubt God's power or God's love for us and for this great university? With your faith and God's power, the five hundred thousand dollars will be raised and our million dollar goal will be accomplished."

At the close of my address, the faculty and trustees joined in the students' cheering. Together, they marched out to more than meet the goal. President Brooks hugged me once again, and Carr Collins, his eyes wet and sparkling, said hoarsely, "Good word, Brother Criswell, good *Word*."

The Trouble with Dante's Divine Comedy

Reaching the million dollar mark in the Baylor Campaign made everyone on the campus feel joyful and a bit lightheaded. Even Professor A. J. Armstrong decided that, rather than a term paper on Dante's *Divine Comedy*, he would ask our class to divide into two groups that would each write and perform a play about the Italian poet's classic work.

The poem took Dante Alighieri at least a dozen years to write, from 1308 to 1320. The plot is simple, the impact exquisite and disturbing. A man, probably Dante himself, is miraculously enabled to undertake a journey to visit the souls in Hell, Purgatory, and Paradise. His guides are Virgil and Beatrice. The first group in our class did a rather boring little playlet about Beatrice and Dante in Paradise.

My group, on the other hand, wrote and staged a "satire" featuring Professor A. J. Armstrong himself. Our little work took place in Dante's imaginary office in the cathedral in Florence. We were there to see Italy's greatest poet on behalf of our "poor lost professor" who had, because of his "exceptional wickedness," been consigned to the very lowest regions of hell.

We did battle with Satan on Professor Armstrong's behalf. The class cheered and applauded. Dr. Armstrong didn't even smile.

"What manner of foolishness is this," he growled before the play had even ended. "Enough!" he said slamming his book closed and dismissing the class.

By my youthful standards, it was a harmless, even creative kind of prank. We harpooned the good professor once or twice as certainly he deserved, but no one dreamed our much beloved teacher would take serious offense. I learned officially that next Monday morning when the scores were posted. It was my only B grade in four years at Baylor.

Professor Armstrong had inducted me into his private literary fraternity, Sigma Tau Delta, two years earlier. I was president my senior year and volunteered dozens of extra hours to help him carry treasures from his Browning collection into the new building named in his honor, where the artifacts would be displayed. I chaired a special visit to our campus of American poet and dramatist Edna St. Vincent Millay, an event that was sponsored by Dr. Armstrong and Sigma Tau Delta. I was one of the professor's favorites, or so I thought, until that Tuesday when I entered his office to plead my case.

"Sir," I said quietly, "I am sorry you were offended by our play. We meant no harm. But if you will check in your record book I have done A or A-plus work this entire semester. My papers and my tests should illustrate that I do not deserve the B you gave me after seeing our 'satire.' "

"Hateful little play," he muttered. "Disgraceful! Demeaning!"

"Again I apologize," I repeated. "We tried to use humor to show our understanding of the *Divine Comedy*."

"You failed!" he grumbled.

"I know, sir, but if you will consider changing my grade even to an A-minus I will still graduate Summa Cum Laude. Your grade will make the difference in an otherwise perfect college record."

"No," he said.

And for endless moments I stood before him, hat in hand, being swallowed by the silence as this great unforgiving man whom I had loved and served faithfully turned his back on me. Because we had been such close friends and because I knew he loved for us students to quote the poet's words, I tried to soften him up one last time.

"O mortal men," I whispered quoting Dante Alighieri, "be wary how ye judge."

Without a second's hesitation, Professor Armstrong answered, this time from the "Inferno."

"Abandon hope, all ye who enter here."

For a moment I thought the good professor might smile. The moment passed and so did I, but not with highest honors, as I had hoped.

The Power of the Word

"Pastor, can you tell me what in the world kind of book this might be?"

Alex Davidson was an affluent cotton farmer and my leading deacon at White Mound Baptist Church in Coryell County. While making my Saturday pastoral rounds one winter morning, I found Alex sitting on his front porch sorting through an old orange crate filled with books.

"Found 'em in a farm sale over near the County Seat," he explained. "Can't figure this one though," he added, handing me a small black book with no title on its cardboard cover.

The binding was cheap and rather primitive. The edges of the pages were rough-edged and didn't exactly mesh. The book smelled damp and felt heavy in my hands. I opened the cover and read the title: *La Biblia en Español.* Scrawled in pencil just below the title I found these words: "Propiedad de Carlos Montoya."

"It's a Spanish Bible," I told him. "Looks like it once belonged to a man named Carlos, Carlos Montoya."

Brother Davidson stood up to get a closer look. We turned the pages. There were little notes in the margins printed in neat, numbered Spanish, and Carlos had underlined many of his favorite verses.

"Somebody loved this Book," I said.

"Yea, but what am I going to do with it?" Alex answered.

"Don't you have a Mexican tenant farmer on your lower thirty?" I asked him.

"Sure do," he replied, "Juan and Maria Sandoval."

We drove to the little tenant farmhouse where Juan and Maria lived with their six young children. Juan rushed out to greet us when he saw Mr. Davidson. Maria hovered over her brood of healthy, happy children as they watched us from the porch and doorway.

"Gracias, Señor," Juan said sincerely, taking the Book and then suddenly looking quite surprised.

"La Biblia," he said turning toward his wife and holding out the open Book in her direction.

"La Biblia?" Maria whispered incredulously, rushing to stand beside her husband. "La Biblia . . . " she said again, this time with real awe in her voice.

"This is my pastor," Alex said quietly.

"*Pas-tor?*" Juan repeated Alex's pronunciation slowly. "Oh, pas-*tor*," he said again, "Like padre, priest!"

Alex looked at me and almost laughed outloud.

"Yea," he said politely, trying not to smile. "Young Brother Criswell here's my family priest."

"Buenos días, Padre," Maria replied, and she whispered loudly to her children who echoed her command in one high-pitched voice, "Buenos días, Padre."

"Buenos días," I replied, wishing I knew enough Spanish to converse intelligently with these dear people.

"Gracias," they said over and over again as we returned to our car. "Muchas gracias!"

Several months later, early one Sunday before our morning worship service at White Mound, the whole congregation was surprised when Juan, Maria, and their children walked up the dusty farm road, turned into the gravel parking lot in front of the church, and stood before us in a perfect little line. The boys were wearing dark pants and white shirts. It looked like Maria had used white feed sacks to sew beautiful little dresses for herself and her two young girls. The children were spotless and smiling. Juan rushed up to greet us.

"Padre," he said. "My English bad, but I ask boss tell you. He tell you yet?"

At that moment, Alex Davidson and his family drove into the driveway in their 1926 Buick. When Alex saw what was happening he rushed to intervene.

"Not today, Juan," he said rather apologetically. "The Padre only comes on weekends. I haven't talked to him yet."

My little congregation was forming in a curious semi-circle, looking on as Alex Davidson tried to explain.

"Do you remember the Bible?" Alex asked, "the Spanish Bible we gave them?"

"Yes, of course," I replied.

Juan and Maria were listening intently to our conversation. Their dark-skinned children were grinning at the white-skinned children of White Mound Baptist Church and the White Mound children were grinning back.

"This could be a mess," Alex whispered. Then he raised his voice and continued. "The long and the short of it," he said, "is this. Looks like Juan and Maria got saved reading that old Spanish Bible."

"Well, praise the Lord," I said, and though I believed with all my heart that such a wonderful thing could happen, I was still eager to know the details.

"Juan tried to explain it all to me, Pastor," Alex continued. "And I think I understand. Apparently, this Carlos Montoya was a Christian convert under Baptist missionaries to Mexico. Somehow his Bible ended up in my orange crate. Looks like Carlos marked the passages that explain conversion and wrote even more notes in the margin, explaining how your sins can be forgiven and how your name can be written in the Book of Life. Now, Juan, Maria, and their children want to be baptized."

Juan and Maria nodded eagerly.

"Si, Padre," Maria said quietly, "to be baptized."

Alex walked me a few steps from the crowd that had gathered.

"You know, Pastor," he said, "it just isn't done around here, white churches baptizing colored folk."

Alex Davidson was a good man. I knew his heart.

"It is now," I said trembling with excitement. "Somehow, by the grace of God, these dear people found Jesus as Lord and Savior through the Word. And that same Word commands us to baptize them in the name of the Father, and of the Son, and of the Holy Spirit. And what the Bible says, we will do."

Alex grinned and absent-mindedly wiped his tough, calloused hands on his suit coat as though preparing for a fight.

"Okay, Pastor," he said. "Let's go do it."

That day Juan, Maria, and their six children were received by the church on their confession of faith. In the nearby Leon River, I baptized the entire family from the largest to the smallest, and the whole countryside looked on smiling and praising the Lord.

But the story doesn't end there. Four weeks later, Maria's can of cooking grease spilled onto her open fire. Flames jumped up the wall and quickly engulfed the farmhouse. Juan just managed to get his wife and children to safety. They were standing together watching the flames consume every precious thing they owned when suddenly, Juan remembered their Bible lying on the little table beside their bed.

"La Biblia," he whispered, and without a thought for his own safety, Juan rushed back into the burning building.

Through that Bible, marked by the loving hand of a stranger, God had given Juan's family new life. From the first day of its discovery, they had read it together faithfully every morning before the day began and every evening as the sun set over Coryell County. In those few short weeks, God's Word had become their family's treasure, and Juan refused to see it burn.

With tears streaming down his face, Alex Davidson told me the whole story the very next Saturday as we drove toward the ruins of Juan and Maria's little home. Already, Alex had provided the family temporary quarters while their new farmhouse was being built. As we approached the end of the farm road, I could see the family standing together near the still-smouldering ruins. Juan rushed toward me, the precious Bible in his hand.

"Padre," he said, "we saved the Word from the burning . . . ."

The Book was blackened by smoke and singed by flames, but the fire had not consumed it. The power of God still dwelt between its damaged covers. The voice of God still echoed from its pages. The Word of God had been rescued "from the burning . . . ."

As Juan placed that precious Book into my hands, I couldn't speak. Tears of gratitude welled up in my eyes. Juan had risked his life to save the Word. As I knelt on the grass that day, I wondered how many others over the centuries had risked and even sacrificed their lives to save the Word "from the burning." One by one, the others knelt beside me.

"Lord," I prayed, and as a quiet echo, Juan began to translate my prayer. "Padre Nuestro," he said.

"Thank you for your Word."

"Gracias, Dios, por la Santa Biblia."

"And thank you for Juan, who risked his life to save it from the burning."

Juan couldn't speak. I said "Amen" and the little family echoed with their own quiet "Amen." I can still remember Juan, Maria, and their children gathered around the one great treasure they had saved from the fire. How precious is the Word to one whose life has been changed by it!

As we drove away, I thanked God for Carlos Montoya, who loved the Word. He read it, underlined it, and wrote messages in its margins that the Holy Spirit used to bring new life to an entire family. Carlos will probably never know the difference he made in the lives of Juan, Maria, and their six beautiful children.

How grateful I am that God taught me early in my ministry that none of us ever really knows the great good God can accomplish through our small acts of faithfulness, especially when it comes to sharing His glorious Word.

Dr. Brook's Last Graduation

Just weeks before graduation, we discovered with terrible certainty that Dr. Samuel Palmer Brooks, Baylor's beloved president, was dying. Even his current biographers don't know exactly what disease slowly sapped him of his strength, crippled his robust frame, and at the close of my senior year, took him from us. For a while during the Great Baylor Campaign, he seemed to be his vigorous self again. Dr. Brooks was determined to leave the university free of debt, and even during those years of the Great Depression wanted to add significantly to Baylor's endowment funds. So in spite of his illness and against his doctor's advice, our president traveled across West Texas by train and automobile, speaking in large churches and city rallies on Baylor's behalf.

That last burst of energy allowed us to reach the million dollar goal, but it may have cost our president his life. As he stood before us one last time in chapel, Dr. Brook's body appeared ravaged by the disease. His face was deeply lined with pain. He knew how much we needed him to lead those morning chapels and was determined to be there for us. His deeply spiritual presence set a tone for the whole university that spread across the campus and throughout the Baptist world. His last chapel prayer was for us students that we "might all belong to the Father by choice and by surrender." In one of his last letters to an unconverted student, Dr. Brooks urged the young man to meet him one day, "where God is, to dwell with Him through eternity."

"Dr. Brooks is coming home!"

The rumor spread across the campus like a prairie wildfire. President Brooks was back in Waco. In April of 1931, his condition worsened drastically. He had been rushed by ambulance to the Baylor Hospital in Dallas and then by train to a special sanitarium in Battle Creek, Michigan. The doctors had failed. Dr. Brooks was determined to die at home, surrounded by his Baylor family. The students' spirit rallied. Dr. Brooks was coming home!

"He has been taken back to the hospital!"

On May 2, 1931, the doctors decided on one last exploratory surgery to see if something might be done to save the life of Samuel Palmer Brooks. When he awakened from the anesthetic, he asked his nurse, "Did they find anything worth saving?" When a delegation of students visited him to inquire of his health, Dr. Brooks replied, "The doctor says I am doing fairly well, but I have internal information to the contrary." Just days later, Dr. Brook's own diagnosis proved correct.

"He is dying!"

The words were whispered from professor to student, from student to staff. The campus grew unnaturally quiet. Everyone was praying and worrying for Dr. Brooks. No laughter echoed across the Quad. No playful pranks interrupted our studies in the dormitories or rooming houses. Classes met. Papers were researched and written. Final exams were scheduled. But the spirit of the place dropped with every bulletin from Dr. Brook's hospital bed. How we would miss that man.

"He is trying to stay alive through graduation!"

From his secretary we learned that our president had determined to greet his one last graduating class, my class. No one believed it. Dr. Brooks was paralyzed from the waist down. He struggled even to breathe. His entire body was failing. Only his strong heartbeat and his determined love for Baylor kept the man alive. He couldn't march in that impressive and colorful line. He couldn't stand before us to deliver one last commencement address. But he determined at least to sign our diplomas and in that way pass on his personal love to us, one signature at a time.

"The diplomas are stacked on his bed!"

A nurse reported that Dr. Brooks had ordered his staff to deliver all four hundred and fifty-five diplomas into the room where he was dying. His secretary filled extra pens and placed them at his side. Slowly, painfully, he began to sign each diploma from the liberal arts college and the colleges of law, medicine, pharmacy, dentistry, and nursing.

"He's finished the A's."

I suppose it was selfish of me, but I joined the other graduating seniors in praying that Dr. Brooks would stay well at least long enough to sign my diploma. I am embarrassed to admit that I was grateful that my name fell so early in that long alphabetical list.

"He's finished the B's."

We were being fitted for caps and gowns. The class picture was taken with an empty chair for our dear missing president. I had finished my last final and turned in my last paper when the good news reached me.

"He has finished the C's."

Dr. Brooks had managed to sign two hundred and fifty diplomas before his strength gave way. He put down his pen and asked his wife to write down the last words he would ever speak to his much-loved Baylor students. We graduating seniors lined up at Waco Hall. The orchestra played the grand processional from "Aida" as we marched to our places, each of us wondering if Dr. Brooks had left a word for us.

The commencement began. One by one the awards were given, the speeches made. Then suddenly, Dean Allen reached into his pocket and pulled out a carefully folded manuscript.

"Dr. Brooks has left this message for the senior class of 1931."

As one person, the entire senior class strained forward in our chairs to hear the words Dr. Brooks had penned for us. They were glorious words. They hang in my office to this day and still inspire me almost sixty years later as they did when I first heard them.

"This, my message to the Senior Class of 1931, I address also to the seniors of all years, those seniors yet to be. This I do because I love them all equally even as I love all mankind regardless of station or creed, race or religion. I stand on the border of mortal life but I face eternal life. I look backwards to the years of the past to see all pettiness, all triviality shrink into nothing and disappear. Adverse criticism has no meaning now. Only the worthwhile things, the constructive things, the things that are built for the good of mankind and the glory of God count now. There is beauty, there is joy, and there is laughter in life as there ought to be. But remember, all of you, not to regard lightly nor to ridicule the sacred things, those worthwhile things. Hold them dear, cherish them, for they alone will sustain you in the end; and remember too that only through work and of times through hardships may they be attained. But the compensation of blessing and sweetness at the last will glorify every hour of work and every heartache from hardship. Looking back now as I do, I see things with a better perspective than ever before and in their truer proportions. More clearly do I recognize that God is love. More clearly do I understand the universal fatherhood of God. More clearly do I know the brotherhood of man. Truths do not change. The truths of life which I learned as a student in Baylor have not varied nor will they vary. I know now that life has been a summary of that which was taught me first as a student here. As my teachers have lived through me, so I must live through you. You who are graduating today will go out into the world to discover that already you have touched much of what the future holds. You have learned the lessons which must fit you for difficulties and the joys of years to come. Then, hold these college years close to your hearts and value them at their true worth. Do not face the future with timidity or with fear. Face it boldly, courageously, joyously. Have faith in what it holds. Sorrow as

well as happiness must come with time. But know that only after sorrow's hand has bowed your head will life become truly real to you, for only then will you acquire the noble spirituality which intensifies the reality of life. My own faith as I approach eternity grows stronger day by day. The faith I have had in life is projected into the vast future toward which I travel now. I know that I go to an all powerful God wherever He may be. I know that He is the personality who created man in His image. Beyond that I have no knowledge, no fear, only faith. Because of what Baylor has meant to you in the past, because of what she will mean to you in the future, oh my students, have a care for her. Build upon the foundations here the great school of which I have dreamed, so that she may touch and mold the lives of future generations and help to fit them for life here and hereafter. To you seniors of the past, of the present, of the future I entrust the care of Baylor University. To you I hand the torch. My love be unto you and my blessing be upon you."

Dean Allen could hardly finish reading the president's words. Most of our class were fighting back tears before the speech had ended. Even my mother and father were wiping tears away when I stood to receive my diploma. What a joy it was to see with my own eyes that Samuel Taylor Brooks had signed it with his own strong hand. Days later he died. Mrs. Brooks told us that on the evening of our graduation, Dr. Brooks had rallied long enough to ask her, "Do you think they will really care when I am gone?"

"Why, my dear," she answered, misunderstanding his question entirely, "telegrams, letters, personal visits, flowers, the resolutions of the State Legislature, editorials in the great papers — the people are showing great regard . . . ."

"Oh, no, no, no," he cut in, "I mean will they care for Baylor? Will they help her on to her highest usefulness?"

And though there are rumors to the contrary, I still love Baylor and will continue to pray that the spirit of Samuel Palmer Brooks and his lifelong commitment to God's Holy Word will one day reign in that great university once again.

9

Southern Seminary

Louisville: 1931-1937

"My son, attend to my words;
incline thine ear unto my sayings.
Let them not depart from thine eyes;
keep them in the midst of thine heart.
For they are life unto those that find them,
and health to all their flesh."
Proverbs 4:20-22

WILL ROGERS, THE DOWN-HOME HUMORIST WHO HELPED brighten my boyhood years, refused an honorary Doctorate of Humanity and Letters from Oklahoma City University in May of 1931, the same month I proudly received my Bachelor of Arts in English from Baylor.

"What are you trying to do," Rogers asked Oklahoma officials, "make a joke out of college degrees? They are in bad enough repute as it is," he added, "without handing 'em around to comedians."

With his tongue planted firmly in his cheek, this wise man, born in Oolagah and raised in Oklahoma Indian Territory, added that he might accept an A. D. (the Doctor of Applesauce Degree).

"Will Rogers only sounds like he's joking," wrote Philip Hyatt, a friend of mine from Baylor who had graduated the year before, "in fact he is serious. College degrees are in bad repute. Going to college, let alone to graduate school, can be dangerous, especially if you choose the wrong school."

I walked along the Brazos River reading and re-reading a letter Philip had sent to me from Brown University, where he was a second-year graduate student in religion.

"Forget the Baptist seminaries," Hyatt urged me. "They're too in-grown, too protective, too provincial. Get a real degree, Criswell," he argued. "Doesn't God deserve the best? Don't our churches and our schools need people with minds sharpened by the finest scholars in the land?"

In those days, I was still a little defensive about some people's view of preaching as a vocation. I was tired of having people think that all preachers are boneheads. I was tired of people asking why I would go into the ministry when I could be a doctor, a lawyer, a teacher, or in some other "legitimate" profession. Philip pressed all my buttons when he urged me to show the world that theology is still "a noble science" and that preachers are as intelligent, well-read, and highly educated as any of their professional peers.

"Also," he added, "we Baptists can be defensive and narrow minded when we should be open to all truth, whatever its source. We're too afraid that our faith can't stand the test of honest scholarship. Well, hogwash, Criswell! Your faith is up to any test. I know you. Go to Yale or join me at Brown, but forget Southwestern or Southern. Expand your horizons. Take the risk."

I had already decided against Southwestern Seminary in Fort Worth. It was a top-notch Baptist Seminary, but I had spent my entire educational lifetime in the schools of Texas. Philip was right in one regard. It was time to widen my educational experience.

"Remember," Philip continued, "that Brown University began in 1764 as Rhode Island College, a Baptist school for men. If it's wandered away from its Baptist heritage, why don't you come up here and we'll set it right together?"

Philip had worked hard to recruit me for graduate studies in Bible at Brown. I admired his intellectual curiosity and his deep spiritual commitment. And his friendship was important to me.

"Besides," he added, "there's a little Quaker church in Centerdale, Rhode Island, just fifteen or twenty minutes from Brown's campus in Providence that wants you to be their weekend pastor. And they'll pay enough to cover all your costs through graduate school."

What a temptation it was that summer to pack my bags and head north to New England! I longed for the exhaustive libraries and demanding classes of those historic eastern universities, and on the surface it looked as though God had cleared the way. I was accepted at Brown and Yale. It was an easy drive to that little Quaker church from Providence or New Haven. Once again, I could pay my bills and pastor at the same time. Everything seemed perfect, but I couldn't shake my uneasy feelings about the decision. Now, looking back, I know for certain that my "uneasy feelings" were in fact the voice of God deep in my heart crying out a warning.

"Don't do it, W. A.," Christy Poole, another friend from Baylor, wrote that same week. "Yale may have begun its life as a bastion of Puritan Christianity, but long ago the university departed from its roots. Now, it's one of the centers of modernism. Why waste the next four years of your life with the enemy?"

Another Baylor grad, Ralph Cooie, wrote from Southern, adding his words against Brown. "It may have started as a school for Baptist boys, Criswell," he warned, "but it's no place for Baptists now, at least not Baptists who are serious about the fundamentals of the faith. Join us at Southern, where you'll find scholarship equal to Yale or Brown and at the same time a real commitment to biblical Christianity."

An Unexpected Visitor

I walked back toward the Baylor campus reading and rereading those three letters. A sudden summer storm boiled up over Waco. Jagged fingers of lightning dashed across the darkening sky. Thunder claps grew louder. Single drops of rain signaled the coming deluge. Quickly, I folded the letters, placed them in my back pocket, and dashed for cover.

The drugstore was empty except for an old pharmacist in the back counting pills into little brown bottles and a waitress sitting idly at the coffee counter polishing her nails and glancing up occasionally as strong winds beat against the windows and rattled the door. She poured me a glass of milk, served it with a piece of lemon pie at a table near the window, and returned to her perch. I sat alone and silent, watching the storm descend on Waco, feeling another kind of storm boiling up inside my heart.

"Lord, please guide me," I prayed. "Help me know Your perfect will. Should I go to a northern university for training or to a Baptist seminary?"

A flash of lightening hit a nearby powerpole. Just seconds later a clap of thunder rattled the windows. The lights in the drugstore flickered out and then almost immediately came back on again. The storm made it hard to concentrate, but God knew I needed guidance and in that same moment provided it.

"Well, look what the wind blew in," a familiar voice whispered coming up behind me. "The Reverend W. A. Criswell himself."

Stephen McKinney stood behind me dripping wet. He and I both entered Baylor as freshmen in 1927. Four years later, we marched side-by-side at the graduation exercises. We were both philosophy minors and had spent hundreds of hours arguing about Aristotle and Augustine, G. E. Moore and Albert North Whitehead. In the beginning, we both had pastored little country churches in Coryell County and we both had played in the Baylor band.

"Waiting for the world to end in a drugstore?" Stephen asked with mock incredulity. "Shouldn't Baylor's 'Savior' be out building an ark or something?"

Sarcasm had been the tone of our relationship during our senior year, but when we were freshmen and sophomores, Stephen and I were close friends, talking and praying together, preaching at the city jail, or preparing for a debate with books and papers spread on our roominghouse beds. Then somewhere in our third year, our conversations took on a sharper edge. Stephen quit pastoring. He dropped out of the Ministerial Association and quit attending meetings of the Baylor Volunteer Missionary Band.

"I'm not going to waste my life preaching," he said angrily one day. "And, Criswell, I'll bet you won't either."

Stephen slid into the booth facing me. He was just one of several Baylor students who thought I would leave the ministry to become a professor, a politician, or a businessman.

"Hey, beautiful," he said to the waitress above the sound of thunder, "I'll take a coffee, heavy cream, heavy sugar, and a shot of Baptist bourbon if you have any back there."

The waitress didn't even grin.

"Well, one of us has to be a grown-up, Criswell," Stephen said staring down at my glass of milk, "since you're still drinking that horrible white stuff."

Our friendship had deteriorated the last two years at Baylor. Stephen got more and more sarcastic and argumentative. Finally, it got too painful to be around him. We had taken the same classes, read the same books, heard the same lectures and sat side-by-side in the same chapel services, but the Baylor experience had moved Stephen in one direction and me in quite another. My Christian faith had prospered at the university while his doubts had multiplied. My confidence in the Bible had grown while Stephen quit reading it altogether.

"Look at us, Criswell," he said, stirring extra spoons of sugar into his coffee. "In just four years, you've become a saint and I a sinner."

"You are not a sinner, Stephen," I mumbled, "and if I am a saint it's only in God's eyes, nobody else's."

"Now, don't be too sure," he said, sipping his coffee and grinning up at me. "I'll bet you got up this morning, read your Bible, and said your prayers, right?"

He paused long enough to make me feel uncomfortable. Finally, I nodded.

"I, on the other hand," he added, "slept late, rolled out of bed nursing a hangover, ate leisurely, and never once thought of God or of my 'Christian duty.' It was wonderful and so less compulsive than your life as Baylor's resident Baptist monk and would-be messiah."

For a long time we sat in silence listening to the storm and wondering why our paths had gone in two such different directions. During our years at Baylor we had struggled valiantly with a whole range of difficult, demanding questions. Now, Stephen had decided on one set of answers, I upon another.

"How can you be sure that God exists, Criswell?" Stephen asked me time and time again during our third-year course in philosophy of religion. "And if God exists today, is He the Old Testament God who smiled on Solomon's seven hundred wives and three hundred concubines and ordered the Israelites to wipe out the Canaanites in a bloody pogrom?"

Those late-night discussions that once we loved became more and more difficult as Stephen's faith began to collapse. Somewhere along the way, he just stopped believing, and though his questions went on, Stephen quit looking for the answers.

"Or did God outgrow his polygamy and genocide stages," Stephen pressed me, "to become the New Testament God of love? And if He is a God of love, why did He need Jesus to die on that ugly wooden cross? It just doesn't make sense, Criswell, not any more. I can't wrap my mind around it."

Stephen grew up a pastor's son. Early in his life he had felt God's call to ministry. When we first met at Baylor, Stephen was deeply committed to the Christian faith and so concerned about the lost. In those days he studied the Bible with his whole heart. He read and memorized it daily, but the more deeply he studied the Bible, the more confused and unsure he became about it.

"Was Jesus really God in the flesh?" Stephen wondered as we studied John's Gospel. "How can we be sure? Did He have power to do those miracles or did His disciples invent them to support their story? Did Jesus really rise from the dead? Why didn't He show himself to anyone but His own disciples? Are they really trustworthy witnesses?"

"I want proof, Criswell," he told me. "I can't believe it just because the Bible says it's so."

Stephen couldn't fall back on faith and so he dangled endlessly on those terrible questions that only faith can answer, the questions of life and death.

"How can we be sure that there is life after death?" Stephen asked over and over again. "No one has come back to tell us, except Jesus, and how can we be sure that His resurrection isn't just wishful thinking?"

For two years the storm raged in Stephen's heart. He couldn't trust God's Word for answers anymore. He couldn't fall back upon the Word as his final authority for faith and practice. Finally, to end the struggle, my friend put down his Bible and walked away from it forever.

"The Bible is just another book, Criswell," he shouted at me one evening when I tried to quote it in reply. "Its authors were artists who wrote in poetry, fable, and myth. Their stories are beautiful and edifying, but you do us all a disservice when you take their words so seriously."

"Stephen," I answered trying to be calm. "You are wrong about the Bible. It is not just another book. It is God's Holy Word, and once you quit trusting it you end up like a blind man groping in a fog."

"You're the blind man, Criswell," Stephen shouted back at me, "when you trust the Bible blindly."

Then he stopped, grinned nervously and tried to end the tension between us.

"One day, my friend," he said quietly, "you'll end up like the rest of us, trusting yourself for answers and treating the Bible like any other book."

"You're wrong, Stephen," I answered softly. "I know the Bible isn't always easy to understand, but I will never end up treating the Bible like any other book. It is the Word of God. The universe is sustained by His Word. We are convicted and converted through it. The Word keeps us from sin. We walk by it, live by it and one day we'll die by it. Our assurance of heaven is only through the Word. Understand it all or not, like it all or not, the Word is our foundation of life, and without it our souls wither up and die."

Stephen's face blanched with anger.

"Oh, Criswell, save that sermon for your little flock," he shouted at me, storming out of my room. "It's too late to preach it to me."

That conversation took place just weeks before graduation. We hadn't spoken to each other since that day. Suddenly, we found ourselves sitting across from each other in the drugstore seeking refuge from the storm.

I don't remember how long we sat in silence in the booth, glancing at each other occasionally and feeling so much pain. Finally, the storm passed. Thunder echoed in the distance. The rain stopped.

"I've got to go," Stephen muttered suddenly reaching for his sweater and gesturing for the bill.

"Don't go, Stephen," I replied sliding out of the booth to face him.

"I'm sorry for the harsh words," he said quietly reaching out to shake my hand. "No hard feelings?"

"Course not," I replied, grasping his hand with both of mine. "But Stephen, don't you want to . . . ."

"Good-bye, Criswell," he said sharply. Then he turned to walk away. "There's no turning back now, is there, for either of us."

Before I could reply, he was out the door and gone from sight.

"Good-bye, Stephen," I whispered to myself. "May God go with you."

I never saw Stephen again. I remember sobbing openly as I walked back across the empty campus to my room. Was this encounter another of God's gifts to me? Was it possible that whatever happened to Stephen at Baylor might happen to me at Brown or Yale? I took the letters from my pocket, placed them in a drawer, took out pen and paper, and began to write.

"Dear Philip, thanks for all your work on my behalf at Brown. But I've decided to spend at least my first year in graduate school at Southern Seminary in Louisville . . . ."

The Beeches

The drive from Waco through Arkansas, Tennessee, and Kentucky was hot, dusty, and plagued by construction crews and detours. After five days on dirt farm roads and a partially completed, cross-country highway, I parked my tired blue Chevy coupe at 2825 Lexington Road in Louisville. Just five years earlier, Southern Seminary moved its campus from downtown Louisville to the Crescent Hill section of that great old southern city on the Ohio River just south of the Indiana border. I unloaded my two suitcases, my duffle bag, and five orange crates stuffed with precious books on the sidewalk outside Mullins Hall.

"Welcome to the Beeches."

I closed the trunk and looked around to return the greeting. No one was in sight.

"Up here, cowboy," another disembodied voice chimed in. This time I recognized the source.

"Christy, where are you?" I said.

"Up here, Criswell, in heaven," he answered. Both men roared with laughter at their own private joke.

Mullins Hall was a far cry from heaven and my monastic cell in that Gothic old dormitory proved to be far less accommodating than a heavenly mansion, but looking up that day into the faces of my two Baylor friends, Christy Poole and Ralph Cooie, was almost as joyful as walking through the gates of pearl on streets of gold.

"Why do they call it the Beeches?," I asked my friends after we had stored all my worldly goods in the little dorm room that would be my home for the next four years.

"Look out the window," Christy said. "What do you see?"

"Red brick buildings with stately white columns," I answered, scanning Southern's new campus, "and in the distance, white paddock fences, houses, and barns on bluegrass fields, rhododendron bushes . . . ."

"And?" both friends asked in unison, trying not to grow impatient with me.

"And beech trees," I added sheepishly, "lots of them."

The campus quadrangle rose up out of a forest of tall, round-headed, wide-spreading beech trees with their steel-gray bark and shining green leaves. Autumn was still weeks away, but already the blue-green leaves were turning yellow.

"Oh, I almost forgot," Christy cut in. "I picked up a letter for you from Coryell County."

On that first day of graduate school in September 1931, I sat on my unmade bed and opened a letter from the generous and caring people of Pecan Grove.

"Our dear Brother Criswell," the letter began. "Enclosed you will find a small token of our appreciation for your faithful and loving ministry among us."

I unfolded their precious offering and lay it on the bed. There were five ten-dollar bills, three five-dollar bills and two one-dollar bills folded carefully and clipped together inside the envelope. That sixty-seven dollar offering represented more than six weeks' pay for a coal miner in Harlan County. Those farmers and ranchers in my little church on Coryell Creek had taken up an offering that left me feeling stunned and unworthy.

"Oh my," I said to my friends. "Will you look at this!"

The boys were speechless. I held the letter in my hands and wept. The Great Depression was at its height. More than four million Americans were unemployed. Bread lines and soup kitchens were common sights, even in small country towns. President Hoover had organized a cabinet-level panel to create emergency aid for unemployed and homeless people who were dying from hunger and the cold. The farmers, ranchers, and merchants of Coryell County were losing their farms and auctioning off their possessions. Yet, in the midst of their despair, they opened up their hearts to me.

"I thank my God upon every remembrance of you," Paul wrote to the people of Christ's church in Philippi after they, too, sent a sacrificial gift to their imprisoned pastor. It seemed appropriate to quote those same words from Philippians as I began my letter thanking the people of Pecan Grove for their gift.

The Mount Washington and Oakland Churches

I had enrolled in Southern Seminary completely on faith. My tuition would be paid by a Baptist scholarship, but I had absolutely no money saved to pay bills for room, board, books, special fees, winter clothing, auto expenses, and offerings. To open that envelope and discover that sacrificial gift made my heart leap and my hopes rise.

Just days later, God provided another surprise gift through a Southern student who approached me in the empty lot behind Mullins Hall.

"Could I ask you a favor?" the young man said rather nervously.

He picked up a towel and began to help me dry my blue Chevy coupe.

"I have a wife and two babies," he said. "We've completely run out of funds and I desperately need a church job to survive."

I can't remember the boy's name. He was tall and lanky with a head of curly blond hair and a face full of freckles. He squeezed his hands together when he talked and grinned self-consciously. His father's fortune in textiles had been devastated by the depression. The boy was lean and hungry and anxious to begin his preaching career.

"I'll pay for the gasoline," he said, "if you'll drive me to the various Baptist Association meetings around the state."

At these Baptist gatherings of preachers and lay leaders, eager young ministers would be presented as candidates to fill empty part-time or even full-time pastorates. I was just twenty-one years old, a first-year student. The seminary had a preacher placement program that began the second year, but I did not want to wait. Over those next weeks as the two of us shuttled north from Henry and Owen counties down as far south as Bowling Green, I kept hoping that God would provide me with a church of my own.

"I've got so many invitations," he said incredulously just five weeks later, "that I can't even fill them all."

"Well, if you don't mind," I suggested rather boldly, "why don't you recommend me for the overflow?"

Preaching was my life. Even though classes had begun and papers and exams were scheduled, I longed to prepare and preach again. After standing behind a pulpit every Sunday for the past three years in those little country churches near Waco, I woke up on those Lord's Day mornings in Mullins Hall feeling sad and wondering when I would preach again. I began almost every morning prayer with one simple, clear request: "Lord, let me preach again . . . soon."

At the very next Baptist Association meeting in Bullitt County, the head deacon of a Baptist church in Mount Washington, Kentucky, just seventeen miles south of Louisville, approached me as I stood beside my little coupe waiting for my friend.

"W. A. Criswell?" he asked tentatively.

"Yes, sir," I answered.

"We need a preacher in tomorrow's service at Mount Washington and your friend in there says he's already scheduled to fill the pulpit at Middletown."

The deacon paused to look me over. I was a skinny kid with a mop of red hair and an overly eager grin. Mount Washington was a classy 'northern church,' all red brick, white columns, and stained glass, carved wooden pews, a massive oak pulpit, and a real pipe organ. It was painfully obvious that I was not quite what the deacon had hoped for. But I stood at attention before him, wearing my rather threadbare dark blue suit and vest, my old but freshly polished dress shoes, a starched white shirt, and a wide, red silk tie that my mother had given to me at graduation. Just thinking about preaching again had me trembling with excitement. The Apostle Paul could not have been more excited by the call from Macedonia.

"Your friend says you're a good preacher," the deacon said hesitantly, his fears obviously unrelieved by what he saw standing there before him. "Says that you are sincere, enthusiastic, and probably available."

"Yes, sir," I replied too quickly. "I mean, yes, sir, I'm available. You'll have to decide the rest for yourself."

The deacon grinned. I preached my heart out. And three sermons later, Mount Washington called me to be their part-time pastor.

Unfortunately, my friend had already volunteered me for another Baptist church we had visited in Oakland, a beautiful little village a hundred and thirty miles south of Louisville and ten miles north of Bowling Green. Oakland was a more 'southern church.' The people were rural farmers and ranchers like my dear and faithful flock in Coryell county. I loved Oakland's little red brick church house with its cupola nestled in those rolling, bluegrass hills outlined with perfect white farm houses, barns, and horse paddocks. It made me feel like I was home again in Pecan Grove.

"Okay, Criswell," the deacon at Mount Washington said. "We've made our decision."

I had asked to spend one Sunday a month pastoring in Oakland and the other three Sundays at Mount Washington. The deacons there needed me full-time but heard my request and tried to understand.

The head deacon was grinning. "W. A.," he said affectionately. "We would rather have your loud voice and lively spirit three days a month than never. So, we approve your plan."

For the next three years, I spent my week in the library and classrooms of Southern Seminary and my weekends pastoring the good people of Oakland and Mount Washington. It wasn't easy. Before the first semester ended, I understood why entering students normally wait a year before they even consider weekend preaching assignments. Southern Seminary was a real graduate school. The academic demands were much higher than at Baylor. The professors were rigorous and determined to graduate men fully equipped "to rightly divide the Word of Truth."

It Pays to Serve Jesus

Those years in seminary were difficult and demanding. Many students became discouraged and barely made it through to graduation. Others quit and gave up their call to the ministry altogether. Often, when I felt tired or under pressure, I would pause to pray, to read a passage from the Bible, or to sing a cheerful gospel song.

One Friday morning, just before a mid-term exam, I was sitting in my room reviewing the various textbooks I had read and the facts I had underlined. Suddenly, I felt like singing, this time not from discouragement, but out of pure joy, knowing that God was with me, sensing His loving presence.

I walked from my room to Mullins Hall to the courtyard in the center of the building. The fall morning was crisp and clear. As I turned my face toward heaven, I began to sing an old gospel chorus that I had learned as a child on the frontier near Texline.

> It pays to serve Jesus
> It pays every day.
> It pays every step of the way.
> Though the pathway to glory
> May sometimes be drear,
> You'll be happy each step of the way.

Standing in the middle of the courtyard, I sang that old gospel song at the top of my lungs. Believe me, bursting forth into song in the middle of Southern's campus was not a common practice for me. My fellow students might have called the little men in white coats if it had happened very often, but on that particular morning, the urge to sing came upon me so strong that I could not ignore it. And so I sang, never once dreaming that another student's life was being changed in the process.

Years later, I was preaching at First Baptist Church in Richmond, Virginia. At the close of the service, Reverend Paul Crandall approached me. He shook my hand, and with tears in his eyes, he told me a story I would never forget.

"Dr. Criswell," he said quietly, "years ago when I was a student at Southern Seminary, God used you to change my life."

For a moment I tried to recall any event in which I might have impacted his life.

"The heavy class load had worn me down," Pastor Crandall continued. "My bags were packed. My resignation letter was written. I was heading for the door when suddenly I heard a voice begin to sing just outside my room in Mullins Hall. I put my suitcase down on the floor and just stood there looking out the window. You were standing in the courtyard singing at the top of your lungs, "It Pays to Serve Jesus." As I listened to your song, God began to speak to my heart. When you finished singing, I got down on my knees beside my bed. I gave my life back to Jesus that day. I renewed my promise to serve Him. Minutes later, I ripped up my letter of resignation, unpacked my bags, and went back to class."

The young associate pastor paused, his face radiant.

"Next thing you know," he continued, "I had graduated from Southern and accepted the call to this great church. God has blessed me ever since," he added. "I will never stop being grateful to God for using you to turn my life around. Thank you, Pastor Criswell. Thank you for singing that song."

Final Exams and Graduation

On May 23, 1934, a posse of Texas Rangers riddled the bodies of Bonnie and Clyde with fifty bullets in an ambush just outside of Shreveport, Louisiana. That same morning I faced another kind of ambush in a small hot room in Southern's "Old Main," where three of my professors had gathered to put me through what seminary students not-so-affectionately called "the grand inquisition."

Clyde Barrow and Bonnie Parker deserved their fate. They had killed at least twelve innocent people over the last two years in a rash of robberies across the Southwest. But I still don't know what I did to deserve the oral exam in Bible and theology that those professors put me through that same day. However, thanks to God and three years in the seminary library, I escaped with my life and was rewarded with the Masters of Theology degree.

Weeks later, I received a call to pastor the First Baptist Church at Paducah, Kentucky, a beautiful and historic town on the Ohio River just minutes from the Illinois border. What a temptation it was to accept the call of this grand old congregation! But I didn't feel ready for a full-time pastorate, not yet. I was twenty-four years old, still unmarried, and eager to earn my Ph.D. Besides, there was a beautiful young woman in my Mount Washington church who had a special hold on my heart, and though she didn't know it, I was determined to stay at Mount Washington until she accepted my hand in marriage.

Bessie "Betty" Marie Harris

Frankly, I didn't have much experience with women. I had always wanted to be a preacher and I had spent almost every waking moment preparing for that day. I noticed girls and felt attracted to them, but my drive toward the ministry overpowered every other drive in me.

During my senior year at Amarillo High School I had an adolescent crush on Pauline, one of the reigning campus beauties. You will remember that the closest I got to telling her of my feelings was to name the resurrected Model-T that I shared with my friend, Drew Crossett, "J. P." after Janet, his heartthrob, and Pauline, the girl of my dreams.

During my four years at Baylor I had only one date, and that was of necessity. As president of the Ministerial Assembly, it was my task to preside over our annual banquet at the elegant old Raleigh Hotel in Waco. At a Volunteer Band meeting I met a young woman who had come to Baylor to prepare to be a missionary nurse. She was kind enough to accompany me to the banquet, and though I thoroughly enjoyed our evening together (and somehow managed to pin that oversized corsage on her borrowed evening dress without injuring either of us), it wasn't exactly love at first sight.

During those first years at Southern, the one experience with the ladies that comes to mind turned out to be a disaster. At a recital in Louisville by the great concert pianist Paderewski, two seminary friends and sat in choice seats near the front of the ornate concert hall. The aisle seat next to me remained empty until just moments before the lights dimmed and the curtain rose. Suddenly, down the aisle came the most beautiful woman we had ever seen, and as the audience applauded Mr. Paderewski's entrance, that beautiful woman in a silk evening gown a mink stole sat down beside me.

Even as the sounds of Rachmaninov's Piano Concerto No. 3 in D minor echoed about the hall, I was planning the speech of self-introduction I would make to the woman at my side. "Don't tell her you're a preacher," a timid little voice said inside of me, "let alone a Baptist, or she'll flee the scene for sure." "Tell her the truth," my conscience replied. "She'll find it out sooner or later anyway."

During all three movements of that great concerto, the battle raged. At intermission, the lights came on and I turned to the lady. With a gesture toward the balcony I said, "Isn't this the grandest congregation you've ever seen?"

She smiled and answered quietly, "You must be a preacher," she answered quietly. "Hope you enjoy the evening."

And with that she was gone. I never saw her again. With my limited experience with women, I didn't know exactly how to announce my growing feelings to Miss Bessie Marie Harris of Mount Washington, Kentucky.

"He's a crazy man," Betty Harris told her mother after our first meeting. "I hope I never see him again," she added. "He embarrassed everybody."

Betty was twenty-one, the church pianist, and a leader of the young people in the Mount Washington Baptist Church. She was a Kentucky "blueblood" with historic roots in that great southern tradition. The first impression I made on Miss Harris proved nearly fatal to any relationship I might later have desired.

"He blew into our little church like a Texas tornado," Betty told someone later, "and I hoped that he would blow right out again without doing too much damage in the process."

In fact, my mistake was innocent enough. The first service I conducted at Mount Washington was a midweek prayer service for the women of the church. I had been introduced to each woman present before the service began and I was proud to demonstrate my good memory for names.

"Miss Jones," I said at the beginning of the meeting, "will you lead us in prayer?"

Miss Jones looked up at me as though she had been branded with a hot iron. For a moment she squirmed in her seat, looking miserable and embarrassed.

"Excuse me, Pastor," she finally blurted out and quickly looked away.

"Miss Smith," I said without a pause, "will you lead us in our prayer?"

Miss Smith was no wallflower. She melted my socks with her fiery hot glare of rage and surprise.

"Excuse me?" she replied not so demurely and it was plain for all to tell that her words meant "No!"

One by one, I asked every woman by name to lead us in prayer, and one by one, exhibiting either surprise, anger, or dismay, each woman said "Excuse me?" and then looked away.

Betty Harris was the last woman whose name I called. She was sitting on the piano bench and when I spoke her name she whirled to face me. She was angry but determined. Her prayer was short and strained. And when she said "Amen" everyone in the room breathed a sigh of relief.

"Women don't pray in church," Betty told me later.

"They do now," I replied.

Years after we were married, Betty Harris laughed as she confessed her first impressions of young W. A. Criswell, but she wasn't laughing that night we met.

"I was sitting on the piano bench watching him embarrass every woman in the room," she reminisced. "I thought to myself, 'Somebody has to stop this man and probably that somebody will be me.'"

Three years later we were married.

"I want to marry your daughter," I said to Mrs. Harris one Saturday night in the Harris' home in Mount Washington, "and I need you to help me corral her long enough to pop the question."

Mrs. Harris managed to maintain her Kentucky dignity while at the same time smiling with delight and brushing away at least one tear that streaked through her defenses.

During my three years as weekend pastor at Mount Washington I was a regular visitor at the home of Mrs. Harris. During my three years at Southern Seminary, her daughter finished high school, earned a one-year teaching credential, and accepted her first position as the school marm of a nine-grade, one-room schoolhouse in nearby Sugar Hill.

Betty had dated several Southern students. I wasn't the first who had been swept off my feet by her southern charm, nor was I the first whose attentions she ignored. But the rules were clear: to be a pastor there must be a pastor's wife, and Bessie Marie Harris, better known as Betty, was the only young woman in the world with whom I could even imagine spending a lifetime. From time to time, I even found myself distracted by her presence as I preached. After playing for the congregational singing, Betty would sit on the front pew grinning up at me. She had dark, shiny hair and olive skin. She was tall, slender. and extremely vivacious. I didn't know much about love or falling into it, but Betty Harris seemed the perfect candidate. So, with my Masters of Theology degree accomplished, I was determined to seek her hand in marriage.

Betty and I had never dated. It wasn't appropriate to date a young woman in a church that I was pastoring, or so it seemed when I was twenty-four. In fact, I was all starch and down-to-business in those days. Betty and her young cousin, Athalee, were the only members of the church who did their best to take the starch right out of me.

Betty was a bit of a prankster then. On one occasion, she found a glass that leaked just enough to drip milk on my vest. "Oh, Pastor," she exclaimed, "you've had a little accident." Somehow she managed to set that glass regularly at my place at table, watching with glee as the single drop of milk rolled down my tie, scolding me for my "sloppy manners," and at the same time choking back her laughter.

On another day, Betty and Athalee rigged an old-fashioned air bulb from a camera shutter that when squeezed just slightly would lift one side of my dinner plate up off the table, dropping food directly into my lap while the two of them howled with glee. And though I responded to her pranks with proper dignity and pastoral reserve, I grew to love her spontaneous, contagious laughter, the fire in her eyes, and her impish, lively spirit. As the days passed, I found myself being drawn inexorably in her direction.

I kept my growing feelings a secret from Betty and her family. Or, so I thought. Forty years later she told an interviewer that she knew it all the time, but I still wonder. If she even suspected my growing affections, she never told me. So, on that special Saturday night, I had to prevail upon her mother to convince Betty to break her date with another man and to keep her home, at least long enough for me to propose our marriage.

"Betty?" her mother asked that night, "won't you join us for dinner?"

Betty had planned to spend the evening with a handsome young schoolteacher from nearby Waterford.

"Sorry, Mom," she answered, "I have a dinner date. We'll have supper tomorrow after church."

"No," her mother said, "you will eat with us tonight."

Betty still remembers how surprised she felt at her mother's sudden insistence.

"Pastor Criswell will be joining us. Please don't be impolite."

"Pastor Criswell?" Betty remembers answering her mom. "He's been eating with us for three straight years. Every time he smells fried chicken or pecan pie he comes knocking at our door. Why should this night be so important?"

I don't understand the power of a single look between a mother and a daughter, but apparently the look Mrs. Harris gave Betty that night said it all. Bessie Marie Harris stayed for dinner and after no little persuasion, she agreed to stay beside me for a lifetime.

On Valentine's Day, February 14, 1935, we were married, the first students to tie the knot in Southern's new colonial chapel. After resigning from Mount Washington, I was hired almost immediately by the people of Woodburn to pastor their little church near Bowling Green. With Oakland and Woodburn to pastor, my new wife and I moved from from Louisville to Bowling Green. We found rooms to rent in the home of Widow Strahm, whose husband had been professor of music at the Teacher's College where Betty would be finishing her degree.

Graduation and the Gathering Storm

I commuted to Southern Seminary to complete my final work in graduate classes and in the library, and I holed up in our rented rooms in Bowling Green to write my Ph.D. dissertation, "The John the Baptist Movement in Relationship to the Christian Movement." For those last years of formal study, under the brilliant and demanding

W. A. & Betty Criswell

tutelage of Professor W. Hersey Davis, I plunged deep into the life and times of John the Baptist and the origins of the movement that he led.

Through a library of ancient books, I lived in my imagination for two years with John the Baptist in the wilderness of Palestine.

I sat with John in the dark, musty caves above the Dead Sea, talking about the Torah with devout, contemplative Jews who had given their lives to understanding and copying its sacred passages.

I overheard the Baptist argue hotly with the zealots, radical and warlike Jews determined to destroy the Roman invaders through acts of terror and bloodshed.

I watched the young and fearless prophet dressed in animal skins, eating locust's and wild honey, moving up and down the banks of the muddy Jordan, pleading with the people to "prepare the way of the Lord."

I was nearby when John baptized Jesus, when the dove appeared in the sky and a voice was heard from heaven saying, "This is my beloved Son in whom I am well pleased."

And I was an eyewitness at John's arrest, his imprisonment, and his beheading by the corrupt and compromising Herod whose adopted daughter demanded the prophet's head on a silver plate.

After two years in my dissertation wilderness, on Tuesday, May 4, 1937, I received my Ph.D. degree in a colorful ceremony at Crescent Hill Baptist Church in Louisville. With the end of six long years of graduate school, I finally had time to look around and see what had happened in my own world while I was living with John the Baptist in the Southern library and in the caves of Palestine.

As in the days when Jesus waded into the River Jordan to be baptized by John, great evil forces were at work. Benito Mussolini's Italian army had conquered Ethiopia and proclaimed "the beginnings of a new and powerful Fascist empire." Japan had invaded China and was threatening the sovereignty of all Asia. And Adolph Hitler had renounced the treaty of Versailles and marched his storm troopers into the Rhineland, launching his "Third German Reich" and propelling the entire world toward chaos, death, and destruction.

My graduation exercises opened with a stately hymn, "The Son of God goes forth to war, a kingly crown to gain; His blood red banner streams afar: Who follows in His train? "

Even as I marched across the platform in my deep blue robe with the black stripes and the mortarboard hat with the dangling gold tassel, I wondered if the world would soon be plunged into a bloody war and what it might cost the body of Christ to remain true to God's Holy Word in spite of nations, flags, and creeds?

The answer came suddenly.

On July 1, 1937, Reverend Martin Niemoeller, a German pastor and a leading critic of the Nazi regime, was arrested and imprisoned by Hitler's Gestapo. Even as the soldiers, dressed in black leather and wearing bright red swastikas on their arms, carried away one of Germany's most respected Christian leaders, his church choir rushed to the scene. Pastor Niemoeller's wife was sitting alone in the shambles of her living room when she heard their voices just outside the window.

> A mighty fortress is our God,
> A bulwark never failing."
> Our helper he amid the flood
> Of mortal ills prevailing.
> For still our ancient foe
> Doth seek to work us woe.
> His craft and power are great,
> And armed with cruel hate,
> On earth is not his equal.

In spite of the Gestapo forces still on guard around the Niemoeller's residence, in spite of the black storm clouds forming over their nation and the world, in spite of the risk to their own lives and the lives of their friends and family, the choir was singing Martin Luther's great hymn of hope and through that hymn telling all the world that God's Word can be trusted. He will triumph over the darkest night.

> Did we in our own strength confide,
> Our striving would be losing,
> Were not the right man on our side,
> The man of God's own choosing.
> Dost ask who that may be?
> Christ Jesus, it is he,
> Lord Sabaoth his name,
> From age to age the same,
> And He must win the battle.

10

The Oklahoma Churches

Chickasha and Muskogee: 1937-1944

"Delight thyself also in the Lord;
and he shall give thee the desires of thine heart.
Commit thy way unto the Lord;
trust also in him; and he shall bring it to pass."
Psalm 37:4-5

"DO YOU KNOW WHY THE STATE OF TEXAS TAXES THEIR own oil wells?" Will Rogers once asked, twirling his lasso and grinning his boyish grin. "So that they can build roads for Southern Baptists to wear out driving to conventions."

The nation's best-known humorist wasn't joking. We Baptists love a good old-fashioned meeting, and during that cold, desolate winter of 1937, Betty and I took time out to attend a little gathering of Baptist preachers in Warren County, Kentucky, that changed our lives forever. My young wife was about to finish her degree at Western Kentucky State Teachers College, and I was preparing to defend my dissertation before the professors of Southern Seminary. In just a few months we would be through with education and ready to begin our life.

"Remember," Betty said to me as we parked in a stand of oak trees near the Baptist church in Smiths Grove, "we're not going to tell anybody that you are about to graduate. If God wants us to have a church of our own, He can make the arrangements for Himself. You aren't F. D. R. and I'm not Eleanor. We're not running for election."

I grinned to myself and nodded. Betty was young and idealistic. She didn't like the way Baptist preachers had to sell themselves to get a job. She hated all the gossip about empty pulpits and who will fill them that went on behind the scenes at almost every Baptist meeting and she urged me "not to play that game."

In fact, that very day as we drove through the rolling, bluegrass hills of Kentucky, we made a covenant with God and with each other. We would take the first church that called us with no questions asked. Betty wanted to stay in the deep south. I had my heart fixed on Texas. But both of us agreed. We would proclaim God's Word where He wanted it proclaimed, and our own feelings would not enter in.

"Onward, Christian soldiers, marching as to war."

We were late. Already B. B. McKinney, the great Baptist songwriter, was leading the morning songfest. We slipped into the back row of that little church jammed with Baptist preachers and their wives from the Warren County Association.

After a time of prayer and sharing, the chairman of our monthly meeting introduced our special guest speaker, John L. Hill, the noted Baptist layman and the chief executive officer of the Broadman Press for the Baptist Sunday School Board in Nashville.

After a stirring address and a rousing discussion with the pastors, the meeting divided into two parts: the ladies remained in the sanctuary for a meeting of the Woman's Missionary Union, and the men gathered for a special program in the parsonage.

From my vantage point in the last row, I could see the local pastor whispering to the association chairman. They both looked concerned and even embarrassed. Our distinguished guests, John L. Hill and B. B. McKinney, were talking quietly in the front row. Suddenly, the chairman walked to the pulpit. The sanctuary grew silent.

"Our morning speaker has not appeared," he said. "So, I'm going to ask Brother Criswell to share with us whatever's on his heart." The giant lump that suddenly formed in my twenty-seven-year-old throat would have made the state of Texas proud.

"You men may not know it," the chairman continued, "but W. A. Criswell will be graduating this year from Southern Seminary with his Ph.D degree."

"How long you been studying for that sheepskin?" the chairman asked as I managed somehow to pull myself up out of the chair and begin the long wobbly walk forward.

"About six years, sir," I answered.

"And that's after college?" he questioned.

"Yes," I replied softly.

"With no time off for good behavior?" he questioned further, and the men laughed and nodded sympathetically.

"And I'm only here today on parole," I said to their applause.

"Gentlemen," I said, trying to look calm and at the same time racing through my repertoire of topics, trying desperately to resurrect an idea that would redeem the time I was about to fill, "I'm going to tell you thirteen good reasons why I don't believe in tithing, and I hope the Lord will lead you to return to your own churches and spread the word."

The men gasped. The chairman looked away. B. B. McKinney was probably thinking up a song to lead when the men in little white coats were called to carry me away. We Baptist preachers believed in tithing. The life of the church and our own livelihoods depended on it. To preach against tithing to a crowd of Baptist preachers was like serving pork ribs at a barbecue for Jewish rabbis.

"Sneak up on them," Miss Hawn told me one afternoon in her little theater in Waco. "Surprise is a speaker's best weapon," she said, pacing the stage and remembering the debates between Clarence Darrow and William Jennings Bryan. "Keep the audience listening at any price."

Those preachers thought a Ph.D. candidate would bore them with long footnotes in Hebrew, Greek, and Latin. I took Miss Hawn's advice to heart. By the time I got to my thirteenth point, the preachers were laughing and applauding vigorously.

"And the thirteenth reason I don't believe in tithing is this," I said, "'Leave me alone. I want to die with what is mine in my cold, dead hand.'"

No one spoke. God's Spirit fell upon the place. I was just as surprised as they were by the impact of those closing words. By listing the terrible consequences of our own selfishness, suddenly it seemed all the more wonderful to obey God's Word and to give back generously from the bounty of gifts God has given to us.

The chairman closed the meeting in prayer. The ministers gathered around me shaking my hand and patting me on the back. B. B. McKinney asked me to repeat my name. He wrote it on a slip of paper, folded it, and placed it in his wallet. John L. Hill asked if I would let him publish my "Thirteen Reasons Not to Tithe" in a Broadman publication.

"Now don't you men forget," the chairman said rapping a chair for attention, "this young lad will be needing a full-time pulpit very soon, and lucky is the church who gets him."

God must have a wonderful sense of humor. Betty and I had just agreed to tell no one that we were looking for a church, and yet when we returned to the sanctuary, the little room was soon was buzzing with the news. Betty's surprised and puzzled look lit up the room.

Chickasha, 1937-1941

God works in strange and wondrous ways. John L. Hill went from that little meeting in Smiths Grove to First Baptist Church in Birmingham, Alabama. The long-term pastor of that large, influential church, Dr. J. R. Hobbs, was very ill. In a long, private conversation with his dying friend, John L. Hill recommended that Dr. Hobbs invite me to Birmingham so that he might hear me preach. The deacons contacted me immediately. Betty and I drove to that great southern city. I preached my heart out. The sermon was broadcast live on a local radio station. Dr. Hobbs heard me and in a meeting in his sickroom that same Sunday afternoon, he took my hand and motioned me to sit beside him.

"Son," he said, his eyes misty and his hands trembling, "in just a few weeks the doctors will tell me whether I will be physically able to continue as pastor of this great church. If the answer is no," he said quietly, "I want you to take my place."

B. B. McKinney went from that same pastor's meeting in Smiths Grove, Kentucky, to lead the music at our Southern Assembly in Ridgecrest, North Carolina. One evening at the close of a service, a pastoral search committee made up of deacons from Chickasha, Oklahoma, approached brother McKinney and asked for his advice.

"We need a pastor in Chickasha," they said. "And you know everybody in these parts. Whose name would you recommend? "

Apparently, B. B. McKinney sat down in an empty pew, paused to think a moment, reached into his wallet, pulled out the folded paper with my name written on it, and handed it to the folks from Chickasha.

"Chickasha, Oklahoma?" Betty said. "That's wilderness, desert sand, coyotes, and cactus."

Certain that God was calling us to Birmingham, I was surprised and dumbfounded when we received the call from Chickasha. And my young wife was brokenhearted. The report from Birmingham had been delayed. Pastor Hobbs was very ill and until further medical tests were completed, the verdict couldn't be certain. We had waited almost eight weeks for the call. And while we were waiting, the letter arrived calling us to First Baptist Church of Chickasha, Oklahoma.

"We made a covenant," Betty said, wiping away her tears, "and we will keep it."

My wife's family roots were planted deep in the south. In 1937, Betty thought that we were moving to the great western frontier. Just forty-four miles southwest of Oklahoma City, Chickasha was actually a growing city of fifteen thousand souls, and the Baptist church with its rather grand neo-classic pillars was the leading church in town, with two thousand members, including many of the faculty of the Oklahoma College for Women.

"God is going to do great things in this place," I said, holding Betty's hand tightly and walking with her to the front of the empty sanctuary, "if we trust Him and preach His Word."

She nodded silently. I could see the questions in her eyes, but just behind the questions, I felt her love for me and her trust for the Lord whom we both loved and served.

"Don't go to Chickasha," John Hill had shouted just days earlier over the long-distance line. "The church in Birmingham is going to call you. It will only be a matter of days until we have the doctor's report."

Surrounded by suitcases and twelve large crates of books, I was standing in our rented rooms in Bowling Green waiting for the mover when the head of Broadman Press called urging me to reconsider.

"But Dr. Hill," I said, "Betty and I told the Lord that we would accept the first church that called us, that we would take that call as a sign from heaven. And now," I added quietly, "we feel obliged to go."

"Son," he said, and I could feel the disappointment in his voice, "then you've got to do it. When God is guiding you," he added, "don't let anybody, including me, get in His way."

Betty and I didn't really feel it then, but God was guiding us. God was honoring our covenant with Him. Looking back years later, it was plain to see that we were not ready for a large, city congregation like the one at First Baptist Church in Birmingham. We were young and inexperienced. That church was struggling to pay off a monumental debt. Various church factions were at war with one another. The people were convinced that no one could fill Pastor Hobbs' shoes or mobilize the congregation once he was gone. And though we felt disappointed and discouraged, God knew best.

Dr. W. A. Criswell begins his pastoral ministry

"I'm going to preach God's Word," I told my wife, "and let the chips fall where they may."

In the empty sanctuary, Betty and I knelt beside the front pew and turned our disappointment over to the Lord. The next morning at 7:00, I was in my new study, surrounded by crates of unpacked books, preparing the first Sunday morning sermon I would preach to my very own church.

The church was packed. The people hushed for the organ prelude and the choir's exuberant call to worship. I looked down at Betty in the front row. Her eyes were wide open and her hands were trembling as she held the hymn book and joined in the singing. After the offering and the announcements, I read my text and began to preach on "Fruit-Bearing Christians!" At the close of the sermon, when I invited people to walk forward to give their lives to Christ, to seek membership or baptism in the church, the aisle filled with people.

Dr. J. W. Bruner had left us a healthy, growing church, and from our first Sunday in Chickasha we never looked back. The church grew in great leaps and, thank God, we grew with it. Without an exception, I spent every morning in my study with the Word. Without classes to take or papers to write or exams to prepare, I was liberated to spend five or six hours every day studying the Old and New Testaments. I was preaching topical sermons in those days: "How to Be a Soul Winner," "The Growing Spiritual Life," "God's Will for Your Family."

But the sermons I liked best were evangelistic. I wanted to win people to Christ, and preaching at the church on Sundays at 10:45 A.M. and 8:00 P.M. or leading the midweek prayer service on Wednesday evenings at 7:45 didn't give me all that much opportunity. I asked God to show me another place in Chickasha where His Word could go forth to people who normally would not darken our church door.

Preaching at the Courthouse

The Grady County Courthouse was not far from the little bungalow that served as our church parsonage. One Saturday evening, Betty and I walked to the courthouse and were amazed to see how many people had gathered on park benches or lawn chairs beneath that great ornate dome.

Old people sat chatting. Young people strolled hand-in-hand. Children played baseball and football or roller skated on the cement sidewalk.

"Thank you, Lord," I said, and Betty looked up surprised. "Oh, oh," she said, seeing the evangelistic gleam in my eye. "Looks like the end of quiet evenings at the courthouse."

The Saturday services at the Grady County Courthouse that we launched that week quickly became a Chickasha tradition. At first, I just took my Bible, walked up onto the lawn, and began to preach.

"Brothers and sisters," I exclaimed, holding up my Bible in one hand and pointing heavenward with the other, "I've got Good News for you!"

Those old farmers and their wives gathered around just as quick as you please. Children and young people sat on the grass. Even prisoners in the nearby jail pressed their faces to the bars to listen.

Remember, nobody had television in the late thirties. And Chickasha radio was half-static and half-nonsense. Even after prohibition ended, December 5, 1933, for all practical purposes, the state was dry. People in our town were glad to hear the Word preached, and they gathered in great crowds to listen.

Every Saturday on the Courthouse lawn, I preached one full sermon in the afternoon while the sun beat down upon my head. In the evening, when the weather was cool and the crowds were quiet, I preached a second gospel sermon. After preaching through two miserably hot summer months in 1938, my deacons asked the county commissioners if they couldn't build me a little pavilion near the jail where I could preach and the people could gather in the cooling shade. That beautiful little pavilion placed me right up against the jailhouse walls.

"Pray for me, preacher," the voice shouted from the top floor of the jail. "I've killed a man and I need God's forgiveness."

It wasn't unusual to hear the prisoners shouting their prayer requests or an occasional obscenity in my direction. I treated the men behind bars in the exact same way I treated the farmers or ranchers who gathered on the grass.

"I'll pray for you, brother, right now," I shouted back, and immediately I got down on one knee and motioned for the people listening to kneel on the lawn or on the steps where they were standing.

"Say these words after me, young fellow," I ordered, shouting over the noise of the crowd so that every prisoner in the jail could hear me.

"Oh, Lord, I am a sinner. I have broken your law and need to be forgiven. Your Word says that the blood of Christ can set me free. I ask you now to forgive me. Come into my heart and free me from my sins. In the name of Jesus, my Savior and my Lord."

I prayed the sinners prayer loudly and slowly, stressing each word and waiting between lines long enough so that the young man locked away in agony and guilt could repeat the prayer on his own and find Christ's forgiveness. When the prayer ended, I heard his voice again. The man was weeping and speaking at the same time.

"Thank you, Preacher," he said. "God has forgiven me."

And the people around me said, "Amen."

A year later, Robert S. Kerr, the governor of Oklahoma, got an unusual request from his State Parole Board to release a model prisoner from the penitentiary in McAllister. Surprised and deeply moved by the report placed on his desk, the governor asked the warden of that state penitentiary to deliver the prisoner to his office in Oklahoma City.

"My parole board wants you pardoned," the governor began his interview, looking directly into the eyes of the young convict standing in manacles before him. "You have been a model prisoner. My toughest warden and his guards have signed the petition to set you free. And yet you have a record as long as my arm: robbery, grand larceny, assault with a deadly weapon, and even first-degree murder. What is it man," the governor asked openly, "that turned your life around?"

Tears in his eyes, the young prisoner told the story of his transfer to McAllister Penitentiary from a jail in Lawton where he had been captured.

"Governor," he said, "I was in a holding cell in Chickasha on the way to prison when I heard a preacher's voice outside my cell. He was shouting to the top of his lungs about the Good News that every man can be forgiven through the blood of Jesus. At the end of his sermon, I yelled through the bars. 'Pray for me, Preacher!' And even as I looked down from my cell, that whole crowd of people got down on their knees to pray for me.

"Governor," the boy, said choking back his tears, "no one ever cared for me like that before. The preacher said a prayer and I repeated it after him. And while we were praying, I could feel God forgiving me. I began to cry. Jesus set me free, Governor. No reason to be in jail now. Jesus lives inside me, and I am a new man because He's there."

The governor's eyes were misty when the young man finished. That distinguished leader of the great state of Oklahoma got up from his desk, walked up to the young man, and held him for a moment in his arms.

"I'm going to pardon you, boy!" the Governor said. "Even though it breaks all the rules, I'm going to pardon you because I can see with my eyes and feel with my heart that Jesus has pardoned you first."

The Outdoor Tabernacle

Crowds of people gathered in the First Baptist Church of Chickasha to see and hear what God was doing. The church grew like wildflowers in the Oklahoma Panhandle, but with every new believer the temperature in our sanctuary seemed to advance a degree. It was crowded, hot, and muggy and the August revival was still ahead. It was time to build again.

"Summer is the grandest time for soul winning," I wrote in our little weekly paper, " The Welcome of the First Baptist Church." "But we shall not be able to reach our largest possibilities as long as we are compelled to stay in our church building for next summer's revival meetings. We need a great, outdoor tabernacle," I exclaimed and the people all answered, "Amen, preacher. Let's build it."

I love to build Christ's body, the church, through the spoken Word, but I also love to build the buildings that house his precious body. When those dear workers from the Lawrence Steel Corporation in their hardhats and overalls began to lift into place the great framework of our tabernacle, the whole church packed a picnic and gathered to watch. The columns went up first, each one fourteen feet high. Then the first truss went across, then the second and the third, each sixty-eight feet long, thirty-six feet high and weighing over two tons apiece. Then the two hip beams were raised, each weighing more than seven thousand pounds.

"And all to the glory of God," I shouted above the sounds of building, and the people shouted back, "All to the glory of God."

What a tabernacle we raised that summer, and every bolt put in place was a cause for saying, "Hallelujah!" When the last beam was bolted and the last shingle pounded home, more than a thousand people could gather in the shade of that great open-air tabernacle to sing gospel songs and to hear the Good News proclaimed.

It was a good time for the people of Chickasha, but it was a bad time for the world. In 1939, the tanks, planes, and goose-stepping soldiers of Adolph Hitler's Third Reich blitzkrieged into Poland. Warsaw was devastated by three weeks of nightmarish bombing. Sixty thousand Poles were killed and another two hundred thousand innocent civilians were wounded in the chaos. Britain and France declared war on Germany. Millions of men, women, and children were about to die in the bloodiest war of all times.

The Birth of Mabel Ann

At that very moment, God gave Betty and me the gift of new life. On June 28, 1939, our daughter, Mabel Ann was born. I rushed to the hospital to find Betty holding our baby proudly and smiling at me. The baby was making wonderful newborn sounds.

"She was born to sing," her mother said to me, and I took my infant child in my arms and wept for joy.

On June 29, 1939, the entire front page of our church paper headlined in "poetry" the birth of Mabel Ann:

> The latest littlest girl
> Has just now come our way,
> And in our pastor's home
> They're mighty proud and gay.
> But some of us oldtimers
> Are feelin' blue and sad,
> For 'stead of lookin' like her maw
> She looks just like her dad.
> But don't you dare let on,
> Cause our Preacher thinks it's gran'
> And all of us are praisin' God
> For little Mabel Ann.

During our last two years in Chickasha, Oklahoma, we watched with growing horror as Adolph Hitler launched his lightning war on our European allies. On May 8, 1940, little Denmark fell in one bloody day. Holland and Belgium capitulated to the German blitzkrieg shortly afterward. On June 4, 1940, three hundred and forty thousand Allied troops were evacuated from Dunkirk to escape Hitler's ruthless advance. Thirty thousand young men perished, were wounded, or were captured that day and a great arsenal of weapons was lost to the forces of the Third Reich. On June 14, 1940, the people of Paris wept openly as storm troopers goose-stepped up the Champs Elysees while German bombs rained down on London, igniting an inferno that threatened to destroy that great, historic city.

During those early days of World War II, our little church in Chickasha continued to grow. Other Baptist churches and associations across the country asked me to come and share the "secret" of that growth. "Preach the Word, brothers," I said over and over again in meetings far and wide. "And God will bring the increase."

I loved to preach, but I have to admit that after just three years in the pulpit at Chickasha, I was beginning to run dry. On Mondays and Tuesdays, I paced the floor in my study trying to find new and interesting topics on which to preach. But there were only so many themes to choose from: "The Fruit-Bearing Christian," "The Faithful Christian," "The Fed-Up and Fighting Christian." I found myself repeating certain topics time and time again. And though the work in Chickasha was growing and the congregation seemed pleased with my ministry, I began to feel restless and ready to move on.

Muskogee, 1941-1944

Just before Christmas, 1940, Dr. A. N. Hall, the esteemed pastor of the First Baptist Church in Muskogee, Oklahoma, died suddenly of a heart attack. This self-educated patriarch of preachers was known about the state as Oklahoma's George W. Truett. On the seventy-five-year-old pastor's desk, Mrs. Hall found the unfinished outline of her husband's last sermon: "My First Five Minutes in Heaven." Apparently, God had been preparing that dear and faithful man for his final journey home.

I had spoken just one time at the Muskogee church for their annual worker's banquet in September, 1940. So Betty and I were both shocked silent when a deacon from Muskogee called us at exactly 1:00 P.M.. on Sunday, January 12, 1940, just two weeks after the pastor's death, to inform us that the pulpit committee had voted unanimously to call us to be their new pastor.

Looking back now, I am convinced that God sent us to Muskogee to help me learn to preach. God had seen me pacing the floor, wondering what topic to preach on next, and God had heard my crying out for His direction. The move to Muskogee was His loving and gracious reply.

I had been instructed in speech, elocution, debate, and declaiming. I had learned Greek and Hebrew and could translate both Old and New Testament passages into Oklahoma English. I had studied biblical exegesis and theology under some of the great minds of the century, but God Himself decided one day that He would have to teach me how to preach. And for that express purpose, He sent Betty, eighteen-month-old Mabel Ann, and me to Muskogee, Oklahoma, to the study of Dr. A. N. Hall, where God put me through a graduate school of His own.

Just fifty-four miles southeast of Tulsa, Muskogee was a town of forty-five thousand souls in the heart of Cherokee country near the Illinois River. Muskogee Baptist Church had approximately fifteen hundred members with an average Sunday school attendance of just under eight hundred. On March 2, 1941, our first Sunday in Muskogee, a curious and enthusiastic crowd climbed the twenty-six steps of the broad granite stairway leading up to that great church with its imposing brick and stone sanctuary fronted by six, two-story, Doric columns, supporting a grand triangular façade. Betty and Mabel Ann sat in the pastor's pew while I took my place in the carved oak chair behind the pulpit.

My title for the Sunday morning topic was "The Surprise Request" and my evening theme was "The Most Tragic Word in the Bible." I didn't know it then, but on the very next day God would enroll me in His own special class on preaching. Not long after, my days of preaching topics would end forever.

Preach the Word!

"Pastor Criswell?"

On Monday morning, as I was uncrating fifteen boxes of books into my new office in the Muskogee Church, Mrs. A. N. Hall suddenly appeared in the doorway and quietly called my name. I jumped up from my knees, slipped back into my suit coat, and dusted off a chair for my unexpected guest. Mrs. Hall was in her seventies, thin and rather frail, but her eyes sparkled and her voice was strong and sure.

"My husband wanted you to have his library," Mrs. Hall began. "He didn't save many books," she explained, "only the volumes that he found precious. Will you accept them, please, with his blessing?"

I followed that lovely lady into her husband's tiny hideaway office on the third floor of Muskogee Baptist Church.

"The pastor prepared his sermons here," Mrs. Hall said as she placed her hands gently on her husband's old leather chair and began to stroke its soft, worn surface. For a moment she seemed almost overcome by memories of her husband sitting there, year after year, the needs of his people flooding his heart, struggling on their behalf to hear the still small voice of God from the Word open and alive before him.

"He called this place his 'Upper Room,'" she told me, "where every day the Master came to meet him, to answer his questions, to shatter his doubts, to bring him hope and strength and inspiration."

There were tears glistening in the old lady's eyes as she opened the leather-bound Bible that lay on the top of her husband's desk. The cover was torn and rather shabby from much use. The pages were dog-eared. Thousands of verses were underlined in various colors. Hundreds of long, carefully penned notes filled the margins.

"This is his library," she said, holding up that precious Bible and handing it to me. "The only other books he kept were volumes that helped him understand its meaning."

I don't know how long I sat alone in Pastor Hall's office, paging through his Bible and scanning the commentaries on his shelves. Actually, I wasn't alone at all. The pastor's gentle, loving spirit filled the place and Christ was at his side, both smiling down on me, waiting for truth to dawn in my heart, eager for me to grasp the lesson that I must learn.

The closer I examined that tattered old Bible, the more dates I noticed written in the margins. The list of days and years began in Genesis and ended in Revelation.

July 2, 1917: "In the beginning God created the heaven and the earth," (Genesis 1:1).

October 4, 1922: "In the beginning was the Word, and the Word was with God, and the Word was God," (John 1:1).

March 7, 1929: "For I am not ashamed of the Gospel of Christ: for it is the power of God unto salvation to everyone that believeth; to the Jew first, and also to the Greek," (Romans 1:16).

February 12, 1937: "He which testifieth these things saith, Surely I come quickly. Amen. Even so, come quickly, Lord Jesus. The grace of our Lord Jesus Christ be with you all. Amen," (Revelation 22:20-21).

Apparently, over four different decades, Pastor Hall had preached on John 3:16 at least a half-dozen times:

"For God so loved the world that He gave His only begotten Son; that whosoever believeth in Him should not perish but have everlasting life," (John 3:16).

Day after day I sat in Pastor Hall's study, seeing the dates and reading the texts in the margins of his Bible and his commentaries. As I sat there immersed in God's Holy Word, my imagination began to fill with the great men and women whose stories are told in the Bible's sacred pages.

Abraham and Sarah were there and the other patriarchs, Isaac, Jacob, and Joseph; Moses was there and Miriam, along with General Joshua and the Judges: Gideon and Samson, Deborah and Barak. Young Samuel was there with the kings of Israel: Saul, David, and Solomon; and with the prophets: Isaiah, Jeremiah, Ezekiel; and the disciples and the apostles, and Lydia, Lazarus, Mary and Martha of Bethany, and Mary Magdelene.

Each man, woman and child from the Old or New Testament who seemed to be gathered in that room with me had a story that needed to be retold, a truth that needed to be rediscovered. And each and every story pointed forward or backward to the greatest story ever told, the story of Jesus Christ, our Savior and Lord. His life, death, and resurrection mark the beginning and the ending of all stories.

"Preach the Word, Criswell," I heard this cloud of witnesses exclaim in growing chorus. "You have said it a thousand times, but you have never really tried it. Preach the Word."

God's seminar in preaching had begun, and the Professor was making His lesson painfully clear. Why should I struggle to think up topics for my sermons and then set out to find biblical texts that support those topics, when I could let those inspiring and informative texts speak for themselves?

In A. N. Hall's little "Upper Room," in my private study in our parsonage, and in that carved oak pulpit in the sanctuary of First Baptist Church of Muskogee, God transformed my preaching. Suddenly, I found myself really proclaiming the Word, book by book, text by text, cover to cover from Genesis to Revelation. I felt new power. Instead of pacing the floor, stressed and anxious, trying to find some new topic to preach, I was pacing the floor with excitement caught up by the might and majesty of God's Word, eager to get on to the next text, to the next story, to the next book, eager to dig out the truth in every line that God's Spirit presented, and working through the Bible's pages that could save the people from their sins and strengthen and comfort them on their journey.

I didn't know it then, but God transformed my preaching just in time. The world was about to plunge into chaos and catastrophe, and only the living Word of God boldly and clearly proclaimed would get us through.

World War II and the People of Muskogee

On December 7, 1941, three hundred and sixty Japanese warplanes pulverized the American military base at Pearl Harbor. Two thousand young seamen and at least four hundred civilians died in the carnage. That same day, President Roosevelt signed a declaration of war. Neutrality and blockades against the warring nations had failed. It was time to fight, and every town and every family in America would feel the horror and the heartbreak of the fighting.

The mobilization of Muskogee began immediately. Camp Gruber at nearby Braggs, Oklahoma, became a training base for the United States Army Infantry. Our air base became Davis Field and housed the Spartan Training School for cadet flyers. A huge gunpowder plant was constructed at Choteau. Transient workers, soldiers, airmen, and their families poured into little Muskogee, filling rental houses, apartments, and sleeping rooms in private homes to overflowing. Mobile home parks sprang up around the edges of the city to hold the overflow.

What an opportunity for the church to be the church! We, too, mobilized on behalf of the war effort, the war that Christ was waging against the Evil One in the lives of every man, woman, and child in Muskogee. I preached the great biblical texts on evangelism. I told the stories of the Bible's great evangelists. I quoted Christ's last sermon to His apostles, "A new commandment give I unto you," Jesus said, "that you love one another. By this will the whole world know . . . ."

The next thing I knew, the laymen and laywomen in my congregation were mobilizing their own "mighty army" and "marching as to war." For example, one layman alone, Don Bankston, the superintendent of the extension department of our Sunday school, was responsible for the salvation of literally dozens of our neighbors. One Sunday morning, when I made the appeal to trust the Lord Jesus and the congregation stood to sing the invitation hymn, two men to whom Don had witnessed came forward at the same time.

When seventy-four-year-old Mickey McFarland walked into the church that day, there had been an audible gasp throughout the congregation. Mickey was a famous gambler from Indian Territory days in eastern Oklahoma. He was a leader of the underworld, the king bootlegger of the state, and the worst man in town; yet there he stood, with

Don Bankston at his side, confessing his sins, trusting the Lord Jesus as his Savior, and asking to be baptized into the fellowship of the church.

The people were still in shock when just behind Mickey, there came tottering down to the front old Bird Doublehead, a full-blooded Cherokee Indian, a hundred and three years old. He took his place by the side of his friend Mickey, accepting the love and the forgiveness of the Lord Jesus and desiring to be baptized.

The whole church became a witness station. And as the war effort expanded, young soldiers and airmen became a primary focus for our churchwide evangelistic efforts. In September 1942, just after the badly outnumbered, sick, and famished Allied forces had been crushed by the Japanese on Corregidor and pushed back sixty miles into Egypt by the savage tank troops of German Field Marshall, Erwin Rommel, we decided that every man in uniform who visited First Baptist would be adopted by a church family, taken home to dinner, and then followed up with cards and letters for the length of the war.

When the harsh realities of rationing caused many of our own families to go hungry, we discontinued the home visit and church women prepared Sunday dinner in the church kitchen for every soldier, sailor, or airman to attend. Fellowship Hall was opened to all service personnel for recreation and study, and our Sunday school classes made trips to Camp Gruber to help furnish and decorate day rooms, to provide fresh, homemade cookies to the boys on the base, and at the same time, to share the gospel with anyone and everyone who would listen.

Quickly enough, the war visited sacrifice and death on our own congregation. First Baptist's finest young men and women, over four hundred of them, served in the various branches of the armed forces. Our church families were devastated by the separation and the sorrow of World War II. More than one of our brave young men returned from fighting in Europe or the Pacific in a flag-draped casket to the stirring sounds of a bugle blowing taps and the quiet prayers of our congregation seeking God's strength for the men and women at the front and for their families left at home to weep.

"Let not your heart be troubled; neither let it be afraid!"

In the face of suffering and death, the Word was proclaimed and people's lives were transformed by its power. In February 1943, after the greatest two-week revival in our church's history, one hundred and fifty-one new members joined First Baptist, ninety-three by baptism, forty-eight by letter, three by statement, and seven by watchcare. Thirteen other people made professions of faith, and during the revival a new Sunday school attendance record of one thousand and twenty-three was established.

The church was growing. We needed a new education building to house our rapidly expanding Sunday school, but war efforts required that our plans for the new building be deferred and existing facilities revamped and renovated. By November of 1943, we proposed a record-breaking budget of forty-three thousand dollars for the coming year. Once again, we set aside one day, Sunday, November 21, to raise the entire amount in gifts and pledges. Imagine the joyful doxology we sang that Sunday night when the church treasurer announced that we had raised $51,276.33.

The Halcyon Days in Muskogee

For Betty, our four years in Muskogee were the halcyon days of our family's life together. The halcyon, a mythical bird that lived in nests floating on the sea, was supposed to have the power to calm the wind and waves. The word has come to mean peaceful, tranquil, or joyous. And though World War II raged around us, Muskogee was our island in the midst of a terrible storm.

Believe it or not, I took almost every Monday off in those days. (No wonder we both look back at Muskogee with nostalgia!) Often, on those precious Mondays that we spent together as a family, I drove Betty and our little Mabel Ann to the banks of the Illinois River, where the water flowed clear as crystal over rocks polished smooth by the current. While Betty unpacked our picnic lunch, Mabel Ann and I waded in the shallows or picked wildflowers and rushed them back to "Mommy" to decorate our colorful picnic cloth.

Betty and I began our little collection of antique Victorian furniture in Muskogee. After our picnics by the river, with Mabel Ann napping in the back seat, we would stop at antique barns and old farmhouses, find a little marble-topped table for fifty cents or a rickety old rocker for a dollar, drive our new "treasure" to the parsonage, and spend the rest of the afternoon and into the evening sanding and varnishing the wood until it shined like new.

During those antique treasure hunts through Muskogee, Okmulgee, and Cherokee Counties, I developed a rather skillful eye at spotting good pieces and a rather impressive skill at refinishing them to their former beauty. My proudest accomplishment was a Victorian rosewood bed that Betty and I found stored in a farmer's attic. After removing a hundred years of white paint and varnish, that beautifully handcrafted bed, complete with intricate carvings of nightingales and baskets filled with fruit and wildflowers, reappeared in all its rosewood luster to stand proudly in the bedroom of our Muskogee manse. Today, fifty years after I rescued and restored the rosewood bed from oblivion, it is still the proud and slept-in possession of a member of the Muskogee church, proof to all the skeptics that Pastor Criswell can do something with his hands besides turning pages.

The Cherokee Nation

During those years in Muskogee, I grew a great affection for the Cherokee Indians. Their history and their customs fascinated me to no end. During the fall each year, a great convocation of Cherokee Baptists would gather to celebrate God's work among them in the past year and to plan for the year ahead. No Cherokee Baptist church could hold that vast throng of Indian Christians, so they met beneath the sky on a hillside or in various campgrounds and public meeting places.

"We should build the Cherokees a great covered tabernacle," I told the people of my congregation and of other congregations around Oklahoma. Roe Beard, a distinguished Baptist missionary to the Cherokees, sought and gained their glad permission for the offerings to be taken. And when the entire budget for a great enclosed tabernacle to be built was collected in the Commerce National Bank of Muskogee, I was invited to the annual convocation to present the funds and our best wishes.

"We will build the tabernacle," our Indian Baptist brothers and sisters said in one voice, "and we will build it now!"

They selected a beautiful sight about four miles east of Tahlaquah on the Illinois River. Every few months, I drove to that site to see what progress had been made. Months passed. Slowly, one wall was erected. More months passed. Another half-wall was built. Finally, after almost a year with little or no progress on the building, I called the head of the Cherokee Baptist Association to ask why so little had been accomplished. He promised that the work would begin in earnest. Months passed. Little progress was made. Finally, at the end of an entire year, I asked permission to address the Baptist convocation of the Cherokee nation.

A great, solemn crowd gathered. Various speakers were introduced. And when it became my turn, the Cherokee chairman ended my introduction with a story in the Cherokee language that I could not understand and at the end of the story, the great crowd roared with laughter.

"What did you say to these people that made them laugh?" I asked the chairman as I stood to speak.

"Oh, I'm embarrassed to tell you," he replied.

"Well, I won't be speaking until you do," I answered, feeling a bit peeved. Finally, the good man gave in.

"Many years ago," he began, "my grandfather walked the Trail of Tears from North Carolina to Oklahoma when the U. S. government moved our people to this place. He received a little piece of land and was plowing it one day when suddenly his ox lay down in a furrow and wouldn't move. My grandfather yelled at him to no avail. Then he kicked and prodded him with a stick. Still, the ox wouldn't move. Finally, my grandfather tied a knot in the ox's tail and pulled on that knot with all his force. The ox jumped up and never stopped plowing until the end of the day."

That wise Indian Christian brother paused and smiled knowingly.

"I've just told my people that you've come to tie a knot in our tail."

The people laughed again and this time I joined in their laughter. In fact, the great tabernacle was built and serves our brother and sister Baptists in the Cherokee nation to this day. From these dear, suffering people, I have learned many lessons over the years, not the least of which is patience. Sometimes building a great church or a great church building requires waiting; other times it requires tying a knot and pulling with all your force.

The Death of Dr. George W. Truett

Again the war interrupted those tranquil days of summer. On Tuesday morning, June 6, 1944, at sunrise, the first four notes of Beethovan's Fifth Symphony were broadcast from General Dwight D. Eisenhower's Allied Joint Command. At the signal, one million brave men set sail across the English Channel to assault the German forces in their massive bunkers along the coast of France. That same day, U.S. B-29 bombers dropped tons of explosives on Japanese military targets, the first Allied flights over the mainland of Japan since Jimmy Doolittle's B-52 raids on Tokyo two years earlier. The Axis and Allied powers had entered the final bloody stages of the war. Tens of thousands of soldiers and civilians alike were caught in the cross-fire. The entire nation mourned our losses and prayed for victory in the days ahead.

Just a few weeks after D-Day, on July 7, 1944, headlines announced the death of a great American preacher and patriot. Dr. George W. Truett, pastor of First Baptist Church of Dallas, had died after a long, debilitating illness. Pastor Truett had first been taken ill in May of 1938. And though he regained his health enough to preach on various Sundays, the old vigor was gone. In 1941 and again in 1942, he was hospitalized or bedridden with serious bouts of illness, preaching only occasionally to his patient and loving congregation who prayed around the clock for their pastor's complete recovery.

Then in 1943, Pastor Truett was stricken with what proved to be his final illness. The Pastor was too weak to preach for at least a year before he died. I was holding a revival in Ridgecrest, North Carolina, when I heard the tragic news. We had known for a long time that this productive and saintly man was dying, but when his death was finally announced at the Ridgecrest meeting, I went into my room, knelt down beside my bed, and wept.

The life and death of a great preacher like George W. Truett was a time for celebration and for sadness. God had honored the life and ministry of this dear man. During his forty-seven years of full-time preaching in Dallas (1897-1944), the pastor had built one of the greatest Baptist churches in all the world. The exceptional power of Dr. Truett's witness had been felt around the globe—in his Sunday morning sermons behind that great, carved oak pulpit in his arched and spired red brick Dallas sanctuary, in tent meeting revivals and humble country encampments, in the halls of the Texas Legislature, in the White House, and even in churches and cathedrals in the great capitals of Europe. Brother Truett was equally at home in the legendary Palace Theater preaching his Easter sermons to standing-room-only crowds or sitting at a campfire on the Texas range sharing the Good News with a lonely cowboy. I was stunned and deeply saddened by the news of Dr. Truett's death.

When the meeting in North Carolina ended, I drove to St. Petersburg, Florida, to hold a revival meeting there. On the drive south, I thought back upon Dr. Truett's inestimable contributions to my life. Even as a child, I had listened spellbound to his preaching. At Baylor and at Southern, his chapel sermons and his occasional classroom lectures had inspired and informed me. In association meetings and Baptist conventions, his voice rang out the Word of God, clear and true. Now his voice was silent, and I wept because I felt sure that no voice would ever ring out the Word of God quite so clear and true again.

That first night in St. Petersburg I had a profoundly disturbing dream. And though I believed then, as I believe now, that on occasion God uses our dreams in special ways, dreams or their interpretation were never of special interest to me. I am certainly not clairvoyant. I don't go to mediums or fortune tellers. I don't believe in soothsayers or necromancers. But this dream left me staggered by its power and by its mystery.

The only time in my entire life that I had visited the First Baptist Church of Dallas was during my freshman year at Baylor when the Baptist Student Union held a convention in the sanctuary of the church. I still remember the theme of that convention, "Christ Adequate," and the sermon on our theme that Pastor Truett preached Sunday morning to the large, enthusiastic congregation.

In my dream, the Dallas church was jammed to capacity exactly as it had been on that Sunday morning seventeen years before. I was sitting in the bend of the horseshoe balcony on the right-hand side of the sanctuary where I had sat as a delegate to the B. S. U. convention. The great choir was in place. A row of men sat in high-back chairs, staring sadly at a casket placed just below the pulpit. The entire stage was ablaze with flowers. A much-loved somebody had died, and the people were weeping shamelessly.

"Why are they all crying?" I whispered to the man on my left.

"The great pastor is gone," he answered, his own eyes filled with tears. "Dr. Truett is dead."

As I sat staring at that lone casket in the wilderness of flowers, I felt a hand on my knee and I heard a quiet voice say, "You must now go down and preach for my people."

Quickly, I turned to see who had spoken those strange words. It was Dr. Truett himself.

"Oh, sir, not I," I answered him. "I could never do that."

Then he tapped my knee again and smiled.

"Yes, yes," he said, "you must go down now and preach for my people."

The pastor's eyes looked deep into mine. I felt a chill, and at that moment, I awakened.

The dream left me dazed. I was still stumbling about St. Petersburg when Betty called me from Muskogee.

"You received a letter," she said, "from First Baptist Dallas. I think you ought to hear it."

That letter from a deacon on the pastoral search committee had reached the parsonage in Muskogee just as I finished my mission in Ridgecrest and began the drive to Florida. Betty had opened the letter, and sensing the urgent need for a reply, had tried unsuccessfully to call me while I was driving through the beautiful countryside of South Carolina, Georgia, and northern Florida.

"W. A.," Betty said excitedly, "did you hear me? I have a letter from Brother Truett's congregation that you must answer immediately."

I didn't say a word, but my heart skipped a beat. For a moment I felt dizzy and faint.

"Dear Brother Criswell," the letter began, "for the last year of Pastor Truett's illness, dozens of preachers have helped to fill the Dallas pulpit. Now that Dr. Truett has gone to be with the Lord, guest preachers, in their kindness, are continuing to preach for the church. Would you consider filling our pulpit on the third Sunday morning in August, the year of our Lord, 1944?"

"No, Betty!" I answered firmly when she finished reading the deacon's request. "I won't go. You know our covenant with the Lord. I don't go to a church that is pastorless and preach. I just don't do it, and I am not going to do it now."

I don't know exactly why I resisted the deacon's simple request with such fervor, but after my dream, I think I was afraid to even get near First Baptist Church of Dallas. I was too young and inexperienced to even dream about pastoring the largest Baptist church in the world. My preaching style was brash and rather loud by comparison to the profound and eloquent Dr. Truett. I was a country boy, a small-town preacher. Dallas was no place for me. I knew that dozens of great Baptist preachers were being considered by its search committee.

Besides, I knew in my heart that every man who preached in Dallas during the next few weeks would be advertently or inadvertently announcing his interest in Dr. Truett's job. I refused to even consider such a bold and arrogant act. From the beginning of our ministry, Betty and I had decided together that there would be no candidating sermons. If God wanted us to change pulpits, He would have to make the arrangements without our trooping about the land.

For a variety of reasons, I said no. Maybe I was scared. Maybe I was proud. Whatever it was, I stood firm even as Betty continued to plead with me.

"They aren't asking you to be a candidate for Dr. Truett's job," she said. "They're just asking you to fill his pulpit for one Sunday morning in August. That's just a few weeks away," she added urgently. "They need an answer now!"

"My answer is no," I said one last time. "I will not do it!"

"Then I will do it for you," she replied, and that very day, my stubborn, determined wife sent a telegram to the deacons at First Baptist Church of Dallas informing them that "I would be glad and honored" to fill their pulpit in just three weeks.

Neither she nor I could even dream where God was leading. It is often that way, you know! God is at work in the lives of those who love and serve Him from the moment they are born. Nothing is coincidence. Good luck or bad luck do not enter in. As wise old Solomon said in his Old Testament book of Proverbs, "Trust the Lord with all your heart and lean not unto your own understanding; but in all thy ways acknowledge Him and He will direct your paths" (Proverbs 3:5-6).

It was no coincidence that on a cold Saturday in February, 1937, Betty and I decided to attend the little meeting of Baptist preachers in Warren County, Kentucky.

It was no coincidence that the guest speaker did not appear or that the chairman asked me to "share my heart" with those gathered preachers.

It was no coincidence that the Baptist lay leader, Dr. John L. Hill, had come from his office in Nashville to sit in the front row that day, nor that something I said or did stuck in his heart.

It was no coincidence that after Dr. Truett's death the search committee contacted Dr. Hill for advice, nor that he told them simply, "There is only one man for you to consider, W. A. Criswell."

It was no coincidence that no one on the committee had even heard my name, nor that after tossing Dr. Hill's recommendation into the wastebasket they returned to him again, only to hear him say one more time, "There is only one man for you to consider."

It was no coincidence that the search committee finally decided "to hear this unknown preacher," nor that even though I didn't want to accept the deacon's invitation, Betty accepted on my behalf.

And it was no coincidence that I dreamed just days after Dr. Truett's death that I heard the pastor's voice in my heart urging me to "go down and preach to my people."

God is alive. He is working to build a people who will share the Good News of Jesus' life, death, and resurrection with the world. Four billion souls are in the balance. They must be reached one dear person at a time. Therefore, every one of us is important. Everyone of us can play an important part. And if we are willing, God will do great things in and through each one of us that we could never dream.

The next time something strange or mysterious or wonderful happens, you dare not think, "Oh, that was just a coincidence." Get down on your knees and look again. It may be God at work in your life, guiding your steps to His ultimate goals for you; just as going to preach at First Baptist Church of Dallas that summer Sunday morning in August 1944 was God at work in my life, guiding me to the place where I would spend the next fifty years in ministry with joy and tears and wonder!

11

The First Decade

Dallas: 1944-1954

"Thou shalt not be afraid for the terror by night;
nor for the arrow that flieth by day...
For he shall give his angels charge over thee,
to keep thee in all thy ways."

Psalm 91:5, 11

"CAN YOU BELIEVE IT?" THE OLD-TIMER MUTTERED, climbing into my father's barber chair in his shop in Fresno, California, where he had gone to retire. "The First Baptist Church of Dallas, Texas, hired them a young, unknown Okie to fill the shoes of the great George W. Truett. And you better believe," he added with a shake of his head, "there ain't no Okie in the world that's up to that!"

My father had just bent down to sharpen his razor when he heard those "fighting words." The old-timer was lying back against the leather headrest when my father rushed around the chair to face him, the newly sharpened razor in his hand.

"God has His ways," my father exclaimed. That poor, frightened California man took one look at the anger in his barber's eyes and must have thought seriously about bolting for the door.

"And I tell you," my father added loudly, trapping the man in his chair, "that boy is going to be the greatest successor any great pastor ever had."

"How come you're so sure?" the old-timer whispered, still eyeing the barber warily.

"Because that boy is my son!" Father replied, leaning forward, gesturing to make his point, the razor still shining in his hand.

"Anything you say," the old-timer answered trembling. Then, after a pause he added, "But I don't think I'll be needing a shave today, thank you very much. Just trim up the sides and I'll be going."

"Fear Not"

Five days later, on October 6, 1944, I sat in Dr. George Truett's high-backed pulpit chair, waiting to preach my first sermon as pastor of First Baptist Church of Dallas. Looking out onto that great sanctuary jammed to capacity, I was thinking to myself, "Ain't no Okie in the world that's up to this!" When the pipe organ played and the huge choir sang, the hair on the back of my neck stood on end. By the time the congregation joined in singing the great opening anthem, I was fighting back my tears. When dear Brother Bob Coleman concluded his short greeting on behalf of all the people and stepped aside, I walked to the pulpit, opened God's Word and began to read. My hands trembled and my heart beat wildly as I read the morning's text:

"For there stood by me the angel of God saying 'Fear not!'"

Suddenly, I sensed the presence of God Himself standing beside me, whispering those same words into my frightened heart.

"Fear not, my son, fear not!"

Once again, the Word of God ministered to me even as I spoke it to my people. "Perfect love casts out all fear," the Bible says, and at that moment, I felt God's love flow into me and that great, dark pool of fear flow out. My hands stopped trembling. My heartbeat slowed, and my sweaty palms grew dry again.

I was God's servant. He had placed me behind that massive, carved oak pulpit. It was His Word the people had come to hear, not mine. And though the Word would travel on the sounds that came up trembling out of me, it would be His voice the people heard, His Word that made the difference. And though I was not then, nor would I ever be worthy to stand behind that great, historic pulpit, God would speak in spite of me, and the people would hear His Word and be blessed.

After explaining the biblical text to the best of my ability, I put down the Bible and shared my heart with the people.

"Some of Job's comforters," I said slowly, quietly, "outside this church are saying that the man to follow Dr. Truett will be a miserable failure because the church was built around the incomparable personality with the silvery hair and the mellifluous voice."

I paused, scanned the congregation from the front row on the main floor to the back of the balcony, and then I added, "They say that the 'Golden Age' of First Baptist Church of Dallas is over; that the church itself will die."

I paused again, and then standing on my tiptoes, I asked those great people the question that would make the difference for the future of their historic church: "Do you and I have the answer?" I could see the reply in their eager, willing eyes and hear it whispered from their lips, "Yes, we do!"

Then I quoted Dr. Truett's own words, "God buries the workman, but the work goes on!"

At that moment, I saw Josephine Truett, the pastor's beloved wife and partner for all his years of ministry, sitting in the fourth row on the right-hand side of the sanctuary. Gracious and thoughtful even in her grief, Mrs. Truett had invited my wife, Betty, and our five-year-old daughter, Mabel Ann, to sit beside her. I shared with the congregation Mrs. Truett's loving words to me on a visit just two days earlier.

"Brother Criswell," she said, her voice tired and still edged with grief, "You will be as my son."

Her voice trembled slightly as she took my hand in hers. "My husband built the church not around himself, but around Jesus Christ," she said confidently. "You don't have to be afraid of the task that God has called you to assume."

My voice wavered from the pulpit as I remembered Mrs. Truett's words of assurance. I had been afraid. And if I were to be totally honest, I was still somewhat afraid. Even before he died, Dr. Truett was a legend in the Baptist world. Betty and my parents were the only people in the world who knew without a doubt that I would not fail. Mrs. Truett's confidence had moved me deeply, and when I get moved, even in the pulpit, sometimes I can't stop the tears from flowing. When I told of Josephine Truett's loving words to me, the tears flowed, but even as I struggled to stop them, feeling somewhat embarrassed and chagrined, I noticed that all across the congregation, other people, too, were weeping.

It seemed an appropriate time to share my personal dreams for that great church: "We'll go on and up with our various works," I promised them. "We'll give more to missions, more than ever before.

We'll have a Sunday school with five thousand in attendance every Sabbath morning. And the services in the church will be in the eye of God—not because of an eloquent tongue and a magnificent personality, but because of God's Word and our prayers, our love, and our labor."

In that sermon I prayed that God would "make of us a colony of heaven planted in the heart of this great city." And I promised my new flock that I would give them "the very best that I had in my heart."

People cried. Handkerchiefs fluttered. And at the close of the service, I was surrounded by hundreds of men, women, and children, all wishing me God's best. And though I felt confident that God would bless my ministry in this great church, I was still dazed by their sudden, unexpected call.

"Get on two phones," Bob Coleman had said when he telephoned us shortly after my "trial" sermon in Dallas. "The people of First Baptist Church of Dallas have voted unanimously to call you as our pastor."

Betty and I were shocked. We hung up the phone, hugged each other, and wept with disbelief. I was thirty-four years old. I had been out of seminary for just eight years. The boundaries of my entire world stretched from Texline, Texas, to Louisville, Kentucky. Dr. Truett was easily one of the best-known and most admired preachers in the nation.

My "golden-tongued" predecessor had spoken in Washington, D.C., at an organizational rally for the League of Nations before the leaders of the world and twenty thousand cheering Americans. He had declined a call to be the pastor of John D. Rockefeller's church in Cleveland, Ohio, at any salary he would name. At the end of World War I, Dr. Truett had been invited to Paris to confer with Woodrow Wilson, David Lloyd George, and Georges Clemenceau while the peace treaty was being drafted. President Wilson respected Dr. Truett immensely and even accepted an invitation from his friend to speak in the pulpit of the Dallas church. Truett was a brilliant, eloquent, distinguished, powerful, and deeply spiritual man. I had legitimate reasons to wonder if these dear people had erred in calling me to replace him.

"You'll do just fine," one dear old lady promised me after the service that day. "You aren't Dr. Truett," she said quietly. "He didn't wave his arms and holler, or pace up and down and shake the Bible at us as you do, but we'll get used to that. Come to think about it," she added, stretching back her memory some forty years, "Brother Truett wasn't very good in the pulpit either when he first came in 1897, but look how he improved. Yes," she said finishing her words of "comfort," much to my relief, "with any luck you'll do just fine."

Preaching at the Palace

That next week, I spent much of my time in prayer. I was a rather brash young evangelist. The only thing I had to offer the dear, faithful people of Dallas was the Word of God. My dream was simple: I wanted to lead the church in a great and constant evangelistic program. I was an evangelist at heart, and I prayed that revival would break open this great church and set its people on fire. The words of David Lloyd George, England's prime minister at the close of World War I, often sustained and inspired me: "It is Christ or chaos!" he said, and I believed those words with all my heart, soul, mind, and strength.

Chaos still threatened to engulf the world. The Allied invasion of Europe was proceeding. Millions of soldiers and civilians were dying in the carnage of bullets, bombs, and bayonets or in the gas chambers and blazing ovens of Büchenwald, Auschwitz, Dachau, and in the dozen or more extermination camps set up across Hitler's collapsing Third Reich.

Just weeks after my first sermon in Dallas, the tanks of Lieutenant General George S. Patton burst into the Saar Basin, Germany's second most important mining and factory region. By January 1945, Soviet troops had swept into Poland, liberating Auschwitz just after sixty thousand Nazi prisoners had begun their death march into Germany. Sensing Allied victory, Churchill, Roosevelt, and Stalin met in Yalta in February of 1945 to strategize the final Allied victory and to decide upon the shape of the new world after peace was realized.

"The peace of the world lies not so much in the hands of the statesmen and diplomats," I said to a reporter on March 11, 1945, "as in the moral hearts of the men who frame them. Treaties will be mere scraps of paper unless backed up by moral and spiritual dynamics. Frankly," I added, "we do more for the future of the world in winning men and women to a spiritual commitment than is done through all the conferences and conventions and leagues of all the nations."

The young reporter from the *Dallas Morning News* was in my office that Friday morning in March to see if I would continue Dr. Truett's pre-Easter, noontime revival tradition.

"He began those holiday revivals April 1, 1917," the reporter reminded me, looking at his notes and then grinning at me again, "in the old Jefferson Theater on Elm Street. Since 1921, he's been preaching at the Palace. You going to try to take his place?"

The reporter raised his eyebrows quizzically. Those pre-Easter revival meetings were held at lunchtime for businessmen and secretaries. The services weren't meant for our seven-thousand-member congregation, but for businessmen and secretaries, merchants and clerks, who worked in the heart of the city.

They were willing to eat their lunches on the run or miss a meal altogether to hear the "Prince of Preachers," Dr. George W. Truett. He was famous. He was a legend both in Dallas and across the nation. His name alone would fill the hall. But I was just an unknown "kid" from Oklahoma, and the reporter wasn't the first one in Dallas who didn't think I should even try to fill it.

"Brother Criswell," one of my skeptical deacons said quietly in the hallway near my office, "there are two thousand seats on the main floor of the Palace and another five hundred seats in the balcony. Are you sure that you can fill them?"

"I can't fill one chair in that place," I answered, "but if we pray and work together as a congregation, God can fill the Palace Theater until it's standing room only!"

My heart was filled with hope. That revival meeting would be my first in Dallas. On Monday, March 18, we would begin a series of services in our sanctuary every night at 7:45. The noontime Palace meetings would begin seven days later and continue through the Easter week.

"This is the greatest responsibility that has fallen upon me since coming to the church last November," I told the reporter. Again I quoted Prime Minister Lloyd George: "It is Christ or chaos," and I promised that "each of my sermons will be centered around the theme that Christ Jesus is the only hope of the world."

With the Great Depression and World War II, the nation and her people were facing a host of devastating problems. Families were divided by the conflict. The divorce rate was soaring. Alcohol and drug abuse were becoming commonplace. Blue-collar crime stalked the streets, and white-collar crime burgeoned in the boardroom. With pictures of the bombed and ruined cities of Europe and the bodies piled high at Auschwitz, cynicism and despair were on the rise.

We didn't know it then, but on the day our revival was scheduled to begin, Anne Frank, the little Jewish poet with the dark, haunting eyes, half-starved and unconscious from fever, fell lifeless from her bed in the Nazi concentration camp in Bergen-Belsen. She was just four-teen years old. Looking back now, her tragic, untimely death was the perfect symbol of the cruel and barbaric treatment of innocent children that left the world cynical and unbelieving. The people of Dallas were no exception. "What kind of God would allow all this to happen?" our neighbors questioned. "How can we believe that God is love when the world is filled with hatred?" one of my Sunday school children asked. And I was hoping and praying sincerely that in that coming two-week revival, God would speak His answer through the Word.

When great miracles are needed, you have to trust God, and then get up off your knees and go to work. If that huge Palace Theater were to fill with strangers, it would require the very best witness and promotion campaign that we could mount. Six weeks before the revival began, we had trained half of our seven thousand members to make personal calls and distribute literature in a canvas of the entire city, with special focus on forty thousand office workers in the heart of downtown Dallas.

God answered our prayers and honored the people's hard work. Night after night, the sanctuary was filled, and at the close of each service, dozens, on some nights even hundreds, of people responded to the invitation to give their lives to Christ, to seek believer's baptism, and to join the church. On the third noonday service at the Palace Theater, the "Standing Room Only" sign went up and extra policemen were hired to control the crowds. And on Easter Sunday morning, 1945, for the first time in the history of First Baptist Church of Dallas, our sanctuary was filled twice for the Sunday morning service.

From those first days in Pecan Grove and White Mound, Texas, it had been my custom to wear to the pulpit a black or dark blue suit with matching vest and tie. During the revival, in the spirit of Easter, for the first time in my life, I preached in an off-white suit and matching vest. Everyone in the congregation noticed, but no one said a word, except for one little girl who entered the sanctuary between services, saw me greeting people in the crowd, and rushed back into the hall to tell her mother, "Quick, come see. Pastor Criswell has a new uniform!"

A Time for Change

During the next thirty days, the entire world was turned upside down. One week after we celebrated the successful close of our Easter revival, President Franklin D. Roosevelt died of a cerebral hemorrhage in his clapboard cottage in Warm Springs, Georgia. Two weeks later, after a speedy trial and execution, the bullet-riddled corpse of Benito Mussolini, the father of Italian Fascism, hung upside down alongside the corpse of his mistress in the city center of Milan, Italy. Just two days later, "the little Führer," Adolph Hitler, the founder of Nazi Germany and the man who launched the bloodiest war in world history, died by his own hand in a bomb-proof bunker below the ruins of Berlin.

On May 7, 1945, Germany surrendered unconditionally, and for the first time in almost a decade, Europeans awakened on V-E Day to the quiet, normal sounds of peace. The Third Reich was dissolved and her leaders were sent to prison, where they would await their trials in Nüremburg for war crimes against humanity.

Days later, after the bloodiest battle in the Pacific war, on June 21, Allied forces completed their occupation of Okinawa, a large, strategic island only three hundred miles from Japan. In August, determined to avoid a costly invasion of Japan, President Truman ordered the atomic bomb dropped on Hiroshima and Nagasaki. Radioactive mushroom clouds towered twenty thousand feet above the devastated cities. In less than ten terrible seconds, one hundred and sixty thousand people died, and a brand new age was born on planet earth.

August 15, 1945, Japan surrendered. World War II was over at last, really over. Our boys were coming home! Crowds filled the streets of downtown Dallas to celebrate V-J Day. Our church became an island in a waving sea of happy Texans. Horns and sirens sounded. Church bells rang. Confetti rained down. People cheered until their voices grew hoarse and wept for joy until their tears could fall no more.

On Sunday, August 19, a happy and grateful congregation filled our sanctuary to overflowing. "To God be the glory," we sang at the top of our lungs, "great things He hath done." There were so many things to celebrate that day, and not just the ending of the war. Pastor Truett had been gone for over twelve months, and First Baptist Church of Dallas was not dead yet. What the people feared had not happened. We were alive, thank the Lord, and growing fast.

During that first year after Dr. Truett went to be with the Lord, eight hundred and eighty-eight people joined our congregation, over two hundred of them by conversion and baptism. Our membership was growing toward the eight thousand mark. Weekly Sunday school attendance was well over two thousand. And our tithes, gifts, and offerings had reached $377,151.00, a new church record.

"We survived," a deacon announced happily when the numbers were announced.

"Survival isn't enough," I replied. "We will go on growing or we will die."

The Dallas church was not really organized for growth. Under Dr. Truett's ministry, a rather mature, middle-to-upper-class congregation gathered on Sundays in our comfortable setting to hear the golden voice of this great man. There was a Sunday school, to be sure, a Training Union, and various counseling and support activities, but in

Dr. Criswell with Dr. Johnson, former president of the Baptist World Alliance

the main we were a preaching place. People drove from the suburbs to hear the "Prince of Preachers" and then drove home again.

I still remember walking through the nearly empty building just days after Betty, Mabel Ann, and I arrived in Dallas. The sanctuary gleamed. The wooden pews were polished and shining. The carpets were vacuumed and the floors were swept clean. The sun streamed through the freshly washed stained-glass windows, painting that great, historic room in a rainbow of colors. The organist was practicing a prelude and fugue by Johann Sebastian Bach, and that elegant auditorium echoed with glorious music. A custodian was polishing the intricate, hand-carved, flowering vines that circled that noble pulpit in the center of the sanctuary. All would be ready for that one hour of the week when the people gathered to sing and pray and hear God's Word proclaimed.

But when I walked out of the sanctuary, the whole world changed. The first large room I entered was dark, dank, and dusty. There were signs that children met there for Sunday school. A few rather primitive pictures of Bible times were pinned haphazardly to the walls. An old flannel graph had remnants of last Sunday's lesson still clinging to its stained and wrinkled surface. The room was a mess, and even when I switched on all the lights, the place was dark and rather grim.

With the help of a custodian, I went from room to empty room, unlocking doors that had been locked for a quarter of a century, or so it seemed, dusty rooms filled with old furniture stacked against the walls and piles of outdated Sunday school material and unread Baptist papers.

Even as I toured that large, seven-story building on the corner of Saint Paul and old San Jacinto Street in the heart of our great city, I began to dream. One day these dark, empty rooms would be freshly painted, carpeted, and furnished. And our people, thousands of them, young and old, single and married, educated and self-taught, in small groups and large, would flood these rooms for fellowship and Christian education, for counseling and training in witness. Night and day, week-in and week-out, their excited voices would echo up and down the hallways. And when this building was filled to overflowing, we would buy, build, or borrow other buildings in the neighborhood until an entire community of Christian believers gathered daily in the heart of Dallas, to find life for themselves and their families and to bring new life to the city. As I walked toward my new office, I determined that this dark and empty place would come to life again or I would die trying.

Change is always slow and costly. Count on it! And there will always be opposition. Good people with a different kind of dream, or no dream at all, will take their stand against you. And not-so-good people, people with a grudge, angry, mean, unhappy people, will rise up out of nowhere and try their best to do you in. It has always been. It will always be. If you have a dream, be prepared to suffer and, if necessary, to die for it. Or quit dreaming now and save yourself the trouble.

"The pastor is young," one deacon said condescendingly, smiling first at me and then at the other deacons gathered in the room. "He means well, but he has so little experience."

"The pastor may be right," another deacon chimed in, "but it's never been done before, and what we have works fine. No use fixing what ain't broke," he added with a flourish.

"The pastor is probably right," a third voice was heard, "but it costs too much, so let's forget it."

Just as peace was being felt across the globe, war threatened to embroil the deacons at First Baptist Church of Dallas. Oh, it wasn't a war exactly, more like a skirmish, but it came upon us suddenly and almost without warning.

Most of the church leaders were excited about the dream to transform our Sunday morning preaching church into a full-time, active, Christian community in the heart of Dallas. I made the changes slowly, carefully, or so I thought, trying to keep every one on board, to help them understand and support each decision along the way. And the first major change seemed harmless enough.

Rather than having one huge nursery where all the infants and children under five years of age were dumped for the duration of our worship service or Sunday school hour, we divided the nursery into age levels: newborns, infants, one-year-olds, two-year-olds, three-year-olds, four-year-olds, and five-year-olds. We trained paid and volunteer staff to care for the special needs of their young charges. The rooms were painted in bright, cheerful colors and equipped with cribs or changing tables, playpens or crawling mats, safe games, toys, and educational tools appropriate for each age level.

The goal was simple: I wanted every young mother and father in Dallas to know that when they attended worship or Sunday school at First Baptist Church, their children would be left in the loving and capable hands of trained workers with safe, suitable, up-to-date facilities. Immediately, the word began to spread. Young parents, glad to see their little children cared for, joined the church in impressive numbers.

The next step was to slowly dissolve the educational system that had evolved during the previous years and replace it with the same age-graded concept used with the younger classes. Under Dr. Truett, the church was organized by tasks: Sunday School, Training Union, Visitation, Pastoral Care, Music, Missions, and Stewardship. I wanted the church organized by ages: Beginners, Primaries, Juniors, Youth, Young Adults, Median Adults, Senior Adults.

In the old days, leaders of each program in the church were responsible for the program at every age level. Under the new system, leaders of each age group would be responsible for everything that happened to the people in his or her care.

"Do you mean," one deacon asked me frowning, "that the Young Adult minister will be responsible for Christian education, training, visitation, pastoral care, missions, and even stewardship for every young adult in the congregation?"

"Exactly," I answered. "Then we won't have various people and programs competing for the loyalty and attention of each young adult. Young Adult leadership will develop a master plan for the spiritual growth and development of the young adults they serve. And so it will be with children, youth, and adults, every age having its own leadership and its own master plan."

"But, Pastor," the deacon replied, "that means that you're dividing the church by age groups into little churches."

For a moment, I paused, trying desperately to explain how and why the new plan must work.

"Do you remember this hymn?" I asked and then quietly and probably off key, I began to sing:

> Like a mighty army,
> Moves the church of God.
> Brothers, we are treading,
> Where the saints have trod.
> We are not divided.
> All one body we,
> One in hope and doctrine
> One in Trinity.
>
> Onward, Christian soldiers, marching as to war.
> With the cross of Jesus going on before.

I am a terrible singer. Thankfully, the deacon recognized that beloved gospel "fight song" in spite of my faulty pitch, rate, and volume.

"Most churches are more like a flock of sheep than an army," I explained, "small enough that one good shepherd, with a helper or two, can see that every little lamb is cared for."

Again, the deacon nodded.

"But we are going to mobilize a great army here in the heart of Dallas," I exclaimed, "and we need to organize immediately to recruit and to train the troops."

The deacon stopped nodding. He liked things the way they were. When I talked about making changes, his back stiffened and his fingers formed into fists.

Why are so many Christians afraid to take risks, afraid to change, afraid to grow? Why can't we just trust the Word, listen for the Spirit's marching orders, and then follow faithfully?

Actually, from the first time I shared my dream, early in my ministry in Dallas, most of the deacons and a large majority of the congregation nodded enthusiastically and smiled broadly in support. On the other hand, from the moment I began to share my plan to build that great community of active, witnessing Christians living and working in the heart of the city, I could see other eyes roll back in skepticism and disbelief.

"The pastor will still be the army's commander-in-chief," I assured them. "And the deacons will continue to function as the by-laws prescribe. But the army will be broken into divisions according to age. I will appoint 'generals' to head up each division, and they will recruit and train the officers, who will recruit and train their troops."

From the start, two leading deacons and their wives opposed me bitterly. They didn't want the church to reorganize. They preferred the old ways. They had key positions that would be eradicated by our new plan. They were not interested in reasoning. They made threats. They spread rumors. I prayed. The deacons prayed. A showdown was imminent.

"My dear brothers," I said, addressing the full fellowship of deacons in an emergency session, "after months of prayer and heartfelt concern, I am respectfully asking you to dismiss these four people from our church."

The room went silent. To withhold fellowship from four key members was no small matter. I didn't take the action lightly. In fact, it broke my heart. But the future of the church was in the balance, and it was time to put the past behind us and move ahead. Christ's church and Satan are locked in battle to determine who will rule the city. God wants His church to win.

Suddenly, the deacon who opposed me most vociferously jumped to his feet and began to shout. For over an hour he ranted and raved, pacing back and forth, pouring out vitriol upon me and the other deacons, boldly threatening to undermine the plan if we decided to implement it, angrily accusing me of this crime and that misdemeanor. Finally, exhausted by his rage, he slumped back into his seat. The chairman of the deacon fellowship stood to his feet and spoke calmly:

"It is time to decide," he said. "All of you who support the pastor, please stand."

Almost every deacon jumped to his feet. Only two men hesitated, but they quickly then joined those standing. The opposition stormed from the room and from the church forever.

During those difficult days, Robert Coleman was my strong right hand. He had been the educational leader of First Baptist Church under Dr. Truett for almost forty years. During that time, Bob Coleman and his team laid the foundation upon which we later built one of the greatest Sunday schools in the nation.

Early in the morning of February 13, 1946, Bob Coleman, my good friend and closest colleague in the Dallas ministry, died suddenly from pneumonia. He was seventy-six years old. I still remember standing alone beside his casket before the triumphant funeral service began, thanking God for Brother Bob's long, productive life, wondering how in the world I would get along without him.

I was determined to replace Bob Coleman with the finest Christian educator in the nation. Dr. W. L. Howse, a professor at Southwestern Seminary, agreed to work part-time on weekends helping to overhaul, reorganize, and modernize the vast educational system serving our historic church.

Much of the credit for the amazing growth that followed must go to the work of Dr. Howse and to the team of educators he helped assemble. In just six years, by 1950, the membership rolls at the Dallas church had increased by 3,923 persons, and our annual giving had broken the five hundred thousand dollar mark, with half of that going to missionary causes outside our local church.

Mom and Dad Criswell

In 1946, my father and mother were living in Los Angeles, near Culver City, where my brother, Currie, had an auto parts store. My mother was seventy-six years old, but she was young in spirit and vigorous. When the manager of their apartment complex on Century Boulevard resigned and moved away, my mother volunteered for the job. When I protested, she explained, "But, son, we can get our rent free, and all I have to do is manage the place!"

Betty and I tried to spend time with our aging parents at least twice a year. We wrote and telephoned them regularly. In 1946, we flew to Southern California to visit my parents in their little apartment. Mother rushed around preparing a turkey dinner with all the trimmings, baking bread and berry pies in her little oven. Father lay on the sofa in the living room talking quietly to seven-year-old Mabel Ann. He loved that little girl with the dark brown, flashing eyes and the strong, sometimes stubborn, spirit of her Grandma Criswell. Annie was bright and articulate. When "Grampa" and Mabel Ann had their conversations, it wasn't easy to know who was teasing whom.

"What's your daddy's job in Dallas?" my father asked, and you could tell by his impish grin that he was baiting little Mabel Ann.

"Oh, Grampa," she answered with a twinkle in her eyes, "Daddy doesn't have a job. He's a preacher, you know that."

My father was dying. He refused to speak of it, but a previously undiscovered mole on his back had proved to be a melanoma. Unknown to any of us, the tiny black mole had metastasized, sending tiny cancer cells into my father's blood stream. The deadly cells multiplied at a furious rate. He died of liver cancer shortly after our last visit.

"Grampa's gone to be with Jesus," Mabel Ann said quietly as we stood by his tombstone in the Forest Lawn mortuary in Glendale, California. "But I will miss him," she added, her lips trembling and her eyes filling with tears. I squeezed her hand and answered softly, "I will miss him, too."

The Menace of Communism

In 1950, my Dallas congregation sent me on a four-month world tour, including visits to South America, Africa, Europe, Asia, and the Holy Lands. Until that trip, the threat of communism to our free society seemed remote. Then, in Europe and Hong Kong, I heard communist speeches and read communist propaganda clearly calling for the destruction of the United States of America. On the journey I met fellow Christian believers who had fled the communist advance. Those dear people who had suffered the loss of their beloved homelands and all the freedoms they once cherished begged me to sound the alarm. Upon my return to Dallas, four thousand members of my flock crowded into the sanctuary or listened on speakers in other rooms across our growing church campus to hear the warning.

"When Judge R. E. B. Baylor, the founder of Baylor University, came to Texas," I reminded them, "he held court with both his Bible and his six-shooter on the bench. With the six-gun he kept law and order. With his Bible he preached the gospel."

"In the way of the ultimate goals of atheistic communism," I exclaimed, "lies Christian America. As long as there is a strong America, the communists will not triumph."

In that sermon, I advocated a return to universal military training. I believed then as I believe now in keeping our defenses strong. "Even the Puritans," I reminded my people, "went to church, leading a child by one hand and carrying a musket in the other.

"But what makes this nation strong?" I asked. "There is no final security in military might. Our ultimate deliverance lies in the answer of God to the repentant cries of His people. However strong we are, we live or die according to God's final Word. A truly Christian nation, God will bless and deliver. But if we reject God, He will reject us. The ultimate answer to the question whether we live or die as a nation will be found not in the words or works of Stalin or Mao, but in our willingness to obey God's Holy Word, to repent of our sins, and to follow the way of life everlasting."

Revival and Renewal

Even as communism began its death march across the planet, God ushered in a time of spiritual revival and renewal in churches, tents, auditoriums, and stadiums all across North America. About that same time, revival came to First Baptist Church of Dallas. From that first pre-Easter campaign in our sanctuary and in the Palace Theater, our congregation was blessed by God with a constant and fruitful outpouring of His gracious Spirit. Not a week went by that people, young and old alike, didn't find Christ as Lord and Savior in our Sunday morning and evening services. And by 1949, the revival meetings at our church were becoming an amazing source of Christian renewal and church growth for the entire Dallas-Fort Worth area.

The closing service of our revival in 1949 lasted for three and a half hours, from 9:30 Sunday morning until after 1:00 in the afternoon. Three hundred and six people joined the church that day, a hundred and thirty of them by conversion. That triumphant Sunday ended a month of meetings where every night but one saw at least one person converted and join the church. During that same time, eight precious young people dedicated their lives to full-time Christian service.

And though my full-time calling was to pastor my beloved flock in Dallas, several times each year I would travel to various cities across the nation and around the world to hold revival meetings. In 1950, for example, I held a ten-week crusade in auditoriums all across the major cities of Japan. When I would give the appeal, so many seekers would respond that I would have to warn them:

"I don't think you understand," I would say. "I want all of you to go back to your seats until I can explain the gospel once again."

Obligingly, the Japanese seekers would return to their seats and painstakingly, I would explain the Good News of Christ's life, death, and resurrection, of sin and salvation, of judgment and of grace. Then the appeal was given again and the aisles would jam with seekers, this time more than before.

In Osaka, Japan, I was the guest of a distinguished Christian businessman and his family. It was a hot summer night. The host had slid open the bamboo doors and walls so that evening breezes could circulate and cool his lovely Japanese home. The family decided to treat me to a traditional Japanese bath. A fire was lit beneath a great iron tub. I had seen others enter those steaming cauldrons only to emerge moments later looking lobster red and wrinkled. The family gathered at a nearby table for tea and sweet deserts.

"Aren't you going to undress and get in while it's still nice and hot?" my host asked in perfect though accented English.

"I can't undress here," I whispered, "not in front of your whole family."

For a moment, that dear man looked confused. Then he smiled, pulled several wall partitions into place and turned politely aside. The partition had large, uncovered spaces through which I could see the family and they could see me. Hoping to offend no one, I hung the giant bath towel over the partition, undressed quickly and was about to climb into the tub when the wife of my host walked directly up to me and asked politely, "Would you like some soap?"

I was a Baptist preacher from Dallas, Texas, and there I stood, stark naked, before that beautiful and innocent Japanese mother.

"Thank you," I mumbled, grasping the soap and noticing for the first time that when I really blush, I blush all over!

I have many happy (if embarrassing) memories from those evangelistic crusades that I held all across America and around the world during my first ten years in Dallas. During one such revival meeting in Charlotte, North Carolina, in 1950, I was invited to dine in the home of William Franklin Graham, Jr., a young evangelist from Charlotte who seemed to have a special gift for mass evangelism.

Immediately, I was drawn as though pulled by a magnet to Billy and Ruth Graham. He was the son of a dairy farmer, a "simple preacher boy" recently graduated from Bible School. She was the daughter of distinguished missionary parents to China. They were both obviously gifted, totally sincere, and one hundred percent committed to proclaiming God's Word, wherever that might lead them. Nobody dreamed that in just seven years, the largest crowd in Yankee Stadium's history, one hundred thousand people, would jam the place to hear the Reverend Dr. Billy Graham call sinners to repentance.

I invited Billy Graham to preach in Dallas on January 7, 1951. By 1953, Billy's evangelistic campaign in Los Angeles had elevated him to national prominence. Through his radio broadcasts, his guest preaching appearances at "Youth for Christ" rallies, and his revival meetings in huge tents and eventually in great stadiums and arenas, Billy Graham's strong and faithful voice moved hundreds of thousands of people to repentance and renewal during that first decade after World War II. When we invited Billy back to Dallas to hold another series of

W. A. Criswell with Billy Graham

meetings at First Baptist Church, the sanctuary could not hold the crowd. We had to hire the largest arena in the city to accommodate all the people who came to hear this dynamic young preacher.

The Cotton Bowl in Dallas holds seventy-four thousand people. As we made plans for the meeting, we prayed. We promoted. We hired busses and chartered trains. We trained banks of telephone callers and sent thousands of volunteers door to door. And when the massed choirs were assembled and Cliff Barrows stood to lead our opening song, every seat in the arena was filled, and the overflow spilled into the aisles and onto the playing field. The headlines read, "Billy Fills Bowl!" In fact, God filled the Bowl, and through Billy's preaching moved thousands of Texans to accept Christ as Savior and Lord.

During that fateful 1953 campaign, Billy was scheduled to preach his last two evangelistic sermons on Sunday afternoon and evening. Sunday morning, at the close of my sermon, the whole congregation was electrified when Billy Graham himself stood and walked down the aisle to request membership at First Baptist Church of Dallas. He has been a faithful member of our congregation to this day.

Billy brought another man down the aisle that Sunday almost forty years ago. Paul Short, a Dallas entrepreneur and entertainment mogul, was one of those Texans who found Christ through Billy's preaching in the Cotton Bowl. He, too, had decided to join First Baptist Church, and until his death was a member in good standing in our congregation.

Over the years, God used Paul Short to minister to me and to my people in so many different and creative ways. He was crucial in maintaining the pre-Easter Palace Theater services. Often, celebrities would accompany Paul to church and thrill our young people with their presence. Paul knew everybody in the entertainment industry from Hollywood to New York City. Through Paul I was invited to hold a series of meetings in the First Presbyterian Church in Hollywood. At a luncheon on my behalf at the Paramount Studios, Paul introduced me to Bing Crosby and a host of famous stars.

"Dr. Criswell," Paul whispered, "see that man who has just entered the commissary?"

I looked in the direction my friend was pointing. A rather grandfatherly man led his entourage of writers and producers to a large table that was permanently reserved for him.

"That's Cecil B. de Mille!" Paul explained.

During the luncheon, I was embarrassed to admit that I hadn't seen many Hollywood movies. In fact, I had preached against them on more than one occasion, but I had seen and been deeply moved by de Mille's monumental motion picture, *King of Kings*, and when Mr. de Mille walked into the Paramount dining room, I watched him with a kind of schoolboy awe.

"Isn't that a Bible he's reading?" I asked Paul as we watched America's leading film director and producer at the table surrounded by his close friends in the industry.

"He reads the Bible every day," Paul explained. "He's a devout Christian believer. In fact," he added, "de Mille was so determined that his depiction of Jesus' life, death, and resurrection in *King of Kings* be true to God's Word that he asked your friend, Louis Evans, the pastor of Hollywood Presbyterian Church, to be his theological advisor on the picture."

Suddenly, Cecil B. de Mille stood and walked directly to my table. We talked for almost an hour. His father, American playwright Henry Churchill de Mille, was also a lay preacher. Cecil's mother was a devout Episcopalian lay leader. He told me that as a young boy he had felt a call to Christian ministry and that he had tried to be true to that call through special motion pictures like *King of Kings*.

"An estimated eight hundred million people have seen and heard the story of Jesus through that film alone," de Mille told me humbly. "Now, I'm working on *The Ten Commandments*," he added, "hoping to give another eight hundred million people a lesson in Old Testament history."

In 1956, Cecil B. de Mille invited me to the studio premiere of his seventieth motion picture, *The Ten Commandments*. Betty and I flew to Los Angeles and rode in a limousine to the Paramount screening room where de Mille, Charlton Heston, and dozens of other motion picture stars and executives had gathered to see this powerful film. Cecil B. de Mille died just two years later. The entire world mourned the loss of this great man's creativity and commitment. Shortly after de Mille's death, I received a letter and a package in the mail from his secretary in Hollywood.

"In Mr. de Mille's office we found the enclosed package with your name handwritten on it. Please accept it with his regard!"

My hands trembled slightly as I opened the package. He had sent me a beautiful, leather-bound edition of the script for *The Ten Commandments*, signed by Cecil B. de Mille. It still stands proudly on a shelf in my library with memories of a man who loved God's Word as I love it. Although I have not seen every film written and directed by Cecil B. de Mille, I am convinced that God used that dear Christian layman, in his own creative way, to bring the Word to life as no preacher has ever done it.

Miss Hattie Moore

In the temple in Jerusalem just before his death, Jesus Himself showed His disciples the kind of spirit God loves best. It wasn't the spirit of the great teachers of the law exegeting the Torah, or the spirit of the preachers and prophets holding forth before the masses, or the spirit of the scribes or the Pharisees or the temple chiefs exercising their great wisdom and power, or the spirit of the rich and noble men tossing large bank notes into the treasury. Jesus loved the spirit of a poor widow who humbly placed two pennies in the offering box and walked away.

"This poor widow," Jesus said, "has cast more in, than all they which have cast into the treasury."

This story is not just about money. It is about the loving, merciful, humble spirit of God that Jesus wants to see in all of us who follow Him. How often I have seen that spirit demonstrated, not by great religious leaders, but by the people in the pews, people who history may not remember, but whose lives really made the difference for Christ and for His kingdom.

Miss Hattie Moore was just such a person. Like the woman in the temple, Miss Hattie was a widow, but she wasn't poor. In fact it was through her gift to First Baptist Church of Dallas that the George W. Truett Memorial Chapel was built. But it wasn't Mrs. Moore's generous giving that left a mark on all of us. It was her loving, merciful, humble spirit.

That spirit was demonstrated best on May 10, 1935, the night Raymond Hamilton was put to death in the electric chair in Huntsville, Texas, for the murder of prison guard Major Crowson. Earlier that day, Hattie Moore saw the picture of Raymond Hamilton's mother, Mrs. Steve Davis, in the *Dallas Morning News*.

"It was such a tragic face," Miss Hattie told me years later. "I felt compelled to find that poor woman and offer her God's comfort."

Quick to obey the leading of God's loving Spirit, Hattie Moore drove through West Dallas in the cold and drizzling rain, searching for the slum house where Raymond's mother lived.

"At first, the poor woman shrank back from me in terror," Hattie told me. "Mrs. Davis must have thought I was a policewoman or a reporter," she explained. "But when I told her that I had come in the name of Jesus to bring her comfort, the poor lady just crumpled up before me. Soon, she was pouring out her bitter story in a torrent of words and tears."

Raymond Hamilton, Mrs. Davis' eldest son, had been the partner of Bonnie Parker and Clyde Barrow, the young couple that robbed and murdered their way across the southwest from 1930 to 1934. Raymond Hamilton narrowly missed dying with Bonnie and Clyde on May 23, 1934, when Texas Rangers finally ambushed and killed the pair in a hail of bullets. A year later, after escaping from prison, Raymond Hamilton, the FBI's "Most Wanted Man" was captured posing as a tramp underneath a railroad bridge on the outskirts of Dallas. He had come home, hoping to see his mother once again. In 1935, Mrs. Davis was sentenced to thirty days in prison for aiding and abetting her son and his two friends, Bonnie Parker and Clyde Barrow.

Floyd Hamilton, Mrs. Davis' younger son, was also a desperado, wanted across the southwest as an accomplice in the crimes of Raymond, Bonnie, and Clyde. He was arrested in Shreveport, Louisiana, on February 5, 1935, after a gunfight with police. Floyd Hamilton was tried and sentenced to Alcatraz to spend the rest of his life in prison. Just weeks later his brother, Raymond, died in the electric chair.

Hattie Moore was with Raymond Hamilton's mother when the boy was executed for his crimes. Day after day, she ministered to that poor woman in Christ's name. Hattie helped Mrs. Davis arrange for the return of her eldest son's body and then provided a funeral service where the woman could grieve in private away from the loud and demanding crowd of reporters and cameramen who plagued her steps. Hattie Moore led Mrs. Davis to Christ and remained her dearest friend.

"Pastor, would you do me this one favor?" Hattie Moore asked me after visiting with Mrs. Davis in 1952. "Floyd Hamilton is serving his life sentence in Alcatraz. Would you visit him there and pray with him that he might find Jesus before he dies?"

Days later I found myself flying from Dallas to San Francisco. Prison officials had agreed to ferry me across the white-capped, windy waters to that cold, stark prison on an island in the bay. The warden received me graciously. We passed down endless corridors, through locked doors and into a steel room in the very center of that maximum security prison. Guards deposited Floyd Hamilton at the door and then locked us in together.

I told him about his mother's friendship with Hattie Moore and about their request that I should visit him in Alcatraz to share with him the plan of salvation.

"Let's kneel down and pray," I said when we had finished talking and the young man seemed eager to accept Christ as Savior and Lord.

"Floyd," I asked, "will you give your heart and life to the Lord Jesus and accept Him as your Savior and ask Him to forgive your sins, write your name in the Book of Life, and take you to heaven when you die?"

"Yes, sir, I will," he answered quickly.

"God," I prayed, "save Floyd Hamilton. Come into his heart."

At the close of my prayer, that young desperado grasped me warmly by the hand. Then he said, "Preacher, if I ever get out of here, which I don't think I will, I'm going to walk down the aisle of your church, confess Jesus as my Lord, and be baptized."

As I stood to leave, he took my hand again and said quietly, "Please, tell my mother that I'm sorry." Floyd Hamilton was a hardened criminal, a convict serving a life sentence on a rock in San Francisco Bay. But when he mentioned his mother, his eyes filled with tears of remorse and his hands began to tremble. "Tell her if I don't see her one day soon, I hope to see her in heaven."

God answered that mother's prayers and the prayers of her forgiven son. Eventually, Floyd Hamilton was transferred to Leavenworth Penitentiary, where he served as the chaplain's assistant and kept the library, a model prisoner. Years later he was released, and true to his word, he walked down the aisle of First Baptist Church of Dallas, he confessed Jesus as his Savior, and he was baptized. And Floyd Hamilton spent the rest of his life going from school to school pleading with young people to avoid the mistakes that ruined his young life.

I buried Hattie Moore on January 2, 1953. Her little funeral was held in the drawing room of the George H. Lewis and Sons Mortuary here in Dallas. There were no great crowds gathered to bid her fond farewell. But I can tell you this, the angels in heaven were lined up along the streets of gold to welcome Hattie home. And when Jesus held out His loving arms to greet her, I am sure He said, "Well done, good and faithful servant."

Hattie Moore, a widow who saw a tragic face in the *Dallas Morning News* and drove through driving rain to bring God's comfort, may have been unknown, unheralded, and unrecognized . But the heart of God was gladdened by her loving, merciful, humble spirit.

12
The Middle Years
Dallas: 1954-1968

"If my people, which are called by my name,
shall humble themselves, and pray, and seek my face,
and turn from their wicked ways; then will I
hear from heaven, and will forgive their sin,
and will heal their land."

2 Chronicles 7:14

THE STRANGER ON OUR STEPS

At 7:48 A.M., I parked my car in the church lot on San Jacinto and walked quickly toward the side door that led directly to my office. Because my working library was at home on Swiss Avenue, I rarely got to the church office during morning hours. Hoping not to be seen and feeling rather guilty about it, I rushed across San Jacinto, looking down at the ring of keys I carried.

"Morning, Pastor."

I turned toward the familiar voice, hoping to get away without a long conversation with our faithful church custodian, when I noticed that he was pointing toward the main steps that lead up into our sanctuary.

"Wonder what's going on?" he said, putting his broom against the wall and hurrying toward the corner. I followed at a distance. A small crowd of businessmen, clerks, and secretaries, interrupted on their way to work, was forming on the steps of the church. A woman gasped. "Call the police," another exclaimed loudly. A postman with a mail bag on his shoulder ran to a pay phone across the street. As I headed for the scene, I could hear a siren in the distance.

"What's wrong, here?" I asked, spotting at that very moment a young man lying prostrate on the cold cement steps.

"He looks sick," someone whispered as I knelt beside the stranger.

"Where'd he come from?" another asked.

"Just staggered across Ervay," a third voice explained. "Saw him start up the church steps; then, boom, he fell . . . ."

"Probably just another drunk," a well-dressed older man exclaimed. "Downtown is crawling with 'em," he added.

The man lying on the sidewalk was in his late thirties or early forties. Though it was a chilly winter morning, he wore no socks and no overcoat, just a dirty blue work shirt and overalls.

"Can we help you?" I asked the stranger. "Do you need medical attention?"

He tried to get up on one knee, and then slumped back onto the concrete steps, too weak to move. As I looked down into his face, he reached out to me. The stranger's eyes were filled with pain and terror. His lips moved, but no words were spoken. Then, after one long sigh, his breathing stopped and all signs of life went out of him.

"A man died on our front steps last Monday morning," I told the congregation in my Sunday sermon. "I saw the crowd gather. I heard the poor man breathe his last breath. I waited while the police took his body away. And I watched the crowd disperse, forgetting the tragedy they had witnessed even as they crossed the street. But we cannot, we must not, forget the stranger on our steps."

At the heart of my sermon that day was a simple truth. Pastor Truett had proclaimed it in Dallas during his decades of service. I proclaimed it during mine. While thousands of churches move to the suburbs every year, God needs at least a faithful remnant of His people to stay in the heart of the city to provide hope, health, and healing to the souls and the bodies of the strangers on our steps. This experience was the beginning of our tremendous mission ministry in the great city of Dallas.

Building the Church in Downtown Dallas

"Why don't you sell this multi-million dollar downtown property and move out to a fine, residential district? You could build a fine cathedral for your people."

How many times we have heard that question asked. When Dr. Truett was asked if he thought First Baptist Church would ever move to the suburbs, he always answered loudly, "No!" And when a reporter or a deacon or a real estate agent asked that same question of me, the same answer rang out, "No! No! A thousand times no!"

"Satan has his throne in the downtown heart of the city," I exclaimed that Sunday morning. "The bright lights are there, the theater district is there, the hotels and night clubs are there, the soldiers and sailors roam the streets down there, the big banking and insurance institutions are there, vice and gambling interests struggle in the underworld there, the whole destiny of our nation and world is determined there. Shall we leave it to sin without a witness to God?

"The thought is unthinkable, much less the deed doable. The lighthouse that shines the brightest for our Savior Christ Jesus ought to shine among those tall skyscrapers downtown. Money is big and sin is big and the world is big, but God is infinitely bigger. His message is the light and the hope of the human soul, and it must be proclaimed and lived out courageously in the heart of the city."

Edgar A. Guest, America's beloved poet, usually writes in rhyme. But in that sermon, I quoted a rare and moving piece of prose by Mr. Guest:

"'I like to see the downtown churches holding their places. It seems good to me that here and there amid the rush of traffic there should remain a building that has no "bargains" to offer and no shop window to display.

"'This is a hospital for sick and weary souls. It is making a battle not for our own sake but for the sake of others. A church in any neighborhood is an asset, but none so much as a downtown church.'"

The church must be more than a great downtown auditorium where the Word of God is proclaimed. I picture the Christian community gathered as a little city within the big city, ministering to every need at every age of every believer, young and old alike. And at the same time, reaching out to every man, woman, and child who lives within the city, bringing the Good News of Jesus to those who now live only in darkness and despair.

We are a family. Consequently, everything that pertains to family life should be centered in the downtown church. Preaching and teaching the Word are central, of course, but the dream is bigger than sermons and lectures, prayer meetings and Bible studies. What do children need to guarantee their spiritual, physical, and mental growth? Provide it! What do young people need to mature in mind and body? Provide it! What do young adults, the middle-aged, and people in their golden years need to continue growing into the fullness of God's dream for them? Provide it!

"Pastor, come quickly!" my secretary was calling from the church office. "The waiting room is filled with reporters and photographers. They all want to talk to you."

It was Friday afternoon, February 5, 1954. I drove from our parsonage on Swiss Avenue and climbed the steps to my office, surprised that the world's media would suddenly be interested in First Baptist Church of Dallas.

On Sunday, our congregation was going to dedicate two new buildings on our growing campus in the heart of Dallas and celebrate the complete renovation of a third. God was honoring our dream. In the words of Augustine, the great fifth-century theologian, we were building "the city of God" at the very downtown center of "the city of man."

In just ten years, our church membership rolls had swelled from 7,804 to over 10,000 souls. Sunday school enrollment had more than doubled to over 6,000 men, women, and children. And annual gifts to the church had increased from $250,000 in 1944 to $1,762,599 in 1953.

The Dallas church was booming, and somehow the press got wind of it. Besides the Dallas and Fort-Worth papers, reporters from *Time* and *Newsweek* were there, along with journalists and recording technicians from *The New York Times* and the Mutual Broadcasting System.

The reporters had asked questions and scribbled my replies as we walked together through the newly remodeled Truett Memorial Building, housing the sanctuary and Sunday school classrooms for forty-five hundred children and their teachers.

"And this, ladies and gentlemen, is our new Activities Building," I said loudly to the flock of noisy reporters following me on the tour. "It is connected to the sanctuary by a tunnel under San Jacinto Street. We started raising money to build this building in 1946," I told them, "but because of the Korean War and the long steel strikes, we were not able to finish it until now."

"How much did it cost, Pastor?" a reporter hollered from the back of the crowd.

Deacon Charlie Roberts

It was the question everybody asked. Property values were high in downtown Dallas. Construction costs were dear. In those days the $1.75 million price tag on our new Activities Building seemed like a very large fortune. In fact, when I first proposed to the deacons that we borrow the money from a bank and repay it over a long period of time, one of my most valued and dearly loved deacons opposed me.

"I move," he said after a long and sometimes even rancorous discussion, "that we set a limit of two hundred thousand dollars on our church indebtedness and then live faithfully within the limits."

There was no way to build "the city of God" in the heart of Dallas with a two hundred thousand dollar debt limit. Great dreams demand great risks! When the deacon continued to oppose us, another deacon, Charlie Roberts, confronted him.

Charlie Roberts was the executive vice-president of Sears under its founder, General Wood. Charlie had already established himself as a dreamer who dreamed great dreams. When the Great Depression threatened to bankrupt the large, national retail chains, Montgomery Ward pulled back to protect its investment, but Charlie Roberts urged General Wood to take the big risk. Because of Charlie Roberts' dreaming, Sears won the day.

When the deacon opposed to our expansion in downtown Dallas continued to mount an attack on the dream, Charlie Roberts went to him and said simply, "Friend, make up your mind. Either help us build or get out of the way."

That confrontation took great courage. The recalcitrant deacon was one of the richest and most powerful businessmen in Dallas. But when he marched angrily into the office of Judge Ryburn, our deacon fellowship chairman, to report the confrontation, Judge Ryburn said quietly, "Charlie Roberts is right. Once you find yourself opposing the majority's dream, you need to decide. Get on board with the rest of us, or find another church."

Every church building in the country has its own story to tell. Usually, it is a story of men and women who believed in the future and of their victory over those who doubt. The real price of a building built to house the work of Christ is not in dollars and cents, but in the measure of sacrifice taken on lovingly, freely, and faithfully by the people who had a dream.

Dr. & Mrs. Criswell with Hershel Hobbs

"The Activities Building will cost us $1.75 million," I told the reporters. "It will house two lovely chapels for weddings, funerals, and other events that don't require our twenty-seven-hundred-seat sanctuary. It will hold additional classrooms, my office, and the offices of twenty-two members of our executive and ministerial staff. The basement contains a craft shop, while the roof garden is designed for summer barbecues and other socials."

Mrs. Minnie Slaughter Veal

Our parking building, now called the Veal Building, was another example of a layperson, this time a woman, who dreamed big dreams for her beloved church. One Friday morning in 1946, I spotted a "For Sale" sign on the Central Christian Church right across the street from our church on Ervay Street. We had just committed more than one million dollars to build the Activities Building. Even the most daring deacon didn't give me much chance for acquiring that new property, let alone for building on it.

"Why don't you ask God for it, Pastor?" Mr. Souther, my educational director, suggested good-naturedly. "Maybe He can afford it."

"Out of the mouths of babes and deacons . . ." the Bible might have said, but didn't. It was good advice nevertheless. I dropped to my knees that day and began to pray non-stop for that precious piece of property.

"Some corporation will buy it," I told Betty, "and build a fifty-story skyscraper on it and we'll never get this chance again."

"Dr. Criswell," my secretary informed me just three days later, "Minnie Veal is on the phone for you."

Mrs. Veal and her three sisters, Mrs. Wright, Mrs. Deloach, and Mrs. Dean, were all daughters of Colonel C. C. Slaughter, a Texas legend. In the nineteenth century, he was the world's largest cattle baron, with three million acres of Texas range land. Much to the colonel's annoyance, one of the world's great oil reserves was also discovered just below the rich and rolling plains he loved. When the colonel died, his daughters inherited that great Slaughter fortune.

Mrs. Veal, the wife of a distinguished Dallas surgeon, was not impressed with money. When her husband died, Mrs. Veal sold the lovely mansion he had built in Highland Park and moved into a little bungalow on Vickery Street in East Dallas.

"I hear that you've been on your knees again, Pastor," she said on the telephone that day.

"Yes, ma'am," I answered, knowing in my heart that Mrs. Veal was calling me at the promptings of our Lord. "I'm praying for the property just across the street from our church."

"How much would it cost?" she asked me.

"They want two hundred and fifty-five thousand for it," I replied.

"Buy it," she said simply. And I so I bought it, in the church's name, without asking or telling anybody.

"What do you want to build on it?" Mrs. Veal asked me several weeks later.

"A parking and recreational building," I told her, and before I had a chance to flesh out the dream, she interrupted.

"How much?" she said.

"About a million and a half," I replied, "or so the architects project."

"Build it," she said, and once again, I did exactly what the wonderful and glorious lady had instructed me. Nobody knew exactly what was going on across the street. They just watched it go up in wonder and amazement.

How often through the centuries God has used great and generous women to help accomplish His will. Almost two thousand years ago,

Lydia, a businesswoman famous for the purple cloth she dyed and exported, opened her door and her pocketbook to help build the first-century churches in Philippi and Thyratira (Acts 16:14). Through the ages, women have lived and died to keep the church alive. And the history of First Baptist Church of Dallas is replete with the stories of faithful, gifted, hardworking, sacrificial women who prayed and paid with their lives to see this church succeed.

In fact, three of our major building were made possible by the gifts of generous Christian women whom God had trusted to be faithful stewards of His creation. Almost a quarter of a century after Mrs. Veal led the way, Mary Crowley, the founder of Home Interior Decorators, gave a million dollars to launch the design and construction of our beautiful Mary Crowley Building, providing much-needed educational space for our growing Sunday school program.

In 1980, Mrs. Ruth Ray Hunt, the wife of H. L. Hunt, gave a three-million-dollar gift toward the building of a center for the church's young people. Less than ten years later, Mrs. Hunt gave another three million dollars to help purchase and renovate the landmark Gaston Avenue Baptist Church to be the permanent home of the Criswell Bible Institute.

"The Lord has been so good to me," Mrs. Hunt said graciously. "The least I can do is give back to His work a goodly portion of it."

Now, I look back on almost half a century of growth by the church in Dallas, and much of that growth can be credited directly to Christian women like Mrs. Hunt, Mrs. Veal, and Mrs. Crowley. Time after time, each of these gracious ladies has answered God's call in our time of need. I thank God for them, and I thank them for helping me throughout the years. Mrs. Veal's building was the highlight of the reporter's tour that day.

"The lower floors will serve the church for parking," I told them, "and the top two floors hold a gymnasium for one basketball, two volleyball, and six badminton courts, with telescopic gym seats for parents and friends to join the cheering. At one end of the playing area will be placed parallel and horizontal bars, traveling rings, twisting belts, striking and training bags, and climbing ropes.

"Besides the gym," I added, and by then the reporter's eyes and mouths were wide open as they followed me through the building, "there will be locker and shower rooms, a four-lane bowling alley, and a ten-thousand-square-foot roller skating rink.

"What's a church need with all this?" one reporter asked, grinning to his colleagues. "Looks like you're building some kind of ecclesiastical empire here."

It is never easy to explain a dream to the critics or the skeptics. The church I wanted to build would be the center of family life for every believer, and a great open door of witness and ministry to those who did not yet believe. If I had my way, we would transform the whole north quadrant of Dallas by our presence. I dreamed of a hospital, a rest home, emergency care centers for the hungry and the homeless, clothing, furniture and appliance distribution depots for the needy, academies, schools, a Bible college, playing fields, and an athletic arena that could serve for revival campaigns as well, even a great Christian university.

"But a bowling alley?" the reporter questioned sarcastically, "in a church?"

"Why should our children be forced to find places to play that are unsafe and unsavory?" I replied. "Why should young people think of church as just a place to worship and study? Why shouldn't they enjoy life here, all of it, to its fullest?"

"Texas, where everything is bigger, has long boasted the biggest Baptist church in the world," the *Newsweek* story began. "And the First Baptist Church of Dallas, with ten thousand members, is bigger now than ever."

"Biggest White Baptist Church in the World Grows Bigger!" one headline read after the reporters finished their tour.

Segregation

On May 17, 1954, the United States Supreme Court outlawed racial segregation in the public high schools of America. In his decision, Chief Justice Earl Warren wrote, "In the field of public education, the doctrine of separate but equal has no place." Mississippi Senator James O. Eastland replied, "The South will not abide by nor obey this legislative decision by a political court."

In December 1955, a brave black woman, Rosa Parks, sat down in the "For Whites Only" section of a public bus in Montgomery, Alabama, and refused to budge. She was arrested, fined, and eventually jailed for protesting the bus segregation laws.

Almost immediately, two black Baptist preachers, Dr. Martin Luther King and the Reverend Ralph Abarnathy, organized a boycott of the city's buses. Hundreds of black men and women were arrested for supporting the boycott. On April 24, 1956, the Supreme Court ruled that segregation in public transportation was unconstitutional.

When a young black woman, known simply as "Miss Lucy" attempted to enroll at the University of Alabama in 1955, she was met by angry crowds throwing eggs and rocks. In her attempt to integrate the university that day, she narrowly missed injury or even death when a large, angry crowd "greeted" her with a barrage of rocks and bottles. Even before she could attend a class, Miss Lucy was suspended by the university's trustees. The college was accused of giving way to mob rule. The trustees claimed they were acting to protect the young woman "from great bodily harm." On February 29, 1956, a federal court ruled that Miss Lucy would have to be re-admitted to the university.

The lines were drawn. Everyone in the nation was taking sides. Angry threats were being hurled back and forth through the ever-present media. The South was in great turmoil. White northern students and clergy were traveling south to join the marches, the protests, the boycotts, and the demonstrations. Fear, anger, and violence prevailed. A tragic conflagration was about to sweep through the South, leaving death and destruction in the ruins.

In a news conference, President Eisenhower said, "It is incumbent on all the South to show some progress toward racial integration." Southerners were outraged. "Why don't the people in the North solve the racial problems in south Chicago, Detroit, Harlem, and even out west in Watts," one Southern senator exclaimed, "before they come down here and tell us how to solve our problems."

At that critical moment in our nation's history, in February of 1953, I had gone to Columbia, South Carolina, to speak to the annual statewide Baptist Conference on Evangelism. With just an hour's notice, the governor invited me to address a hastily assembled joint session of the South Carolina legislature. There was no time to prepare. My speech was impromptu. I had never spoken publicly about the Supreme Court's decision before that day. I would never speak publicly about it again.

I wasn't a political figure. Nor was I interested in speaking to political issues. I had no political ambitions. I was a pastor. My first concern was the health and the growth of Christ's body, the church, black and white. And I was not convinced that the Congress or the courts could help the growth of the Christian church by law or mandate.

"Desegregating where we live," I warned the South Carolina legislators, "is stirring up our people over a cause that, as of now, is not wisely presented."

In that off-the-cuff speech, I tried to explain why at that time in my life I believed in allowing black and white churches to continue "separate but equal." I knew many black Baptist pastors, and I thought I understood their position: "It is a kindness and a goodness to them," I explained, "that they go to a black church, while we seek to develop our own people in our churches."

Never in my life did I believe in separating people on the basis of skin pigmentation. Racism was, is, and always will be an abomination in the eyes of God, and should be in the eyes of God's people. And where we who call the name of Christ have knowingly or unknowingly contributed to racism in any form, we have sinned and need to beg God's forgiveness.

In my speech that day, my real concern was in helping the churches become more effective instruments at reaching people for Christ. At that time, it seemed pragmatic that the best way to reach black people was with a black pastor, black deacons, black Sunday school teachers, and a black style of worship. It seemed the same for white churches as well.

In my admittedly unwise and untimely address before that joint session of the South Carolina legislature, I pled for the continued right to free association in our homes, our schools, but especially in our churches. Reporters rushed to typewriters and telephones. The next thing I knew, banner headlines labeled me a "hateful segregationist."

In fact, black people were free to attend First Baptist Church of Dallas for decades before the Supreme Court's decision in 1954. I had inherited an "open door" policy from Dr. George Truett and never once contemplated changing it. In fact, we never even thought of doing anything but accepting everybody and anybody that God gave us.

During seminary, I had attended black Baptist meetings regularly because the worship services and the powerful preaching thrilled my soul. I had visited the great black Baptist churches in Dallas and was stirred deeply by what God was doing in the lives of these dear brothers and sisters in Christ. In 1946, I attended the Abyssinian Baptist Church in New York City, pastored at that time by Dr. Adam Powell, Jr., the only black congressman in Washington D.C. In my weekly "Pastor's Pen" to my people in Dallas, I shared how much I had learned from these dear people and their creative Christian commitment.

I knew and loved black pastors all over Texas and across the country. In fact, it was a black pastor in Dallas, Reverend Ernest C. Estell, pastor of St. John's Baptist Church, who defended me even as the press was quoting and misquoting my South Carolina speech.

"I can hardly conceive of Dr. Criswell taking any kind of stand against first-class citizenship for Negroes," he said. "I would like to express doubt that Dr. Criswell ever made such statements."

Making that speech, at that time, in that great, domed capital of South Carolina before reporters just itching for a controversial story was one of the colossal blunders of my young life. Looking back, I wish with all my heart that I had not spoken on behalf of segregation in any form or in any place. In the following weeks, months, and years, as I prayed, searched the holy Scriptures, preached the gospel, and worked with our people, I came to the profound conclusion that to separate by coercion the body of Christ on any basis was unthinkable, unchristian, and unacceptable to God.

The 1960s

Once again, the world was turning upside down as the people of First Baptist Church entered the new decade and its ninety-second year of service to the people of Dallas. The Soviet Union had launched a "cosmic rocket" carrying the hammer-and-sickle past the moon into a permanent orbit around the sun. Soviet Premier Nikita Khrushchev, banging his shoe at the United Nations, took center stage in the "Cold War" race for nuclear supremacy and world domination. An American U-2 spy plane had been shot down over the Soviet Union, dishonoring President Eisenhower and driving relations between the two countries into a tailspin. Fidel Castro's Soviet-backed communist forces had conquered Cuba.

At that moment in history, a young, charismatic Catholic from Massachusetts was running against Vice President Nixon for the American presidency. Once again, I found myself thrust into the political arena. *Newsweek* magazine declared that I was "waging a spirited fight against Kennedy, while studiously avoiding the guttersniping that was employed against Al Smith in 1928."

It was true. In those days I was not convinced that a committed Catholic should be elected president. To hundreds of millions of Catholic believers around the globe, the pope's word was law. Rome, the center of Catholicism, was a sovereign state with obvious ambitions to increase its worldwide sphere of influence. Already, Catholic cardinals, bishops, and even priests exercised undue influence over other "sovereign" governments throughout South America, Europe, and the Philippines. We had never elected a Catholic president. We had no guarantees that a committed Catholic in that office would fully protect the nation's most cherished freedoms: freedom of conscience, freedom of worship, freedom of the press. So I raised the questions and took the second major political stand of my ministry.

On January 20, 1961, John F. Kennedy placed his hand on a Bible and swore "to preserve and protect" the nation's freedoms. Immediately, our thirty-fifth president found himself in the midst of a "Cold War" that was heating up dramatically. On April 12, 1961, Soviet cosmonaut Yuri Gagarin beat the Americans into space. Just two and a half weeks later, the U. S. launched astronaut Alan Shepard, Jr., on a fifteen-minute ride a hundred and fifteen miles above the earth.

On April 25, the American-backed invasion of Cuba's Bay of Pigs was easily defeated by Castro's Soviet-trained forces. Five months later, Soviet-backed troops helped build the wall that would divide Berlin and escalate East-West tensions even further. One hundred and fifty thousand free West Germans roared their support for President Kennedy months later at the wall when our president gave his famous "Ich bin ein Berliner" ("I am a Berliner") speech.

The two great nuclear powers stood glaring at each other across that "Cold War" wall and in other hot war theaters around the globe, especially in Vietnam. In 1962 and 1963, President Kennedy assigned more troops to back our allies in Saigon. He even ordered American forces into Thailand to search and destroy insurgent bases there. Finally, on October 28, 1962, the Cuban missile crisis sent the world screeching toward nuclear war. But in the showdown, our young president refused to compromise, and with a final, empty threat, Mr. Khruschev ordered his missiles out of Cuba.

The whole world mourned when our young president was killed by an assassin's bullet while he and his wife rode in a motorcade not far from our church in downtown Dallas. During his brief one thousand days in office, Mr. Kennedy kept his promise for a pluralistic America and proved himself to be a profile of courage in times of "Cold War" conflict.

You can imagine the horror in our hearts as we watched those films of the tragedy repeated over and over again: the bullets striking down our governor and our president; Jacqueline Kennedy in her blood-spattered pink suit and hat reaching out to pull a secret serviceman into the speeding limousine; young "John John" Kennedy saluting his father's funeral cortege; the "eternal flame" burning in remembrance.

"To the family of John Kennedy, I send our sincerest, heartfelt sympathies," I said to the press and in that next Sunday morning sermon. "In times like these, the world has but one hope," I exclaimed. "That hope is the life, death, and resurrection of Jesus."

The World's Only Hope

In 1963, after seventeen years and eight months, I finished preaching through the entire Bible, book by book, chapter by chapter, line by line. It was preaching the Word that seriously that changed my life and the lives of the good people at First Baptist Church of Dallas.

We were there, together, at the Creation, when God said, "Let there be light." We stood side by side in awe and silence as God bent down and made the first man and the first woman out of the dust of the earth. As a congregation, we walked with Adam and Eve in the Garden of Eden and heard God's loving voice say, "Be fruitful and multiply." Together, we saw Evil in the form of a serpent whisper disobedience in the ear of Eve, and we wept when that first couple broke God's heart and began the plague of sinfulness that would reach out and touch us all.

We cringed in horror when a jealous Cain slew his brother Abel, and we watched with incredulity as sinfulness spread like a giant stain across all of God's creation, until God Himself cried out, "I will destroy man whom I have created from the face of the earth . . . for it repenteth me that I have made them." And we sang with joy when Noah found grace in the eyes of the Lord. "Build an ark," God whispered. And in that loving, forgiving act, God, the Father of us all, launched His plan to save the world from its sinfulness.

The thirty-nine Old Testament books and the twenty-seven books of the New Testament are a dramatic, eyewitness account of God at work, reaching out to save creation, and among the fallen creatures are you and I. The Old Testament stories of the patriarchs, the priests, the kings, and the prophets are stories of God's plan of redemption through the ages. "I will build myself a nation. They will hear my voice and follow me. And through them I will save the peoples of the earth." And the New Testament story of Jesus' life, death, and resurrection and of the men and women who followed Him—the greatest story ever told—is the climax of that age-old story of God working to save us all.

To hear those stories, one by one, is to have your life transformed, your spirit renewed, and your hope born again. And in the midst of a great "Cold War" between the superpowers, East and West, in the midst of growing nuclear tension and calamity, the Word gave us strength for our journey and comfort and guidance along the way.

On my twentieth anniversary as pastor of First Baptist Church of Dallas, our membership had grown to 13,291 souls. Our Sunday school rolls had swelled to 8,322 men, women, and children, and our offerings that year went over the $1.5 million mark. On Anniversary Sunday, songs of praise echoed out from the crowded sanctuary and across the growing city.

The Last Visit with Mother Criswell

"You look tired, son," my eighty-seven-year-old mother said to me during one of my visits in 1964. She was living in a rest home in Los Angeles. The minute I walked into her room carrying flowers and an envelope of pictures of Betty and Mabel Ann, she climbed out of her bed and rushed to my side.

"You lie down," she said steering me to her bed.

"Mother," I protested vainly. "I am fine. You are the one to be in bed. Not I."

"Son," she repeated with that look in her eyes that from my childhood had stopped me in my tracks. "Lie down."

"Yes, Mother," I said grinning, hoping no one would pass the open door of her little room and see that fragile, old woman ordering me around like a child.

"Mother," I muttered, "I'm fifty-five years old myself you know."

"You look a hundred," she said, placing a light blanket over me and sitting down beside the bed. "Besides, I have all of eternity to rest."

"Mother . . ." I replied.

"Shhhh," she answered, stroking my arm and leaning back in her chair beside me. I only did lay down to humor her, but in her loving care I fell into a deep sleep. When I awakened, she was still sitting there, still stroking my arm, still praying for me as she had for more than half a century.

"Do you feel better now, son?" she asked.

"Much better, Mother," I answered, taking her in my arms and holding her as we both cried silently with gratitude for our years together.

Several months later, Mother lay down in that same bed, closed her eyes, and went to be with Jesus. Today, her body lies beside my father's remains in the Forest Lawn Cemetery in Glendale, California, but her spirit is alive and well in heaven.

I have often imagined that moment just seconds after she died when Jesus welcomed Mother home.

"Anna Currie Criswell," our Lord Jesus exclaimed, His arms open in welcome, "enter into the rest prepared for you."

Finally, after a lifetime of hard work and struggle, much of it on my behalf, Mother got her chance to rest.

Dr. Criswell with Auca Indians in South America

The Jungles of Peru

When Jesus said, "Go, ye, into all the world," He must have had Cameron Townsend especially in mind. "Uncle Cam," the founder of Wycliffe Bible Translators, decided early in his life that he would see that God's Word was translated into every language or tribal tongue in the world.

God was very generous to make Uncle Cam my friend. Often, he and I would travel across the earth visiting mission stations to teach and preach the Word, to encourage missionaries and the national Christian leaders they were developing, and to bring home a mission's report to the people in North America and Europe whose generous gifts supported Uncle Cam and his Wycliffe team.

In 1964, Uncle Cam and I made a three week tour of Wycliffe mission fields in South America.

"You have to visit the village of Tariri," Uncle Cam told me as he walked to the little airplane that would carry him to Lima from Wycliffe's home base in Yarinachocha, Peru. "You will enjoy meeting the Shapra chief," he added, giving me one more reason for staying the extra day in the Amazon jungle. "Before his conversion, he was a legendary figure among Peruvian tribes for his brutal killings and his merciless head-shrinking."

Cam Townsend was a tease. The visit to Tariri would be as safe as a trip to downtown Dallas, or so I thought.

Early the next morning, Floyd Lyon, the young missionary pilot for Jungle Aviation and Radio Services, described the journey.

"There's almost two hours of flying time between the Ucayali and the Maranon Rivers," he shouted over the sounds of the noisy engine. "We'll be out of touch with civilization for the entire time over a jungle without a place to land, or without a person to meet you if you did land."

The wild world below us was deep green and endless, scarred only occasionally by a river or a stream. The plane's loud drone had me dozing comfortably when suddenly the engine coughed, backfired with a loud explosion, and went silent. The only sounds that followed were the loud beating of my heart and the wind whistling through the struts and around the windows as the little plane spiraled toward the jungle.

"Mayday, Yarinacocha!" the pilot shouted into his microphone. "Mayday!"

We were between the rivers, out of range of any known missionary station or jungle outpost. If we survived the crash, it was unlikely that anyone could find the wreckage. Suddenly, the radio crackled.

"Give me your position," an unknown voice demanded. "I will relay."

"Thank, God," Floyd muttered under his breath as he wrestled to gain control of the airplane.

"Look, there," he said, pointing at a wisp of smoke rising up from the endless green. "And there," he shouted excitedly. "Thatched roofs . . . and a stream," he said. "God's given us a place to land."

The "stream" was hardly a place to land. Only the sun glinting off the water made it appear through the almost impenetrable jungle overgrowth. It was shallow and filled with jutting rocks and logs.

"We can't get in there," I shouted to the pilot.

"We have to," he answered dropping the airplane's nose toward the center of that tiny stream.

At the last possible second, he jerked the wheel back into his lap. I braced myself. The plane shuddered, leveled out, and zipped across the treetops toward the waiting stream.

We hit a sandy bank, bounced into the stream, jolted across the rocks and logs toward the dense foliage, lodged against a sand bar in the creek, and stopped dead in the water.

Floyd turned to me with an impish grin. "Thank God. We're safe!"

"Let's thank Him now," I said.

When we raised our heads, there were dozens of native faces pressed against the windows.

Are these the headhunters Uncle Cam was "joking" about? I asked myself.

The friendly Christian natives that God had placed in our sandy path were graduates of a Wycliffe Bible training school.

The Amazon jungle covers an area nearly as large as the continental United States. There was not a road through it in those days. If you tried to chop your way through the dense and dangerous foliage with a sharp machete you might make thirty feet a day. But God heard our "Mayday!" An unknown stranger relayed it to home base, and while we were sitting in an unnamed village on a tiny stream surrounded by millions of acres of jungle, the rescue team was already headed in our direction to take us safely home.

"Trust in the Lord," the Bible says, "and He will direct your paths."

Integration

That speech on segregation that I made before the South Carolina legislature haunted me, and my congregation, for more than a dozen years. We knew that our church doors had been open to any visitor of any color, but we had never made it an official, stated policy that any believer, black, white, or yellow, could become a member of the church. We knew that racism was wrong, but we had never really taken a stand to right that wrong. And even after the Supreme Court's decisions, after years of rioting and bloodshed, after endless laws, speeches, and sermons, neither our country nor our church seemed to be getting any closer to healing the deep wounds that racism had inflicted on each of us.

In 1957, nine black students were turned away from Little Rock High School by hundreds of white people screaming threats and racial epithets. President Eisenhower said he was forced to call in federal troops "to prevent violence and bloodshed."

In 1960, black Americans began sit-ins all across the South to integrate restaurants, coffee shops, and cafes. Angry, violent clashes followed. Innocent people were injured and killed in the confrontations.

In 1962, when James Meredith tried to become the first black student to enroll in the University of Mississippi, a massive riot erupted. Mobs of angry whites stormed onto the campus. At least three people died, and fifty more were injured in the fighting.

In 1967, "black power" advocates Stokely Carmichael and H. Rapp Brown were calling for a violent black revolution in America.

"We have no alternative," Carmichael declared, "but to use aggressive armed violence to own the land, houses and stores inside our own communities."

On April 5, 1968, Dr. Martin Luther King, Jr., my fellow Baptist minister, was assassinated on a motel balcony in Memphis, Tennessee.

"Brothers," I said to my deacon board on Tuesday, June 4, 1968, "we must face this issue and face it now."

The deacons had assembled for their monthly business meeting. I had spent the last weeks in restless, agonizing prayer.

"Pastor, tell us what God has placed on your heart," the chairman said to me. "Bare your soul to us," he added, "and let us listen."

They were good men, all! And I poured out my heart to them.

"Do you remember," I asked, rehearsing the history of our open door policy, "when we invited the children from the Buckner Home to worship and study here with us at First Baptist Church?"

They nodded and smiled.

"One of you said to me during that discussion, 'But, Pastor, there are colored children in the Buckner Home.' And I answered, 'We shall welcome them—white, red, black, yellow. We shall welcome all of the children.' Do you remember?"

Again, the deacons nodded and smiled. Those children, all of them, had filled the church with wonderful, noisy love.

"But what happens when that little boy whose skin is black becomes a young man," I asked, "and here on a Sunday morning finds Christ as Lord and Savior? What happens then? When he walks down the aisle to give his heart to Jesus, to request baptism, to become a member of our church, what exactly will I tell him?

"'Go back, young man, I didn't really mean you!' And what will I say to God? 'He was black, Lord. He belonged in a black church, not in ours.'

"In a thousand years, I couldn't find the words to speak to God or to that young man because there are no words to explain it. It would be wrong. And I am done with preaching and worrying even as I preach that someone who is black might respond to my invitation."

Suddenly, my eyes filled with tears. There was so much more to be said, but the energy just went out of me. I didn't know what the deacons would say. Before I could even settle back in the folding chair, a deacon jumped to his feet.

"Mr. Chairman," he said excitedly, "all of us rise to our feet."

And as one man, the deacons stood.

"We shall stand by you, Pastor," the deacon said, his voice strong and sure. "To the last man, we shall support this conviction that God has placed on your soul!"

Our chairman walked to the front of the room. For a moment, it looked like he was going to speak. Then, suddenly, his eyes filling with tears, the dear man turned and knelt at the front altar. In just seconds, the rest of the deacons were streaming forward to kneel beside him. All of us were weeping as we knelt, each praying his own private prayer for forgiveness, for guidance, and for strength.

"Dear Lord," a new voice called out, and I could tell exactly who it was by the beautiful, accented English that he spoke. "Bless these dear men."

It was our Nigerian missionary deacon who led us in our prayer of consecration and commitment.

"Give them wisdom, Lord Jesus," he prayed. "Give them courage."

And even as he prayed, the room echoed with the sobs of grown men who could feel Christ's loving, forgiving presence among us, guiding us into His certain future.

A Centennial Celebration

The year 1968 was a year marred by tragedy. On New Year's day, simultaneously in one hundred Vietnamese cities, communist forces launched their Tet Offensive, bloodying soldiers and civilians alike, blasting their way even into the fortress-like U. S. embassy in Saigon. In April, Dr. Martin Luther King was assassinated. Presidential candidate Robert Kennedy was shot and killed in June. In August, riot police battled mobs of protestors outside the Democratic convention in Chicago.

And in November, in spite of all the bloodshed and horror across the nation and around the world, we gathered in the sanctuary to celebrate the centennial year of First Baptist Church of Dallas and my twenty-five years as her pastor.

It is a well-established Christian tradition to celebrate Christ's light in the face of darkness, to renew our commitment to His life in the presence of death. In spite of everything, God was at work in the world, redeeming the lost, and we were celebrating one hundred years of His presence among us and among those who preceded us at First Baptist Church of Dallas.

God had blessed us in so many ways! Our annual fall "Round-Up," begun in 1945, had expanded from a church-wide extravaganza under a big tent on the downtown campus to a dude ranch, and finally to a "First Baptist Only" night at Six Flags Over Texas. Our annual stewardship campaign, held usually just after the fall "Round-Up," had increased every year but one. During our centennial year, church offerings passed the two million dollar mark, and half of the total $2,220,141 gathered in 1968 went to missions outside our own church program.

Our junior board, established in 1947, had mobilized hundreds of fine young men into more active Christian service. Our Family Camping program, begun in 1949, now serviced hundreds of families and thousands of children and young people. In 1958, we purchased the eleven-story business and professional building just across Patterson Street from the sanctuary. The Burt Building, named for R. E. Burt, who agreed to sell this valuable property to our congregation for far below the market value of a million dollars, helped house our rapidly expanding Sunday school program that had grown to 8,655 men, women, and children by the time of our centennial celebration.

The traditional pre-Easter revival meetings, once held in the Palace Theater, had been moved to our church sanctuary and were continuing from strength to strength. We were experiencing regular, church-wide revivals in our congregation, and by 1968, our church membership roles had grown to 14, 825 souls.

"With 14,825 members," the *Time* story began, "the First Baptist Church of Dallas is the biggest Southern Baptist church in the U. S."

Betty and I still have the *Time* magazine picture of the two of us wearing Uncle Sam hats and sitting in rocking chairs in the church gymnasium on a stage before several thousands members of our loving congregation.

The walls of the gym were hung with garlands of colorful Texas wildflowers. An enormous American flag covered another entire wall. Many speeches were made. Many compliments given. My eyes teared up with gratitude when retired Judge Pierce McBride called me "the greatest pulpit man in the world." It wasn't true, but it felt so good to hear it.

And most of the people who deserved the real credit were long since gone. In my imagination I could see the dear folks who had invested their lives in mine standing against the back wall of the gym, smiling at me. My father was there, in his barber apron, still waving his freshly sharpened razor and shouting above the noise: "He's going to be the greatest successor any great pastor ever had! You'll see."

Pastor John Hicks, the man who led me to the Lord, was there with Brother L. S. Hill and Brother Campbell, my pastors in Texline. They were standing side by side, smiling and shaking their heads in wonder. Georgie Abbott was present and I could hear him whispering, "Not bad, little Bible Reader. Not bad at all."

Evangelist Whaley was present with his songleader, young John R. Rice, still wearing his silver Baylor belt buckle and exclaiming, "Your Bible is the sword of the Lord, Criswell. Keep it sharp and swinging!" And the dear old pastor from the Cimarron Encampment was still holding out his crippled hand to me and saying quietly, "Stay in the Word, young man. Don't let anybody keep you from it."

Mrs. Sells was there: "E-nun-ci-ate, Mr. Criswell," she commanded loudly. "Ev-e-ry syl-la-ble musssttt be cle-ar." And Miss Martha Folks Hawn stood nearby. I could still hear her advice after I had preached a sermon in her little theater in Waco: "From this moment," she said loudly, "and for the rest of your life, when you stand up to preach, do exactly what you feel like doing. I'm not promising that people will like it," she added, "but I am telling you this: They will listen!"

My friends Christy Poole and Alvin Daves were there. How I wished that Alvin hadn't drowned and that both of them could share this moment with me.

The great preachers who God used to shape me were all standing together: Wallace Basset, G. L. Yates, L. R. Scarborough, Robert G. Lee, and chief among them George W. Truett. And the great teachers gathered nearby: Samuel Palmer Brooks, A. J. Armstrong, W. Hersey Davis, A. T. Robertson, all of them wide-eyed and open-mouthed, no one saying what every one of them must have felt: "If God can use W. A. Criswell in such a way, He can use anybody."

And my mother was there, with flour on her apron and a freshly baked pie in her hands. How many pies she must have baked and how many heads of hair my father must have cut to support me through those long years of education! "Good work, W. A.," my father was saying. "Now rest, son," Mother added. "I have all eternity for resting."

Suddenly, the lights dimmed and the memories faded. As Betty and I sat hand in hand, our daughter, Mabel Ann, walked into the spotlight and began to sing.

"To God be the glory! Great things He hath done."

Annie sang like an angel. She was a grown woman now, and as she thrilled the congregation with her song, I remembered holding tightly to her little hand as we waded in the shallows of the Illinois River on our Monday family picnics in Muskogee, Oklahoma. How quickly the years had passed! God had done so much. If only there had been more time.

13

President,
the Southern Baptist
Convention
1968-1970

*"But when they deliver you up, take no thought
how or what ye shall speak: for it shall be given
you in that same hour what ye shall speak."*

Matthew 10:19

1968, HOUSTON

On June 6, 1968, I was elected president of the Southern Baptist Convention by fifteen thousand Messengers gathered in Houston, Texas, for our 111th annual meeting. Sitting in a balcony high above the convention floor, crowded by delegates from all fifty states, my wife Betty, my daughter Mabel Ann, and I wept when the results were made known. Shortly after the ballots were counted, convention officials led me to a large conference room where members of the world's press were waiting.

"Like a lamb unto slaughter," a friend whispered good-naturedly as we entered the noisy room filled to capacity.

"Go get 'em, Criswell," another friend exclaimed.

215

With our more than eleven million members, Southern Baptists made up the largest denomination in the United States. Dozens of journalists, cameramen, and sound technicians were assigned to cover our meeting at this crucial moment in the nation's history.

Flash bulbs lit up the room even as we entered. I sat down at a little table covered with microphones and portable tape recorders. Strong television lights were switched on as cameras began to roll.

"Dr. Criswell?"

Reporters leaned forward in their chairs and seemed with one voice to cry out my name.

I was not popular with the liberal press. One reporter described me as "a cross between Billy Sunday and King Kong." Another labeled my theological position as "only slightly left of the Flat Earth Society." A third described my preaching style as "a sort of symphonic bellow."

I didn't mind their cracks and potshots at my preaching. In fact, I rather enjoyed them. Preachers are also public figures. Like everybody else, we have to take our chances with the press, but I felt angry and helpless when reporters impugned my integrity or lied about me or my church in a newspaper article or television story.

"Criswell weeps all the way to the bank," one reporter wrote cynically after seeing me show my emotions during a Sunday morning sermon, "while his church board is obliged to rent an armored car to transport each Sunday's collection receipts to a Dallas bank."

In fact, most of those reporters didn't know a thing about me or about my values. They were surprised when I expressed my sympathies publicly to the entire Kennedy family upon young Bobby's tragic and untimely death. They were surprised when I informed them that First Baptist Church had black members already on its rolls. And they were surprised when the man they had labeled "an avid segregationist" signed the strong racial statement adopted by the Messengers.

"Every Southern Baptist in the land should support the spirit of that statement," I exclaimed. "We Southern Baptists have definitely turned away from racism, from segregation, from anything and everything that speaks of a separation of people in the body of Christ."

"Dr. Criswell," a New York reporter began her question, looking down at her pad quizzically and then back at me. "Do you really believe the Bible word for word? For example, do you think Jonah really did get swallowed by a fish?"

"Yes, I do," I replied directly. "I believe that a fish literally swallowed Jonah. And if there isn't a fish big enough to do that, I believe that God could have made a fish for that purpose. And if He'd wanted to, He could have made it big enough to have a whole suite of rooms waiting for Jonah in the fish's belly with a television thrown in for good measure."

The reporters laughed and wrote furiously.

"What's your goal for the nation's largest denomination?" a newsman asked.

"I would like to lead our convention into a great evangelistic and missionary effort," I replied. "I want to get lost people to God."

"But what about social action?" the same man shouted, implying that I had no social concern. "What about the poor, the homeless, the hungry?"

"You cannot divorce faith and works," I shot back at him. "You cannot divorce morality and ethics from evangelism and missions. You can't put a man's head over here and his heart over there."

"What about the split between Baptist conservatives and Baptist moderates?" another reporter asked.

"Oh, we Baptists are too soft to split," I replied grinning. "I want to call the convention to unity in Christ. When disunion and divisiveness enter," I added, "the church is hurt, the witness destroyed, and Satan triumphs."

For an hour the reporters bombarded me with their questions and their cynical asides. Finally, I was escorted from the room.

"Good work, Criswell," my friends said surrounding me. "They thought they had you on the grill, but you won them over with your openness and your honesty."

In fact, in the days following that press conference I discovered again that few reporters are "won over" by the facts, let alone by "openness or honesty." *The San Francisco Chronicle* writer began his story by calling me "an arch-segregationist" and *Newsweek* magazine, after informing its readers that early in my ministry I had "followed literally the example of Saint John by preaching from any handy creek or river and dunking converts, clothes and all . . ." claimed that "Criswell still defends racial segregation."

There was no way to explain my real feelings at that moment. I loved the Southern Baptist Convention. Her pastors and her teachers had shaped my professional life. Her dear, generous people had paid my college and my seminary tuition. Eight of her churches from Pecan Grove to Dallas had trusted me with their pulpits. The Southern Baptists were my home and family, but I had never aspired to leadership of the Southern Baptist Convention.

I was a preacher and a pastor. For years I was asked to run for high office, and for just as many years I had declined. I didn't want to spend more Sundays away from my people and my pulpit. I didn't want my family or my flock to be the victims of lies, half-truths, and hyperbole in the world's press. I didn't want my church divided by controversy and contention. I wanted only to pastor my flock, not to lead the eleven million member denomination. Finally, God and a handful of my friends intervened. I had been elected to a one-year term as president of the Southern Baptist Convention. I would do my best. The rest was in God's hands.

I walked out of that press conference and returned to my room. I got down on my knees and prayed. While I was kneeling there, I remembered Jesus' last words to His disciples as they sat in the Upper Room just before His arrest and crucifixion.

"A new commandment I give unto you, that you love one another; as I have loved you, that ye also love one another. By this shall all men know that ye are my disciples, if ye have love one to another," (John 13:34-35).

My goals for the Southern Baptist Convention were simple: that we learn to love—to love the Lord, to love the lost, to love the Bible, to love the right, to love all humanity, and to love each other. It was the heart of my message to the executive committee three months into my first term as president of the Convention and the heart of the message I preached in churches, great and small, that first year all across the nation.

Why I Preach That the Bible Is Literally True.

During my first term in office, I also wrote a little book for Broadman Press, our Sunday School Board publishing house, entitled *Why I Preach That the Bible Is Literally True.* When the book was released, a great controversy rose up surrounding it. Sixty-four Baptist professors of religion condemned the book. In a long resolution, they "deplored" and "protested" its publication and promotion by the Sunday School Board.

At first, I thought the whole affair a kind of tempest in a teapot. It was hard to believe that Baptists could disagree about the basic issue of the book: "Is the Bible the Word of God?" In the text I answered the question forthrightly: "If the Bible is the Word of God," I maintained, "we have an absolutely trustworthy guide for all the answers our souls desire to know . . . . But if the Bible is not the Word of God, if it is the mere product of man's speculation, if it is not altogether trustworthy, then we are all in a trackless wilderness not knowing where to go or to turn."

In the book, I explained why I believe and why I preach that the Bible is literally true. I ended the book with an appeal to my fellow Southern Baptists to continue preaching in their own pulpits that the Bible is literally true.

The sixty-four Baptist professors said one problem with my book was its "denial of the historical-critical method of Bible study." After they announced their condemnation of *Why I Preach That the Bible Is Literally True*, headlines in the *Dallas Morning News* announced it to the world: "Criswell's Book Gets Chilly Reception!"

In fact, my Southern Baptist brothers and sisters rushed to defend what I had written. Jack Gritz, editor of the Oklahoma "Baptist Messenger" summarized what I believe were most Baptists' feelings: "Nowhere in his book has Criswell denied the validity of the historical-critical approach to the Bible as the professors claim. He has challenged some uses of this approach. The truth is that with an earned doctorate of philosophy degree in New Testament from Southern Seminary at Louisville, Kentucky, and with thirty years of preaching from the Greek New Testament behind him, Criswell knows more about the historical-critical approach to the Bible than do most of the professors."

I knew that Old and New Testament writers wrote both literally and figuratively. In the book I tried to show the difference.

"If the literal meaning of any word or expression makes good sense in its connections, it is literal. But if the literal meaning does not make good sense, it is figurative. Since the literal is the most usual signification of a word and therefore occurs much more frequently than the figurative, any term ought to be regarded as literal until there is good reason for a different understanding; and that understanding will become clear as well, as we read the context and background of the passage in the Bible."

Sides were taken. Hard words were exchanged. At first, I felt blue and downhearted. Think of it! Our Sunday School Board castigated for publishing a book by a pastor who believes the Bible and whose preaching of the Book has been blessed beyond compare! It was a startling, jarring development to me.

As I prayed and worried, God helped me to see how foolish I was to be depressed by all the fury. I resolved to dismiss it from my mind, go right on preaching that blessed Book to my people, and say nothing in rebuttal.

Can We Trust the Word?

The real issue soon surfaced. Can we trust the Bible or can we not? Whatever method we use to study it, can we depend wholly upon God's Word as our guide to Christian faith and practice, or should we look somewhere else for truth? Can we build our lives and our eternal destinies on the Word's rock-firm foundation, or is the Bible just another book of sand?

Too many professors—not all of them, mind you, but too many— live in ivory towers. They spend their days in libraries reading books. That isn't bad unless the process blinds them to the real world where real people have their dead to bury and their prodigal sons to pray over. Professors are paid to be smart, but some of them get too smart to be helpful. They learn the ancient languages, and they should. They dig into the ancient texts, and that's right for them. But instead of affirm- ing the Word, they raise erudite questions about this Old Testament passage or that New Testament parable. Instead of building confidence in the Word, they show off their own picayune discoveries. Instead of demonstrating the Word's eternal trustworthiness, they take every chance to tear it down.

Before long, their poor students wonder if the Bible can be trusted. They begin to fear that no one short of a Ph.D. can even begin to understand it, let alone apply it to the problems of their world. Too many exercises in Greek or Hebrew exegesis leave them feeling stupid and uninformed. Sermons criticized by their peers leave them feeling worthless and untalented. Harshly graded exams and scholarly papers finally do them in. Innocent students become confused and afraid. They lose sight of their own precious gifts and of God's certain call. Their hearts grow faint and their hope withers. Soon, but for the grace of God, they leave the ministry forever.

Tell a man whose heart is broken and whose hold on faith is slipping that the Bible is not to be taken literally, and you may destroy him. Tell a woman whose marriage is in jeopardy or whose child is born handicapped that Jesus didn't really mean exactly what He said and you could kill her hope forever.

Worse yet, it usually follows that when someone gives up his faith in God's infallible Word, he also gives up the gospel! Then sadly, when men and women, boys or girls don't hear from the pulpit that Jesus died for our sins, that through His blood we can be forgiven, that we can have our name written forever in the Book of Life, the lost stay lost forever.

In February, 1971, one of my deacons, Jim Ray Smith, introduced me to a young Texas businessman who wanted to join our congregation. And though I've heard similar stories a thousand times or more, that young man's confession nearly broke my heart.

"Dr. Criswell," he said, "I found Christ through the witness of a friend nearly four years ago, and immediately I joined a church in my neighborhood and began to read the Bible."

That young layman standing before me was Jack Pogue, a Dallas real estate broker. His eyes sparkled and his words tumbled out of him.

"After I found Christ," he said, "I bought a Bible and read it the first time cover to cover in forty days. Then I read it a second time, and a third, and a fourth. I was hungry for the Word. I loved every minute that I spent reading it, and I longed to belong to a church where the Word was preached, where Christ was honored and His plan of salvation was made clear."

Suddenly, the young stranger paused. His expression changed from excitement to sadness.

"But my preacher didn't even seem interested in what the Bible had to say," Jack continued. "He preached about social issues exclusively. I was hungry to hear sermons from the Word. I had questions about what the Bible said. There were passages I could not understand. I needed answers, but my preacher wasn't preaching from the Bible, and I was growing more and more discontent."

"Then, one day," he continued, "when I was doing business with one of your deacons, Jim Ray Smith, he began to talk to me about Christ and the Bible. As we talked, questions poured out of me about the Bible from Genesis to Revelation. And almost every answer your deacon gave me began with 'Dr. Criswell says . . . .'"

"Finally, I asked him, 'Who is Dr. Criswell?'"

That very day, my faithful deacon invited that eager young seeker to worship with us, and the next Sunday morning, Jack Pogue sat in the balcony of our sanctuary hoping, praying that his heart-cry would be answered.

"Dr. Criswell," he said to me that Sunday morning, "when you stepped up to preach, you held your Bible out for all of us to see and then you said these words: 'For forty-three years I've been preaching from this Holy Book, and I will not stop preaching from it until the day I die.'"

"I had been attending a church for four years," Jack Pogue told me that day, and I could tell he was fighting back the tears. "And never once did the pastor hold up the Word and preach from its pages. Never once did he make the plan of salvation clear. And the last Sunday I was there he said from the pulpit, 'Jesus was a good man. He was like God in many ways, but He wasn't God.' And when he spoke those words, I said to myself, 'I'm getting out of here and I'm going to find a church where the Word is preached.'"

That young Texas businessman was shocked that his own pastor had never made the gospel clear. Jack had been a faithful layman. He had attended church every Sunday. He had given generously of his money. But in all those years, no one in that church had proclaimed Jesus Christ as Lord and Savior or explained to the congregation how sinners can find forgiveness for their sins.

In May of 1971, Jack Pogue joined First Baptist Church, and for these past twenty years that dear man, out of love for Christ, has served our church faithfully. Endowed by God with special gifts, Jack has been one of my closest friends and co-workers in the ministry. And it all began because I simply preached the Bible. Like thousands of spiritually hungry men and women before him, Jack Pogue's life was changed forever by the preaching of God's infallible Word.

"Dr. Criswell," Jack said to me shortly after he had joined our church, "imagine the millions of church members in this country who have never heard how they could be born again." He paused and looked puzzled. "Why?" he asked. "How can so many preachers preach on so many things, and never once mention that we are lost, and that only Christ can save us?"

My new friend learned the reason soon enough. When young pastors attend schools that no longer teach the infallible Word of God, they lose track of God's will for the world. They forget that the Old and New Testaments are the history of God at work redeeming humankind, and that at the heart of Jesus's own story is the blood He shed to redeem the lost. When pastors lose hold of God's infallible Word, they also lose hold of the gospel. What then do they have left to preach?

Instead of proclaiming God's plan of salvation, these poor, lost preachers ride their own personal hobby horses to death! They'll ride war and peace until it's threadbare. Then they'll pick up civil rights and ride that into the ground. Then along comes ecology, hunger, or nuclear arms to fill another futile Sunday.

None of these subjects is bad. God's Word speaks clearly and boldly to each of them. But these hobby horse preachers quit preaching the Word a long time ago. They continue forever quoting facts from the newspapers, statistics from UNICEF or UNESCO, and heart-warming stories from World Vision or World Relief. They forget about God's Word altogether.

And the poor, hungry layman or laywoman who has heard it all on radio or has seen it all on television or has read it all in the daily papers or in the weekly news magazines, yawns and mutters under his or her breath: "Preacher, we have seen and heard all this before, only more effectively and more dramatically, in the media. We came to church to hear what God has to say to heal our broken lives and to give us reason to go on living. Preach the Word or let us alone!"

"Don't you ever doubt, Dr. Criswell?" a seminary student once asked me in a graduate class I was teaching. "Don't you ever have doubts about the Word?"

Feeling the young man's pain and remembering myself the long, difficult years of study and preparation, I answered simply.

"No, son," I said quietly. Then, after a long pause, I added, "Trust the Word. Never quit believing it, all of it. Use your brain to the limit," I said, encouraging the young man to use every intellectual power at his command to study the Word. "But what you cannot understand, accept on faith, and God will honor your faithfulness."

The class was silent. I waited for one long moment, and then in my own croaky baritone, I began to sing a little chorus I had learned from the children in our Sunday school:

> We'll talk it over, in the by and by.
> We'll talk it over, my Lord and I.
> I'll ask the reasons.
> He'll tell me why.
> When we talk it over, in the by and by.

1969: New Orleans

During my first term as president of the Southern Baptist Convention, 1968-1969, America had been torn by rioting over racial equality and the war in Vietnam. The Democratic convention in Chicago had erupted in violence. Huey Newton, leader of the Black Panther Party, was convicted on manslaughter charges for murdering an Oakland policeman. Black activist James Foreman had presented a "Manifesto," demanding millions of dollars in "reparations" from America's churches "for their role in the suffering of black Americans."

Two U. S. athletes at the 1968 Olympic Games had been suspended for giving the "black power salute" on the winner's stand.

Anti-war student activists had seized college campuses from New York to California, demanding an end to America's involvement in Vietnam and insisting on greater involvement in the control of university affairs.

The restless, warring spirit of the 1960s hung like a storm cloud over the 1969 Southern Baptist Convention in New Orleans. As the end of my term approached, the controversy over *Why I Preach That the Bible Is Literally True* had widened from the battle of the Bible to a full-fledged war between Baptists who held to the fundamentals of Southern Baptist belief and those who did not. Like all Americans, Baptists were also concerned about racial conflict and the war in Vietnam. The 16,800 Messengers who gathered in New Orleans in June of 1969 didn't know what to expect during our 112th annual meeting. Threats were made. Rumors were flying.

"Dr. Criswell," a reporter asked as Betty and I arrived at the New Orleans convention center, "is it true that black power advocate James Foreman is on his way here to make demands on convention delegates?"

"Dr. Criswell," another journalist shouted above the noisy crowd, "will you meet with the Baptist Students Concerned who support the Black Manifesto demands and want to liberalize church action?"

"Dr. Criswell," a third chimed in, "what about the E. Y. Mullins Fellowship of liberal professors who are determined to oust you from the presidency? How will you answer their charges?"

"No comment," I answered each reporter, barely managing to escape them through a backstage doorway.

It had been rumored that black activist James Foreman was en route to New Orleans to disrupt our meeting. I was afraid the convention platform would be turned into some kind of riotous brawl, but even as I presided over the opening session, Louisiana Governor McKeithen, a personal friend and a visitor to our Dallas church, called to inform me that if Mr. Foreman tried to enter Louisiana, he would be stopped at the state line. And though Mr. Foreman had visited Northern and American Baptist church conventions, apparently his trip to New Orleans was just a rumor and our convention proceeded smoothly.

The thirty-five Young Baptists Concerned were heard by convention leaders and their requests "to liberalize church literature, provide sex education in Sunday schools, end racial discrimination through the denomination, and channel church funds directly to Negro-administered economic and anti-poverty organizations" were referred to the resolutions committee and returned in various forms to be considered by the full convention.

Twice-elected president of the SBC

The E. Y. Mullins Fellowship, an organization of dissident Baptist professors, formed to "liberalize Baptist seminaries and to advocate the historical-critical method of Biblical interpretation," opposed my re-election and supported the candidacy of William C. Smith, a University of Richmond religion professor.

It was not my wish to run for a second term, but there was too much at stake to flee the scene of battle. Forces were at work from within the Southern Baptist Convention to redefine what it means to be a Christian and a Southern Baptist. The fundamental teachings of God's Word and loyalty to the historic Baptist creeds were at stake. This was no time to quit. I was re-elected, 7482 votes to 400, for a second term, and the 16,800 Baptist Messengers concluded the week of heated, heartfelt deliberation with a worship service that filled the stadium to capacity and sent God's praises echoing across New Orleans.

1970: Denver

During my second term as president of the Southern Baptist Convention, 1969-1970, America managed to place astronauts Neil

A. Armstrong and Edwin E. Aldrin, Jr., on the moon. But back on earth, our nation was coming apart at the seams.

On November 15, 1969, paratroopers guarded the Pentagon and the Justice Department as two hundred and fifty thousand anti-war activists marched on Washington, D.C. To make matters worse, just two weeks later, a platoon of American soldiers was accused of massacring 567 civilian Vietnamese in the little village of Mylai. Violent anti-war protests escalated across the nation.

On May 18, 1970, just weeks before our 113th annual meeting of the Southern Baptist Convention in Denver, the Kent State shootings shocked the nation. On that normally tranquil Ohio campus, two young men and two young women protesting President Nixon's expansion of the war into Cambodia were killed by nervous and inexperienced National Guardsmen.

The old decade ended in a paroxysm of radical protest and cataclysmic change. Five hundred thousand young Americans gathered in a huge, open field near Woodstock, New York, to listen to rock music, to smoke marijuana, to make love, and to lie naked in the grass.

"The old American values are bankrupt," said one rock musician, who later died of a drug overdose, "and there are no new values to take their place."

Another war between old values and the new was being waged by a handful of professors and student activists in various seminaries and colleges across the Southern Baptist Convention. The historic Southern Baptist commitment to the centrality of the Bible in all matters of faith and practice was at stake. Even the traditional Baptist confessions of faith adopted over the centuries that had guided the Southern Baptist Convention for its one hundred and twenty-five years of Christian growth and service were being questioned. Fundamental Christian values were "up for grabs."

I began my second term in office with a speech before the executive committee that made my feelings clear:

"I think we ought to take those Baptist articles of faith of 1925 and 1963," I exclaimed, holding those precious documents in my hand, "and we ought to say, this is what it is being a Baptist. If you don't believe that, you are not a Baptist."

There was no reason to sugar-coat the issue. I believed in unity with all my heart, but there was a limit to the amount we could compromise to stay together. As for me, allegiance to God's Holy Word and to the historic Baptist confessions of faith was not negotiable. I didn't mean to sound angry or belligerent, but it was time to decide.

"Baptists who do not believe in the inerrant Word of God and who do not accept convention-adopted statements of faith," I urged, "ought to leave the Southern Baptist Convention and find another organization."

Shortly after that speech, Dr. William C. Smith Jr., the man who had run against me in New Orleans, left the Southern Baptist Convention. He told a reporter:

"Criswell's call that all those who don't accept Baptist statements of faith should get out was the last straw. . . . I don't feel any bitterness or vindictiveness," he said. "I just feel like a Boy Scout. I enjoyed it, but now I've outgrown it."

In June of 1970, fourteen thousand Messengers representing 11.4 million Southern Baptists gathered in Denver to celebrate our 125th anniversary. The lines of conflict had been clearly drawn. Baptists would have to choose. Would we re-commit ourselves to the fundamental values of the Bible and the Baptist faith, or would we not? From the opening gavel, tempers flared. Angry accusations were hurled back and forth like missiles, and good people on both sides were wounded in the fray.

W. R. White once said, "Sometimes fundamentalists have the best theology and the worst spirit of anybody in the world." That meeting in Denver proved him right again. The loving spirit of Christ was missing from too much of our deliberation, and to this day I regret it. I wish that the people who believed the most about the Bible had the most loving spirit about what they believe, me included. But so many times the opposite is true. The war of words must have grieved our loving Father, for it certainly broke my heart.

In spite of all the fury, the Denver meeting ended without division. The naysayers and the prophets of doom were wrong. No separatist movement was launched. No great crowd of people bolted from our ranks. In fact, the vast majority of the fourteen thousand pastors and laymen proved themselves again to be committed to the fundamentals of the Christian faith.

In our Denver meetings, Southern Baptists re-committed themselves to the lordship of Christ, to the centrality of the Bible, to the historic Baptist faith, to increased efforts at worldwide evangelism, to deeper concern for the human needs of those who suffer, and to unity within the Southern Baptist Convention.

"The Southern Baptist denomination has infinite potential," I told a reporter after our closing session. "Our people are really Christ-committed, Bible-loving, and missionary-hearted. Our leaders are God-anointed. They love the Lord, and they love the Book."

"What developments within the Southern Baptist church are you most concerned about, Dr. Criswell?" a reporter asked.

"I'm not worried about Southern Baptist pastors or their people," I replied. "Once again they have proven their commitment to God's Word as their sole rule and guide for faith and practice.

"But I am worried about the growing number of professors in our Baptist colleges and seminaries who no longer support an infallible view of Scripture or the historic Baptist statements of faith which spell out what the Bible says about the nature of God, the nature of man, salvation, believers baptism, the virgin birth of Christ, and so on.

"Will our next generation of students be fed upon the Word," I wondered aloud, "and upon the historic Christian faith, or upon the professor's heretical notions? The future of the Southern Baptist faith is at stake. Unless these professors truly teach the Word, the next generation could be lost."

"What happens next for W. A. Criswell?" a voice asked softly.

"I'm going to lay down this burden," I said with a great sigh of relief, "and I am going back home to my wonderful people in Dallas. And for the rest of my life, I am going to do exactly what God has called me to do: to preach the infallible Word of God and, through the Criswell Bible Institute, to teach thousands of young preachers, evangelists, and missionaries to do the same."

The Call to Preach the Word

God first called me to preach when I was just a boy living with my family on the wide, empty prairies near Texline. Since that day almost seventy years ago, I have doubted God's call only once.

When I was just seventeen, for one long terrible moment the heavens turned to brass. It seemed for all the world that God had deserted me. I was a freshman at Baylor, preaching my first outdoor revival in Pecan Grove beneath the little wooden tabernacle on Coryell Creek. I had preached my heart out to those dear farmers and their families, but no one had responded to the invitation.

"If anybody here will come down this aisle and ask God to save him," I said boldly, my adolescent voice quivering with emotion, "and God doesn't save him, I will quit the ministry and never preach again!"

As the volunteer quartet repeated its hymn of invitation, a young, bow-legged cowpoke about my age got up out of the last row of seats and shuffled forward.

"Preacher," he said, so loudly that everyone could hear, "I'll take you up on that proposition."

"Everyone be seated in the spirit of prayer," I commanded the little congregation.

"What's your name?" I asked the farmhand.

"Jim," he replied quietly, looking down at his stained jeans and scuffed boots.

"Jim," I said, moving out from around the pulpit to stand before him face to face, "You really want to be saved?"

"Yes, sir," he answered quickly looking at me, his dark eyes flashing, "more than anything."

"And you are asking Jesus to forgive you and come into your life right now this moment?"

He nodded, gripping his hat so tightly that his knuckles turned white.

We knelt together. The whole congregation looked on, half-praying, half-worrying for the both of us. With my hand on Jim's shoulder, I asked Jesus to save him and save him now. At the end of my short, fervent prayer, I stood up.

"Jim, if God has saved you," I said reaching out my arm to him, "take me by the hand."

The poor cowpoke stayed on his knees. For a moment he tried to hide his face. Then, suddenly he looked me in the eyes beseechingly.

"Preacher," he whispered, "there ain't nothing happened to me. I'm just the same."

The congregation grew tense. Jim looked desperate and embarrassed. I knelt beside him once again.

"You want to be saved?" I asked.

"Yes, sir," he whispered.

"You want Jesus to come into your heart right now?" I said again.

"Yes," the boy mumbled, nodding sincerely.

"O God," I prayed, save Jim right now. Fill his heart with your loving presence."

At the close of my second prayer, I stood again and reached out my arm to him.

"Jim," I said hopefully, "if God has saved you, if He's come into your heart, take me by the hand."

The boy looked stunned.

"I swear, Preacher," he whispered loudly, "there ain't nothing happened to me. I'm just the same, just like I was."

A third time I got down beside him on the tabernacle's hard, cement floor. A third time I asked him the question and a third time he answered, "No."

"Lord," I prayed and this time my heart was beating wildly. I could feel the congregation's worried look. And the poor cowboy was hardly breathing.

"You heard what I said, God. If anybody would come and ask You to save him and You don't save him, I'll quit the ministry. Does this mean, Lord, you want me to give up preaching your Word? You said, 'Whosoever calls upon the name of the Lord will be saved.' And we're calling upon Your name now. Save Jim, Lord, and save him now!"

The whole congregation said "Amen." I stood beside Jim again and reached out to him. But before I could speak, he whispered desperately:

"I swear, Preacher, I don't feel nothin'. I'm just as I was. What should I do?"

There was nothing else to do, not that I knew. I made a promise. God had answered. We sang a closing hymn and the congregation departed in a kind of embarrassed silence. I rode to the Davidson farmhouse in the back of their Model-T Ford. One of their older children began to tease me.

"If nobody gets saved," the oldest boy mocked good-naturedly, "I'll quit the ministry."

When I didn't respond or even smile, the whole family realized how seriously I had taken that whole event. For me, the one primary goal of preaching was reaching the lost. I had failed. I walked quickly to my room in the Davidson home and dropped to my knees in agonizing prayer.

"Lord, you promised. Now, I don't know where to turn. You said in your Word that 'whosoever calls upon the Lord will be saved.' That boy called upon You and You didn't save him. I made a promise, Lord, and it looks like I'm going to have to keep it."

Light from the full moon streamed in my open window. God was out there somewhere, but I felt no comfort. I tried to pray, but my prayers bounced back off the ceiling. Finally, after tossing and turning half the night, I fell into a restless sleep. In the morning, in the Davidson's car, we drove back to Coryell Creek. I was determined to keep my promise, but I wanted one last chance to be alone in God's tabernacle, to say good-bye to everything I dreamed.

"Say, Preacher!"

Alex Davidson slammed on the brakes just at the edge of Pecan Grove. The cowboy was riding toward me on a frisky mare. He was standing in his saddle and shouting frantically.

"Preacher," he yelled, "I've been looking all over for you."

Christmas services at First Baptist Church of Dallas

He reigned in, leaped off his horse and ran up the road in my direction. Mr. Davidson parked the car beside Coryell Creek as I turned to face him.

"What's the matter, Jim?" I asked, perplexed by his sudden appearance.

"I've been saved!" he shouted running up to me and grabbing me in his arms.

I pulled back from his embrace, put my hands on his shoulders and looked him directly in the eyes. This was no time for jokes, even one meant to make me feel better. But the look on that boy's face said, "This is no joke!"

"When were you saved, Jim?" I asked him, feeling a terrible lump in my throat and tears damming up behind my eyes.

"On the way home last night," he answered, and the words were tumbling out of him. "I was riding home in the moonlight asking Jesus to come into my heart over and over again. Suddenly, something happened. I don't know exactly what it was, but He was there, I could feel Him, in my heart, just like you said. I yelled right outloud, and before I knew it I was crying like a baby. I'm saved, Pastor. Don't you doubt it for a minute."

For a moment we stood there looking at each other both of us trying not to cry. Finally, Brother Davidson and I shook the young man's hand and praised the Lord. Then we drove up and down the country road honking the horn madly. Farmers and their families gathered at Coryell Creek that very day to hear Jim's confession of faith and to watch us wade together down into those peaceful waters.

"Jim," I said, placing my left arm around his waist and lifting my right arm up toward the heavens, "I baptize you in the name of the Father, and of the Son, and of the Holy Spirit."

As that happy young man went down beneath the waters, I knew in my heart that I would never doubt again my call to preach the Word. I lifted Jim back to his feet. Our tears mingled in the water, and the people of Pecan Grove said in a chorus of gratitude and praise, "Amen and Amen!"

Going Home to Preach the Word

After that experience as a teenaged preacher in Pecan Grove, never again did I doubt my call to preach the Word. Using the Bible as my text, I have spent most of my lifetime struggling to bring to life the primary doctrines of the Christian faith: the inspiration of the Word, the virgin birth, the deity of Christ, the death of Christ, the blood atonement, the resurrection of Christ, the power and presence of the Holy Spirit, the reality of Christ's body the church, the second coming of our Lord, the Great Judgment, the separation of the sheep from the goats, heaven and hell.

Being president of the Southern Baptist Convention required hundreds of days on the road, flights across the nation and around the world, and too many Sundays away from my pulpit in Dallas. The deacons and I prayed that God would not let our church stand still or even fall back because of my two-year term in office. God heard our prayers, and the church in Dallas prospered.

During those years of the presidency, between 1968 and 1970, our membership grew from 14,468 to 15,929 souls. Our Sunday school enrollment jumped from 8,414 to 9,449 men, women, and children, and our total offerings went up from $1,926,904 in 1967 to $3,464,250 in 1970.

Nevertheless, how glad and grateful I was when the presidency ended and I could get back to preaching God's Word without interruption.

14

Obeying God's Call to Study and to Preach the Word

Dallas: 1970 to the Present

"O God, thou hast taught me from my youth:
and hitherto have I declared thy wondrous works.
Now also when I am old and grayheaded, O God,
forsake me not; until I have shewed thy strength
unto this generation, and thy power to every one
that is to come."

Psalms 71:17-18

STUDYING THE WORD

In obedience to God's call, I have given sixty-three years to studying and preaching His infallible Word. Almost half a century of that time has been spent at First Baptist Church of Dallas, working and praying mornings in my office, at home on Swiss Avenue, studying God's Word on my way to proclaiming it in the carved oak pulpit in that great, brick sanctuary on Ervay and San Jacinto Streets.

The best hours of my life have been spent studying the Old Testament text in ancient Hebrew and the New Testament text in Koine Greek. In the large extension on our home that the people of First Baptist built to house, my growing library, I have collected the finest commentaries covering all sixty-six books of the Bible, and they are constantly open and in use.

To help me be a better student, I also have theological dictionaries, biblical encyclopedias, volumes of Word studies in English, Greek, and Hebrew, histories of the life and times of the people of Palestine, biographies of great biblical lives, books of poetry and related fiction, volumes on the liturgical arts and music, records of archaeological digs, letters and papers, dissertations and theses, and hundreds of history books: Jewish history, histories of the Christian church, histories of missions, Baptist histories, and histories of the church in America.

I use every method possible to break open the meaning of each God-given text. I don't ignore the results of hundreds of years of responsible biblical scholarship. Quite to the contrary, I am informed and inspired by it. Nevertheless, this I believe and this I proclaim: God's Word is perfect, literal, inerrant, infallible, and totally trustworthy.

Although Bible scholars argue endlessly about the authorship of the first five books of the Old Testament, when I read Moses' ancient text, I hear God's voice, and my heart leaps and my pulse quickens with His saving faith. "In the beginning, God created the heaven and the earth. And the earth was without form, and void; and darkness was upon the face of the deep. And the Spirit of God moved upon the face of the waters. And God said, Let there be light: And there was light" (Genesis 1:1-3).

Whatever biblical scholars may say about two, three, maybe four authors of Isaiah's writings, God's one great prophet, Isaiah, still speaks in one prophetic voice to me. "Come now and let us reason together, saith the Lord: though your sins be as scarlet, they shall be white as snow; though they be red like crimson, they shall be as wool" (Isaiah 1:18).

If Matthew, in his description of our Lord's birth, left out the chorus of angels to wide-eyed shepherds in the fields; if Luke didn't write about the wise men's journey to the stable in Bethlehem; if Mark and John ignored the star, the angels, the wise men, and the shepherds altogether and jumped right into the action thirty years later, those four unique Gospels still tell one, whole, glorious, trustworthy, life-changing story about God, who humbled Himself to dwell among us and in whose life, death, and resurrection we are redeemed. "In the beginning was the Word, and the Word was with God, and the Word was God. The same was in the beginning with God. All things were made by him; And without was not any thing made that was made. In him was life; And the life was the light of men" (John 1:1-4).

The Criswell Bible Institute

In 1970, out of the struggle to preserve and proclaim the centrality of God's infallible Word to Christian faith and practice, the Criswell Bible Institute was born. "We will not study about the Bible," I exclaimed. "We will study the Bible itself."

In the beginning, I thought we would be teaching the Bible primarily to laymen and laywomen in the evenings on our church campus. Weekly sermons and Sunday school classes, no matter how biblically based, were not enough to satisfy the people's growing hunger to learn more about the Bible. Clergymen could not win the world by themselves. We needed to equip an entire generation of Christian lay people to "rightly divide the Word of Truth." Remembering that Baylor University began with a class of less than fifty students, we were amazed when five hundred lay students enrolled for our first year of classes.

There were two other reasons that compelled me to begin our Bible Institute. First, while I was president of the Southern Baptist Convention, I learned that more than half of our denomination's thirty-seven thousand preachers had never graduated from college. At this time in their lives, they could not take seven years off to earn their college and seminary degrees. Besides, they had learned much from life. It would be a waste of their time and money to begin their studies as college freshmen. They needed an opportunity to study the Word, to develop pastoral and preaching skills.

In Chicago, the Moody Bible Institute was founded to meet just such a need. During my regular visits to Chicago to preach and to teach on the Moody campus, God placed it on my heart to create a Bible institute like the Moody Bible Institute in the heart of the South that would also minister to lay and clergy alike.

My third reason to launch the Criswell Bible Institute grew out of another tragic discovery made during those years as president of the Southern Baptist Convention. Everywhere I traveled, I had the opportunity to hear other Southern Baptists preach. To my surprise, almost none of them were doing expository preaching. Most preachers were still selecting a topic and then finding verses that helped support or illustrate that topic.

Southern Baptists claimed to be people of the Book, but we were not living up to our claim. And our seminaries, for the most part, were not preparing preachers to preach the Word expositionally. Even in those early years, it was my dream that one day our Criswell Bible

Official White House photo with George Bush

Institute in Dallas would held equip this new generation of preachers to preach the Word.

In 1972, Dr. H. Leo Eddleman, a respected Southern Baptist educator, accepted our invitation to become president of the Criswell Bible Institute. Recently retired as president of the New Orleans Baptist Seminary, Dr. Eddleman was a distinguished Baptist pastor, missionary, and scholar, fluent in Hebrew and Arabic, and an enthralling expositional preacher.

In 1975, Dr. Paige Patterson, another distinguished preacher, teacher, and evangelist, became the second president of Criswell Bible Institute. Under his sixteen years of leadership, CBI has witnessed amazing growth. From just twelve men studying full-time for the Christian ministry in 1975, we now have twenty-six faculty serving more than four hundred full time students, one hundred of them enrolled in graduate degrees: the Masters of Arts, the Masters of Divinity, and the Masters of Missionology, a unique and rare program for training Christian missionaries.

Already, the Criswell Bible Institute has more than five hundred graduates on the field, most of them pastors, some evangelists, and many missionaries. Already, in just twenty years, our precious CBI graduates, trained to preach and teach the Word, are serving Christ in forty-six states and seven countries. To God be the glory! Great things He hath done!

In 1972, Jack Pogue, my dear friend and long-time associate, founded the W. A. Criswell Foundation to help support the Criswell Bible Institute and the First Baptist Christian Academy. In November of 1990, thanks to the generous support of Mrs. Ruth Ray Hunt, First Baptist Church of Dallas, and the W. A. Criswell Foundation, we moved CBI faculty and students to our beautiful, newly-renovated Gaston Avenue Campus. I want to spend the rest of my life training a whole new generation of pastors, evangelists, missionaries, and Christian workers to be committed to preaching and teaching God's infallible Word with all their hearts, souls, minds, and strength.

These precious students are called to preach and teach the Word. They are willing to sacrifice everything to obey God's call, but they don't have funds to pay high tuitions or fees. The least we can do is to underwrite their education by keeping our tuitions low and our grants and aid programs generous. President Paige Patterson, the W. A. Criswell Foundation, and I have launched a massive campaign to fund and endow the Criswell Bible Institute.

"Often, lay people don't have soul-winning gifts," Jack Pogue said quietly as he tried to explain why he has committed his life to the financial and spiritual health of Criswell Bible Institute. "Most of us can't preach or teach the Word like these gifted young people who study at CBI. But when we invest our money in their educations, we make possible the preaching and teaching of God's infallible Word in cities and towns across the nation and around the earth.

"After all," Jack said happily, "when CBI students graduate and take their places in local churches or on the mission field, we who helped to make their education possible have a part in every soul they win to Christ. What better way is there to invest our money for eternal good!"

Preaching the Word

What a joy it has been to spend my life preaching and teaching the Word. Using the Bible as my foundation and authority, I have spoken to every imaginable issue during these past decades. How grateful I am in looking back upon these memories that God's Word went out, often in spite of me!

In 1971, in Washington, D.C., before the 92nd U. S. Congress I preached a sermon entitled "Drugs Is Spelled D-E-A-T-H." Using Romans 12:1-2 as my text (". . . that ye present your bodies a living sacrifice . . ."), I exclaimed to that great assembly that "God's way is spelled L-I-F-E," and the hall crowded with the nation's leaders erupted in applause.

Again in 1971, after meeting with Pope Paul VI in Rome and with Rabbis Yinon and Nathan in Jerusalem, using Titus 2:10 as my text, I said to my dear congregation, "Can we not, in true faith, hold out our arms like the arms of the cross—out, out, out—until we embrace all mankind . . . asking all men everywhere to share with us the life that we have found in Christ Jesus?"

In 1972 when we founded the First Baptist Academy to train children from kindergarten through high school, I quoted an Old Testament proverb at the dedication: "Train up a child in the way he should go: and when he is old, he will not depart from it" (Proverbs 22:6).

Now more than ever, we need Christian kindergartens, elementary, junior, and senior high schools where God's Word is at the center of the curriculum. When we began our Academy, we never dreamed that in just two decades our student body would grow to its present size of just under one thousand students from kindergarten children through seniors in high school.

Sometimes, over the years, in my exuberance to communicate, I said and did exactly the wrong thing, or the harsh thing, or the unloving thing. For example, in 1975, during a grueling, three-hour, statewide television debate with atheist Madlyn Murray O'Hair, I lost my temper and upon her fifth interruption, I shouted to the harassed reporter who sat between us, "Will you keep her trap shut until I reply?" It wasn't what Jesus might have done perhaps , but the audience applauded in relief.

In 1976, when President Gerald Ford announced his plans to attend our church on Stewardship Sunday, reporters asked me if I was going to change my sermon text from 2 Corinthians 8:1-9.

"No," I answered quickly. "Presidents need to hear God's Word about stewardship just like the rest of us." As the president flew back to Washington, D.C., that day, he called me from Air Force One to say how much he had been blessed by the preaching of God's Word. Today there is a little brass plaque in our sanctuary where the President of the United States heard the call to make sacrificial gifts to God with a grateful heart.

In 1976, after my daughter Ann sang a moving gospel song, I preached to the students at Southern Seminary. "If I had it all to do again," I confessed to them, "I would still preach the Bible as the verbal, inspired word of God. If you want to succeed in ministry," I assured them, "keep your heart fixed on Jesus and your mind centered on God's Word."

In 1977, upon the sixth anniversary of our School of Prophets, I shared this central theme with the ministers who came to Dallas for a time of inspiration and information: "Let the true pastor never turn aside from his great calling to preach the whole counsel of God, warn men of their sins and the judgment of God upon them, baptize their converts in the name of the Triune God, and build up the congregation in the love and wisdom of the Lord."

Using 2 Chronicles 7:14 as my text in 1978, when Dallas Cowboy kicker Rafael Septien became First Baptist's twenty-thousandth member, I reminded our people that God's Word makes it perfectly clear what must happen if this great nation is to find renewal and rebirth. "If my people, which are called by my name, shall humble themselves, and pray, and seek my face, and turn from their wicked ways; then will I hear from heaven, and will forgive their sin, and will heal their land."

In 1979, before a Southern Baptist Convocation on Peacemaking and the Nuclear Arms Race, I confessed that "it is my earnest prayer that some solution can be found for the illimitable waste spent on armaments that could be so desperately useful for the poor and the lost of the world." Using the words of the prophet Zechariah, the Word of God burst forth in our hearts anew: "Not by might, nor by power, but by my spirit, saith the Lord of hosts " (4:6).

In 1980, during a time of financial crisis for our church and for our community, I stood before the more than six hundred members of Mrs. Criswell's celebrated Bible Class and quoted the text from God's Word that has given me so much hope over the decades: "Trust in the Lord with all your heart and lean not unto your own understanding; but in all thy ways acknowledge Him and He will direct your paths" (Proverbs 3:5-6).

That year, when one of our dear, loyal laymen committed suicide after losing his business in tragic bankruptcy proceedings, I remember walking into his funeral saying that text over and over to myself and feeling God's comforting presence even as I quoted it.

In 1982, I broke a lifelong tradition and finally shared my fears with the good people of Dallas. That sermon titled "My Traumatic Perplexities" was based on the incomparable words of Jesus found in John 15:12-14: "This is my commandment, that ye love one another, as I have loved you. Greater love hath no man than this, that a man lay down his life for his friends. Ye are my friends, if ye do whatsoever I command you."

During that sermon, I shared my deepest fears with the good people of Dallas: that we weren't leading more people to Christ; that liberalism and secularism were snatching Baptist educational institutions from their moorings; and that all too often our own church membership "acted as a country club, gathering our own together, offended by the soil, dirt, and filth of the falling, hungry masses around us."

On that Sunday, I shared these moving words from Vachel Lindsay's "General William Booth Enters Into Heaven."

> Every slum had sent its half-a-score;
> The round world over, Booth had groaned for more.
> Tranced, fanatical they shrieked and sang:
> "Are you washed in the blood of the Lamb?"
> Hallelujah! It was queer to see

Bull-necked convicts with that land made free.
Loons with trumpets blow a blare, blare, blare.
On, on upward through the golden air!
Are you washed in the blood of the Lamb?

In 1983, in a Sunday morning sermon, I elaborated on my growing concern for the future of Baptist colleges and seminaries. At the heart of that sermon were the words of Jesus from John 8:31-32: ". . . If ye continue in my word, then are ye my disciples indeed; and ye shall know the truth, and the truth shall make you free."

"Almost all of the great old universities of the world were established by the church," I recalled that day, "to train the ministers and godly lay people in the truth of God's Word. Over the decades, the great old schools have lost the faith. Today, they are infidel institutions. And now," I added, "the same terrible process is happening to us. The liberals are taking our institutions away, one by one. And when the Word is lost, there is no truth. And when there is no truth, we are no longer free."

In 1984, after the Republican National Convention nominated Ronald Reagan and George Bush as their candidates for the nations highest offices, I closed the convention with a simple prayer for God's health and healing for the nation "through God's Holy Word." I still pray daily that somehow the Bible will find its way back into our schools and that prayers will once again be heard in our classrooms.

In 1985, I proclaimed to twenty-five thousand Southern Baptist preachers: "Whether we continue to live as a denomination or ultimately die lies in our dedication to the infallible Word of God." Jesus made it joyfully clear when He said: "If a man love me, he will keep my words: and my Father will love him, and we will come unto him, and make our abode with him. He that loveth me not keepeth not my sayings" (John 14:23-24).

In 1986, at the dedication of the Ruth Ray Hunt Youth Building, made possible by a generous gift from Mrs. Ruth Ray Hunt, a dear and precious lady whose loving presence has made an inexpressible difference in the life of our church so many times over these past years, I quoted this text to the young people present: "Let no man despise thy youth; but be thou an example of the believers, in word, in conversation, in charity, in spirit, in faith, in purity" (1 Timothy 4:12).

The future of the church and of the world is in the hands of these dear young people. We must sacrifice everything to pass on to them our love for God's Word and our trust in God's promises.

In 1989, in an interview with a journalist I said, "My liberal critics call me a 'funny-damn-mentalist.' But do you know," I said to him, "if I were to begin my life all over, I would do it all again. I would commit myself again to God's infallible Word and until the day I die, I would give my life again to proclaiming it."

For these last sixty-three years, I have poured everything I had into preaching God's Word. For me, preaching is the trust of God mediated through a man's voice, life, heart, mind—in fact, his whole being. My heart is broken if souls are not being won, but when even one person steps out of his pew and walks down the aisle to kneel at the altar and give his or her life to Jesus, I am in ecstasy.

The Old Mourner's Bench

We didn't always have a kneeling altar at the front of our sanctuary in the Dallas church. The old mourner's bench was only a footnote in frontier history when I began preaching here. Then, early in the 1970s, the executive leader of our Southern Baptist Convention in California invited me to speak to their annual meeting at a campground in the redwoods near Santa Cruz.

"To see a man, woman, or child born again is the preacher's greatest joy," I exclaimed to that great crowd of pastors and evangelists. "The angels sing and the heart of God leaps for joy when just one person finds Christ as Savior and Lord."

At that moment, only halfway through my sermon, a preacher sitting in the back row stood up, walked down the aisle, and knelt at the rough-hewn, wooden mourner's bench that stretched across the entire front of the tabernacle.

At first, I pretended not to notice him kneeling there, sobbing his heart out. I just kept on preaching.

"When you are called by God to preach," I said, trying to keep the group's attention, "obey the call whatever it may cost you."

At that the poor man wept even more bitterly. Suddenly, another man rushed to the front of the tabernacle, knelt down at the mourner's bench and began to cry.

"Many are called," I said, "but so few answer with their lives."

Another man rushed forward, and then another. I kept on preaching, but in just a matter of minutes, the place was in chaos. Both sides of the mourner's bench were crowded with men on their knees, crying out before the Lord. I had never seen anything like it. When most of the seats were empty and the altar was filled, I quit preaching and got down on my knees beside them. The voice of God was speaking so loudly in the hearts of those dear men, it was time for me to be silent.

"Dear Dr. Criswell," the letter began just a few weeks later, "I am the man who stood up while you were preaching and knelt down at the altar crying." It was a letter of apology and explanation.

"I have never once in my life made such a spectacle of myself," he confessed. "If you knew me, you would be amazed and surprised that I would do such a thing.

"My wife and I have pastored a little church for the past ten discouraging years," he went on to explain. "I came to your meeting ready to quit, to give up, to walk away from my call, and to get a secular job that would support me and my family.

"Then our executive secretary called to offer me a free trip to hear you preach at Beulah Park. I needed a vacation. My wife and I agreed. We would leave the ministry upon my return.

"Then you stood to speak. Suddenly, through your sermon, God's spirit got hold of me. I couldn't wait until you were finished to kneel before Him, to seek His will and way for me. Please forgive me for interrupting your meeting, but God has turned our lives around. Revival is breaking out in our little church and we feel hope again."

My own tears fell rather freely as I sat in my study reading that man's wonderful letter. From that day, I determined to ask the deacons to build a mourner's bench at the front of our great church, a place where people could kneel and do business with the Lord as that young pastor had done. But a mourner's bench was a strange, old-fashioned notion. For several months in a row, I lost my courage to tell the deacons. Then, finally, one night at the end of a deacon's meeting, I stood and told them the whole story.

You could hear the flies buzzing when I sat down. The stony silence seemed to go on forever. I could imagine their concerns. I was proposing a rough, wooden mourner's bench for a great, stained-glass church in the heart of downtown Dallas. Nobody moved to support the idea. Everyone liked our sanctuary exactly as it was. Then, our oldest deacon stood slowly to his feet.

"When I was a child," he said, "God got hold of me at a mourner's bench in a camp meeting in the Oklahoma Panhandle. And if God has laid on our pastor's heart the need for a mourner's bench in our church, then I move we do it."

Without another question, the deacons approved the idea. Months later when the architects and carpenters had finished their work, I was disappointed to realize that we didn't have a rough-hewn mourner's bench as I had dreamed. We had a beautiful, hand-finished altar railing that blended in with the rest of the sanctuary furniture as though it had been there through the ages.

But on that first Sunday morning, my disappointment vanished. At the close of our service, a young man walked to the front of the church, knelt down at that beautiful railing and, weeping, gave his life to Christ. Suddenly, his parents were kneeling there beside him and the whole church joined in their prayer of praise.

On that day I discovered that it didn't matter if a mourner's bench was rough-hewn from unfinished planks or lovingly hand-crafted, carved and polished. What really matters is what happens when people kneel at that altar railing to pray.

In 1970, when my son Cris was just eleven, he knelt at the front of the sanctuary after a Sunday evening service. God gave us this precious child when he was only one year old. Born, June 24, 1959, Cris entered our family in the summer of 1960. He entered God's family ten years later in my study, standing on his tiptoes and peering up at me over my desk.

"I want to be a Christian, Daddy," he said quietly, and once again my heart leaped for joy.

The Word had been central to our family's life together. We had studied and memorized verses from the Old and New Testament during our quiet family times before we knelt beside Cris's bed for evening prayers. After our traditional pancake breakfast on Saturday mornings— I prefer my flapjacks burned, buttered, and basted with real maple syrup—Cris, Betty, and I would share the verses we had memorized that past week. On Christmas morning, before the stacks of presents were unwrapped, we would quote in chorus the entire nativity story from the Gospel of Luke.

Betty and I longed to see Cris accept Jesus as Lord and Savior. And once again God proved faithful to His promise. What a joy it was that Sunday evening when Cris was only eleven years old, to kneel beside him at the front of the Dallas church sanctuary as our son confessed his faith before the entire congregation.

A young life transformed, a family reunited, an old woman's life made new again, an alcoholic delivered from addiction, an entire row of derelicts kneeling together, the world's richest man entering Christ's

Receiving honorary degree from Liberty University, with Jerry Falwell

kingdom with his precious family, a state senator seeking God's guidance, a teacher answering God's call to the mission field, a frightened soldier seeking strength for his journey, an unwed pregnant girl finding healing for her broken heart, my own children acknowledging Christ as Lord and Savior—Sunday after Sunday they come from across the sanctuary to stand or kneel and give their lives to the Lord.

Looking back over these past years, my happiest moments have been spent preaching the Word and at the close of every sermon praying with the people who have heard God's voice and have opened up their hearts to Him.

For a lifetime the same fire that burned in Jeremiah's bones has burned in me. I wish that I had spent more time with my family during these past busy decades. But there was so much work to be done, so many lost souls waiting to hear Christ's name. When I neglected family or friends, it wasn't because I didn't love them or need them or miss them. It was because I had heard God's call and was consumed by my sincere desire to obey that call with my whole heart.

I pray daily for my precious family, trusting God to hold their lives safely in the palm of His loving hand. I pray for my wife, Betty, thanking God for her love and for her faithfulness; for Mabel Ann, our daughter whose gift of music has blessed many people; for Cris, our son, who has always been a joy to us. As he grew up he was active in Sunday school, in missions activities, in chapel choir, and in all church meetings. He is a man now, a dedicated Christian businessman in Washington, D.C. , where he is an agent in commercial real estate and the teacher of his own Bible class. We pray daily for our grandson, Paul Daniel Jackson, a student at A & M University in College Station, Texas, and for his precious father, Dr. Kenneth Jackson, a noted oral surgeon in Dallas.

> *Thank You, Father, for allowing me a lifetime in Your Word. Thank You for standing beside my desk all these decades, informing, correcting, inspiring, and directing me.*
>
> *For my blunders along the way, I ask Your forgiveness. The errors, Lord, were mine. Sometimes I got in a hurry. Other times I let my mind wonder and my brain rest. Yet other times, I was tired, lonely, or afraid. Still, Lord, You never failed me.*
>
> *Thank You, too, for Your people sitting in the pews, smiling at me, listening with their brains and with their hearts, confronting me when I was off target, commending me when You spoke clearly to their needs.*
>
> *Thank You, too, for my wife, my family, my friends, my deacons, my staff, and my congregation. Even when they needed me, they waited patiently as I searched the Scriptures, studied and wrote at my desk, or struggled on my knees before the open window.*

And God Brings the Increase

In spite of my own failures and weaknesses, during almost half a century in Dallas, God has honored the preaching and teaching of His Word. Our people have been faithful to our Lord and Savior Jesus Christ, and their hard work and sacrifice has led to great growth and amazing change.

Over the years, through our Sunday and midweek services, through our revivals and special meetings, through our Sunday school classes and our family and small group programs, through KCBI, our 100,000 watt FM radio station, through our tape and television ministries, through our thirty-two missions to various language and cultural minorities across Dallas, and now through the Dallas Life Foundation, purchased to help us meet the physical and spiritual needs of five hundred homeless people a night, and through the witness of our congregation where they live and work and play, tens of thousands of men, women, and children have had their sins forgiven and their names written in the Lamb's Book of Life. And hundreds, maybe thousands, of people, young and old alike, have given their lives to preach and teach the Word.

There is no way to measure the number of lives changed through the prayers, sacrifices and hard work of the people of First Baptist Church of Dallas. But we have seen amazing, incomprehensible, unbelievable growth. God has kept His promise: "Give, and it shall be given unto you; good measure, pressed down, and shaken together, and running over" (Luke 6:38).

In 1989, First Baptist Church celebrated 27,500 members and over 13,000 men, women, and children on our Sunday school rolls. And that same year, our annual giving to all causes exceeded $16,000,000. How can I say thanks to all the people, lay and clergy alike, who have made this ministry possible?

Especially, how can I say thanks to my beloved wife, Betty, who always helped me and the churches we have served by teaching weekly Bible studies and a Sunday morning class? Today, "Mrs. C's" class at the church in Dallas has an enrollment of more than five hundred members. For years, this wonderful class alone has given an annual gift to our church budget of more than a million dollars.

Preachers get far too much credit for the growth and renewal of a church. The people who work with us, clergy and laity alike, are the real heroes of this story. I thank God for all the people who stand beside me faithfully in this ministry and I beg their forgiveness that their precious names are not written down in this book with all the gratitude and love I feel. But I can see them now, even as they read this page, smiling, knowing their pastor's heart, content that God has written their names in the book that really counts, the Book of Life.

Together, we have given our lives to this ministry. How do we really measure the success of those years? Do we measure success by counting up the number of people who respond to an invitation or by adding up the new members of our church? No. Great missionary preachers have spent their lives proclaiming the Word faithfully only to die with no converts at all. Still, God honors their faithfulness.

Do we measure success by adding up the offerings or by increasing our church budget every year? No. There are countless faithful preachers who must struggle to support themselves and their families with a part-time job, and thousands of faithful churches who find it hard to survive the hard financial times. Still, God honors their faithfulness.

Do we measure success by beautiful new buildings and church sanctuaries that echo with the sound of pipe organs and great, robed choirs? No. Faithful witness is often done by humble Christian servants in a Quonset hut, a canvas tent pitched in the desert, or on the street corners of our lost and dying cities. Still, God honors their faithfulness.

The truth is, we don't measure the success or failure of our preaching, our teaching, our giving, or our years of Christian service. As the Apostle Paul explained to the Christians in Corinth: "We are laborers together with God," he said. Somebody plants. Somebody waters, "but God gives the increase." We are not called to measure success or failure, but to preach, teach, and live the Word as best we can. This is our task, to be true to Christ, to win the lost to Jesus, and to obey God's infallible and inerrant Word, so that when our Lord comes to take us home, He will find us faithful and true, standing on the promises of God.

Standing on the Promises

Late one afternoon, I entered that great sanctuary of First Baptist Church of Dallas. No one sat in the twenty-seven hundred seats nor stood against the walls or in the hallways. Even the choir loft was empty. The organ was silent and the instruments of the orchestra were all locked away. The television cameras and microphones were covered. The red glow of a Texas sunset illuminated the auditorium in pale pink light as I sat in the front row looking up at the great carved pulpit that had been my home these many years

"How long, Lord," I wondered silently, "before I open my Bible and preach the Word in this great place for the very last time?"

God was silent, but He was there, for I could feel His loving, sympathetic presence.

"Lord," I whispered, "You know that dying holds no fear for me. To rush from this world into Your open arms will be a moment of triumph and praise. But, dearest Father," I continued, "there are times I wonder if all of heaven could hold the joy that preaching Your Word has brought to me. Is there anything in eternity, Lord, that even compares to kneeling beside someone at this mourner's bench who is finding forgiveness for sin and accepting Jesus as Lord and Savior?"

The room was silent, but the Spirit of God was moving on my heart and His voice echoed these words of the Apostle John from his book of the Revelation: "And God shall wipe away all tears from their eyes; and there shall be no more death, neither sorrow, nor crying, neither shall there be any more pain."

No one wrote of heaven with the eloquence and grace of the Apostle John. As I was thinking about his words in Revelation, suddenly, I remembered a letter that I had received from a precious grandmother, writing of her grandson's tragic death.

"He was only seven when he died," she wrote me. "The doctors discovered that my grandson had leukemia when he was two years old, and for most of his young life he was hospitalized in great pain and terrible suffering."

Her letter had reached my study shortly after Easter.

"During the Christmas season last year," she wrote, "I walked into my grandson's hospital room to find him watching you on television. He was so engrossed in your sermon that he didn't even hear me enter the room. So I waited silently and watched his face as God spoke through your sermon directly to that little boy's heart."

My text for that sermon had been that same wonderful promise from the Revelation of John. With tears streaming down my face I shared from my heart what God had promised. "Talk to Jesus. Ask Him to forgive your sins. Let Him write your name in the Book of Life, and one day you will join Him in heaven where God Himself will wipe away the tears from your eyes; where man will die no more; where there is neither sorrow, nor crying, nor pain."

"I could see tears in my grandson's eyes," his grandma wrote me. "I longed to interrupt, to hold him in my arms, but it seemed wiser to wait. When your sermon was over, my grandson turned to me and said: 'Grandma, how can I talk to God?' I answered his question in the only way I knew. 'Honey,' I said to him, 'you talk to God just like you talk to anybody else.'"

"He smiled and took my hand," she said. "We had a lovely visit and on the next day when I returned, his smile lit up the room. For the first time in years, his eyes were sparkling. His body was frail. His health was failing, but there was a new energy about him, a kind of hopefulness that even the nurses and doctors had noticed.

"'Grandma,' he exclaimed the moment I came into the room, 'last night I talked to God. He came down from heaven and put His arms around me. He told me that soon He would come back from heaven again to take me home to be with Him forever.'

"I stood there looking down on him," the grandmother wrote. "He was so sure that God had visited Him that I, too, believed it. His face lit up the room with joy. I could barely hold back my tears.

"'Grandma,' he said, leaning towards me and whispering, 'when God comes after me, I want you to tell Mommy and Daddy not to cry. Give my crayons to Mary and my books to John, but,' he added mysteriously, 'don't give my shoes to anybody.'

"That was shortly after Christmas just last year," the grandmother told me, "and just two weeks ago, on Easter Day, my grandson died. As the whole world paused to celebrate the resurrection of Jesus, the Lord God Himself put His arms around my little grandson and took him home forever. We never did find out why my grandson wanted to keep his shoes. Maybe he was thinking he would need them for the long journey home.

"Thank you, Pastor," she concluded her letter, "for preaching the Word in a way that even a seven-year-old boy could understand it."

As I sat alone in the quiet sanctuary, God answered my question with that touching memory. There is only one joy greater than preaching or teaching the Word, and that joy is this: One day soon we will see the Author of the Word face to face. If we trust Him as that little child trusted, one day God Himself will hold us in His arms and take us home. In the meantime, all He asks of us is that we go on loving the Word and sharing it in our own ways, that we remain faithful to the Word, that we win the lost to Christ. And when our trials come, when we feel pain and suffering, when our tears flow again, it is our joy and comfort to lift our faces heavenward and to go on standing on the promises of God.

Dr. Criswell studies his beloved Bible

A Personal List
Some of the Greatest Passages and Promises in God's Word!

Where we came from:	*Genesis 1, 2*
Where the saved are going:	*Revelation 21, 22*
Where the lost are going:	*Luke 16:19-31, 2 Thessalonians 1:8-9; Revelation 20*
How to get to heaven:	*John 3; Acts 16:31; Romans 10:9-13*
The meaning of the death of Christ:	*Romans 5*
The coming of the Holy Spirit:	*Acts 2*
Great examples of conversion:	*John 9; Acts 8:26-39; 9:1-10; 16:16-34*
The Ten Commandments:	*Exodus 20*
The Sermon on the Mount:	*Matthew 5-7*
The Golden Rule:	*Matthew 7:12*
The two Lord's prayers:	*Matthew 6:9-13; John 17*
The precious love chapter:	*I Corinthians 13*
The Good Shepherd:	*Psalm 23; John 10*
Old Testament prophecies of the coming of Christ:	*Isaiah 9:2-7; 53; Psalm 22; Zechariah 9:9; 12:10; 13:6*
The birth of Christ:	*Matthew 1; Luke 1,2*
The death of Christ:	*Matthew 27; Mark 15; Luke 23; John 19*
The resurrection of Christ:	*Matthew 28; Mark 16; Luke 24; John 20, 21*
The coming again of Christ:	*Matthew 24; Zechariah 14; 1 Thessalonians 4:13-18; Revelation 19*
The final judgment:	*Revelation 20*
The ordinance of baptism:	*Matthew 3; 28:18-20; Acts 8:26-39; Romans 6:3-5*
The ordinance of the Lord's Supper:	*Matthew 26:26-30; 1 Corinthians 11:23-26*
The heroes of the faith:	*Hebrews 11*